S

To John
with thanks for
great inspiration

Julia

# THE **EU** AND SECURITY

## A HANDBOOK FOR PRACTITIONERS

LARS-ERIK LUNDIN

SANTÉRUS
FÖRLAG

www.santerus.se

© 2015 Lars-Erik Lundin and Santérus Publishing, Sweden
ISBN 978-91-7359-095-2
*Cover*: MAC Rhino
Santérus Förlag, Stockholm, Sweden also publishes books
under the imprint Santérus Academic Press

info@santerus.se
Printed by BOD, Germany 2015

*This book is dedicated to my family and above all to my wife
and companion since more than 40 years, Inger Bäcklund*

*I have enjoyed constant support and encouragement
over many decades of travel and overtime work*

# Contents

# Acronyms

| | |
|---|---|
| ACP | African, Caribbean and Pacific |
| ASEAN | Association of Southeast Asian Nations |
| AU | African Union |
| CBRN | Chemical, Biological, Radiological, and Nuclear |
| CFSP | Common Foreign and Security Policy |
| CHG | Civilian Headline Goal |
| CIMIC | Civil-Military Co-operation |
| CNN | Cable News Network |
| COREPER | Comité des représentants permanents, is the Committee of Permanent Representatives |
| COREU | Correspondance Européenne |
| COTER | Commission for Territorial Cohesion Policy and EU Budget |
| CRT | Civilian Response Teams |
| CSDP | Common European Security and Defence Policy |
| DAC | Development Assistance Committee |
| DCI | Development Cooperation Instrument |
| DDR | disarmament, demobilisation, and reintegration |
| DJC | Development Cooperation Instrument |
| DG DEVCO | The Commission's Directorate-General for International Cooperation and Development |
| DRC | Democratic Republic of the Congo |
| DTIB | Defence Technology Industrial Base |

| | |
|---|---|
| EC | European Community |
| ECHO | European Community Humanitarian Office |
| ECOWAS | Economic Community of West African States |
| EDA | European Defence Agency |
| EEAS | European External Action Service |
| EIDHR | European Instrument for Democracy & Human Rights |
| ENI | European Neighbourhood Instrument |
| ENP | European Neighbourhood Policy |
| EPC | European Political Cooperation |
| ESDP | European Security and Defence Policy |
| ESS | European Security Strategy |
| EUPM | European Union Police Mission |
| EU | European Union |
| FAO | UN Food and Agriculture Organization |
| FPI | Service for Foreign Policy Instruments |
| FSJ | Freedom, Security and Justice |
| FYROM | Former Yugoslavian Republic of Macedonia |
| G8 | Group of Eight industrialized nations |
| HLG | Helsinki Headline Goals |
| HR | High Representative |
| IAEA | International Atomic Energy Agency |
| IEDS | Improvised Explosive Devices |
| IfSP | Instrument contributing to Stability and Peace |
| IPA | Instrument for Pre-accession Assistance |
| ISS | Internal Security Strategy |
| JFDS | Joint Framework Documents |
| JSSR | Justice and Security Sector Reform |
| MDG | Millennium Development Goals |
| NATO | North Atlantic Treaty Organization |
| NGO | Non-Governmental Organisations |
| NPT | Non-Proliferation Treaty |
| NSA | National Security Agency |
| OCT | Overseas Countries and Territories |

| | |
|---|---|
| ODA | Official Development Assistance |
| OECD | Organisation for Economic Co-operation and Development |
| OPEC | Organization of Petroleum Exporting Countries |
| OSCE | Organization for Security and Co-operation in Europe |
| PFP | Partnership for Peace |
| PI | Partnership Instrument |
| PSC | Political and Security Committee |
| PSI | Proliferation Security Initiative |
| SALW | spread of small arms and light weapons |
| SCR | Common Service for External Relations |
| SSR | Security Sector Reform |
| TEU | Treaty of the European Union |
| TFEU | Treaty of the Functioning of the European Union |
| TTIP | Transatlantic Trade and Investment Partnership |
| UK | United Kingdom |
| UN | United Nations |
| UNDP | UN Development Programme |
| UNIDO | United Nations Industrial Development Organization |
| UNMIK | United Nations Mission in Kosovo |
| UNODC | United Nations and its Office on Drugs and Crime |
| US | United States |
| VP | Vice-President of the European Commission |
| WEU | Western European Union |
| WMD | Weapons of Mass Destruction |
| WTO | World Trade Organization |

# Academic Preface

Observers of the European Union, scholars and other interested readers will from the outset want to know the genre of this book. Clearly, more than anything else it should be regarded as a *handbook* written on the basis of decades of discussions with interlocutors, both practitioners and academics, within and outside the EU institutions.

It is intended to help practitioners and students to create a strategic perspective for themselves.

It is also hoped that the book will inspire future research. But it is important to be clear about the limitations of the book from an academic perspective.

The analytical framework of the book is not derived primarily from the scholarly literature. Although a conscious effort was made to relate to this literature, including theoretical work, the book was not written with a dedicated ambition to improve on any particular theory beyond a strong emphasis on the need for a comprehensive approach to security.

Ideally, other scholars should be able to replicate scientific works on the basis of available material or at least attributable sources.[1] Case studies[2] are needed based on a systematic selection of material that helps test well-defined hypotheses. The present study has clear limitations in this regard.

1  See the discussion of methods of observation in Harrison, L, & Callan, T: *Key research concepts in politics and international relations*, SAGE, 2013
2  See the analysis of the case study concept in *Ibid.*

Much of the analysis in the following chapters is based on the author's personal experience over the years, some of which cannot be explicitly attributed to identifiable sources. In the discussion of problems of impact, the study presents different examples that are linked to processes where the author can claim to have some comparative advantage in terms of experience in his professional career. This obviously entails a risk of bias. However, it can be considered progress if some, either as scholars or practitioners, take inspiration from questions that are put forward.

Thus, the *material* was not collected in a single systematic effort according to predefined hypotheses. Notably, interviews were undertaken in several contexts over a number of years and were partly designed for the purpose of other, closely related studies. The interview results have not been coded systematically but have for the most part been recorded.[3]

References to the literature primarily suggest further reading and give examples of the point that is being made. References to interviews are often not explicit due to a commitment to protect the respondents.

## Key Concepts: The EU, Security and Impact

The character of a handbook requires that all concepts be used in accordance with EU official documents. This affects the use of key concepts such as *the EU, security* and *impact*.

First, the vision of the EU as an actor[4] thus differs depending on the context. Sometimes it is quite clear that EU action will need to be implemented through a consensus procedure along a single line of command with clear time limitations and real-time control from member states' representatives in Brussels. Sometimes the effort is much more differentiated, with less clear time limitations, and is deployed using different decision-making procedures in both intergovernmental and community contexts, perhaps also including efforts by member states themselves.

3   For a brief description of the methodological aspects related to interviews see *Ibid.*

4   For examples of a great number of different perspectives on this issue in the literature – see the bibliography.

Second, the book illustrates that the concept of security[5] also varies depending on the context. Again, this has to do with the fact that this is a study based on declared EU policy objectives, not an analytical construct of what these objectives should be in terms of security.

Third, the book demonstrates that the *models for impact assessment* differ widely, far beyond the technical methodology developed for impact evaluation in the literature..[6]

EU member states have instructed their citizens and governments and the EU institutions to comply with the Treaty of Lisbon, with the Treaty establishing the European Atomic Energy Community (Euratom) and with a number of other international commitments. They have also put resources at the disposal of the EU institutions until 2020. But they have not prescribed a single actor to implement these commitments, and they have not defined a single coherent objective for the work in terms of security. Rather, they have allowed a considerable amount of flexibility in the interpretation of the treaties and other commitments both in terms of the evolution of EU actor capability, ways in which EU actions are securitized and ways in which impact assessment is to be made.

This ambiguity also means that the question *"security for whom?"*[7] cannot be addressed in the same way throughout the book. Sometimes it is obvious that measures of success are intermediate, referring to the situation in a particular conflict area, the policies of other governments, the compliance with international commitments, the interdiction of dangerous flows into the Union, the protection of important flows of energy, trade etc.

The EU treaties refer to both values and interests. This means that the EU is not supposed to work only for the security of citizens or the member states. Notably, the EU and its member states provide more than half the development assistance in the world.

5   For a conceptual overview see Buzan, B, & L Hansen, *The Evolution of International Security Studies*, Cambridge University Press, 2009 and specifically as regards the EU in international organisations see Jørgensen, K E, *The European Union and International Organizations*, Routledge, 2009.

6   As an example of the latter see: Khandker, S, G B Koolwal, & H Samad, *Handbook on Impact Evaluation*, no. 1, 2009, pp. 1–239.

7   See Weaver, O, J Sperling, & J Hallenberg, 'European Security Identities', *Journal of Common Market Studies* vol. 34, No. 1, 1996.

A key concept employed in the study is impact. The question was put during the writing of this book if it is possible to discuss problems of impact if case studies evaluating earlier impact have not been undertaken. In this regard most readers will agree that both the academic literature and the political discourse in the EU are clear enough: even if EU documents are often somewhat self-congratulatory when evaluating earlier policies, a massive literature is available on shortfalls in terms of EU impact on security. This book contains many examples of such shortfalls that have been either publicly described or discussed in interviews. There are also dedicated efforts underway to deal with some of these shortfalls in major policy areas as well as through reviews of existing structures, notably the European External Action Service itself,[8] and policies in the context of the financial framework for the period 2014 to 2020.

Areas where *the lack of sufficient impact has been criticized* include (in no particular order):

The Common Security and Defence Policy (CSDP), which is shown throughout the book to be in difficulty, ranging from poor capacity building, isolation from other policy areas, bad micromanagement in terms of procedures, lack of strategic and long-term objectives beyond capacity building, etc.[9]

Neighbourhood and enlargement policies that are often stovepiped, where the comprehensive approach has not yet been systematically applied, uniform strategies have not been developed, and there is a lack of serious impact assessment including agonizing reappraisals.[10]

Policies based on conditionality such as sanctions, clauses etc. where the literature shows very uneven and sometimes

---

8    See EEAS, *EEAS Review*, 2013.
9    G Grevi, D Helly, & D Keohane, 'European Security and Defence Policy The first 10 years (1999–2009)', 2009, reviews the impact of a number of different ESDP missions and enumerates close to a hundred different problems of implementation during the first decade.
10   See for example Lehne, S, 'Time to reset the European Neighborhood Policy', Carnegie, 2014.

unprincipled performance in areas such as WMD proliferation and human rights.[11]

Policies relating to so-called strategic partners where the concept itself seems to have created considerable confusion when governments or policies in the partner countries have changed dramatically.[12]

When dealing with good and bad flows, problems in creating a coherent framework of internal and external policies covering many different types of flows ranging from transnational threats, cyber security, maritime security and the protection of energy supply.

Finally, the eternal problem of conflict and crisis prevention where crises in many areas time and again demonstrate a lack of contingency planning and sufficient efforts before the crisis has escalated to try to defuse and prevent them.

It is important to note, as the index shows, that these different types of partial failures of EU policies are not dealt with in any specific chapter of the book. Many of them reappear in chapters throughout the book from different complementary perspectives. It is argued that it is necessary to apply most if not all of these perspectives in order to optimize outcome. The fact is that individual parts of the EU structures, whether a geographical directorate in the European External Action Service, a thematic unit in a line directorate general in the Commission, or an EU delegation to an international organization are nearly never competent to apply all these perspectives. The EU therefore needs to develop a comprehensive approach.

Ideally, again, the book should have been based on clear-cut assessments of the actual impact of EU policies. Such annual assessments do exist, such as the rating of the success of EU and member states' foreign policies by the European Council for Foreign

---

11   See for example Grip, L, 'The EU non-proliferation clause: A preliminary assessment', SIPRI, background paper, 2009; Zwagemakers, F 'The EU's Conditionality Policy: A new Strategy to achieve Compliance', IAI Working papers 12, 2012.

12   See Schmidt, A, 'Strategic Partnerships – a contested policy concept; a review of recent publications', SWP, 2010.

Relations (ECFR).[13] The present study is not an attempt to replicate such studies, certainly not with an academic ambition. References to impact in this study are by necessity provided by way of examples derived from the literature or from interviews.

## Inspiration for Future Research

The chapters and the extensive bibliography illustrate that there is a serious body of literature that deals with various issues brought up throughout the book. But several problems were discovered that may be useful as a guide for future research:

> First, practitioners express a recurring dissatisfaction with existing research in a number of different areas. They often argue that research is too general to be useful for actual policy-making and that it is often made available too late to be effectively taken into account. The fact that the EU academic network for conflict prevention, created a decade ago, was discontinued indicates a serious problem in this regard.[14] It remains to be seen whether the EU Non-Proliferation Consortium will encounter the same fate. In the Horizon 2020 research programme, administered by the European Commission, there is significant funding for relevant academic research.[15] It will be interesting to see whether this investment will be more successful than previous similar attempts. Much will arguably depend on the interaction between stakeholders and researchers throughout the process.
>
> Second, it is noteworthy that research on the EU and security in an overall context is still seeking its frame of reference. A large part of the discourse on the EU as a peace project before the arrival of the Common Foreign and Security Policy (CFSP) was not explicitly securitized. Issues relating to integration within and outside the EU have for various reasons not been

---

13   See ECFR, European Foreign Policy Scorecard 2014, 2014.

14   Rummel, R, 'Die Europäische Union lernt Konfliktprävention', Konflikt-
     prävention zwischen Anspruch und Wirklichkeit, Wien 2007, pp. 39–59.

15   Including calls related to the EU as a global actor; border security and external
     security, including conflict prevention and peace building.

discussed systematically from a security perspective. And when the CFSP and the ESDP/CSDP did arrive in the late 1990s, the approach was entirely intergovernmental, with very limited interaction with the existing community framework. It was only when the Lisbon Treaty entered into force a decade later that the conditions were created in terms of both legal basis and resources for a more explicit comprehensive approach. This is obviously reflected in the literature and it will most likely take another decade for a substantial body of literature to be developed from a comprehensive perspective.[16]

In certain specific areas examined in the book there also seems to be a gap in available analytical research. One notable such area is the literature on *flows*. There is a great deal of material on transnational organized crime, financial flows, energy flows, migration flows, etc. But whereas generic models for integrated border management have been developed and described in the literature this does not seem to be the case as regards a holistic analysis of good and bad flows. It is for instance noteworthy that issues relating to WMD proliferation are not well integrated with other related issues in the literature.

The tension between different schools of thought as regards norms, power, crisis management, functional analysis, etc. also lead to questions concerning how EU security actions are to be assessed in terms of impact. Hopefully, chapters 6 and 7 in particular will generate new research. Sometimes the literature assumes that the issue is the role of the EU. Alternatively, the issue is defined as the extent to which EU partners comply with what the EU or the international community dictates. In other contexts a study may deal with the extent to which a recipient of assistance is enabled to do what is necessary in line with jointly agreed objectives. But the literature is more seldom based on systematic surveys of perceptions.[17] The proof in many situations after all is the extent to which populations

16  For recent contributions to the comprehensive approach analysis see in particular High Representative & European Commission, 'Joint Communication to the European Parliament and the Council. The EU's comprehensive approach to external conflict and crises', 2013 and other examples listed in the bibliography.

17  For a recent example of surveys of relevance which also include Russian perceptions see German Marshall Fund of the US, 'Transatlantic Trends 2014', 2014.

in other countries, as well as within the EU, find EU policies in line with their concerns and priorities and the extent to which these policies help to provide hope for the future. Restrictive policies and military force always have to be deployed with this clearly in mind.

Finally, it is noteworthy that an *evaluation of evaluations* and lessons-learned exercises undertaken so far in the EU is warranted. The evaluations undertaken ex-post of the impact of important EU assistance policies typically cover a long period of time and are still not well focused on security, with a few exceptions.[18] Questions addressed in these evaluation studies often seem to be standardized, with limited effort to address more critical questions. For example, it may be asked whether earlier evaluations of EU policies in countries affected by the Arab Spring addressed the issues that are now obvious in those countries. The present book gives a few examples in this regard. Second, lessons-learned exercises in the intergovernmental domain are often classified and not systematically subjected to academic discussion. Third, there seems to be a glaring lack of systematic application of ex-ante impact assessment in external relations, starting with the establishment of the European External Action Service itself and the communication on the comprehensive approach. Neither of these important exercises was accompanied by an analysis of the financial implications or the need for change-management capabilities, including consequences for staffing.

✤❧✤

The unique contribution of the present book is the combination of different overlapping perspectives to better identify links between various problems of impact. It is meant to show the very wide and differentiated scope of links between various aspects of EU security-related policies. The need to explore more thoroughly and more strategically the potential added value of the EU for security is demonstrated. Such an effort has seldom been made in the past few decades, certainly not with an open mind to both the intergov-

18   See chapter 6.

ernmental and Community frameworks for cooperation in the EU and not taking into account the overall civilian and defence-related potential of the Union.

This is an exploratory study to encourage further analytical and empirical work in a number of areas. Those engaged in scholarly work on the EU as a normative power and other major research traditions may find that the study starts at the wrong end. It addresses some of the main theoretical issues only in the final chapter and mainly through linking up with some of the most important theoretical discourses rather than discussing them in depth.

The present author has published some dedicated studies elsewhere on different aspects of issues dealt with in this book. These contributions range from follow-up to the European Security Strategy, the need for a comprehensive approach in EU external action, effective multilateralism, the EU and non-proliferation, inter-institutional cooperation between the Organization for Security and Co-operation in Europe (OSCE), the EU and other regional organizations in Europe, the UN and regional organizations outside Europe, the democratic legitimacy of EU security policies, etc.[19] The present study is informed by these other contributions referenced in respective chapters, but the structure of this book is adapted to the questions that are developed relating to problems of impact.

This is a study where a practitioner's experience meets theoretical analysis, rather than the other way around. The added value of the book is at the same time not the descriptive empirical material on each issue but rather the attempts to establish links between various problems of impact and to provide a broader scope for analysis. There are many books, studies, articles, and reports on

---

19   L-E Lundin, 'From A European Security Strategy to a European Global Strategy: Ten Content-Related Issues', *UI Occasional Papers* vol. 11, 2012,  L-E Lundin, 'From a European Security Strategy to a European Global Strategy: Take II: Policy options', *UI Occasional Papers* vol. 13, 2013,  L-E Lundin, 'The EU as a regional organization. Effective multilateralism in conflict management' in P Wallensteen, & A Bjurner (eds.), *Regional Organisations and Peacemaking Challengers to the UN*, L-E Lundin, 'The EU, the IAEA and the Comprehensive Approach' in S Blavoukos, D Bourantonis, & C Portela (eds.), *EU and Nuclear Nonproliferation*, Palgrave, 2015,  L-E Lundin, 'Effective Multilateralism: the EU Delegation in Vienna' in J Bátora, & S David (eds.), *European Diplomacy post-Westphalia*, Palgrave, 2015.

individual issues in the literature that go deeper and contain more solid descriptive analysis. A number of very useful and important edited volumes provide many perspectives on security issues. Sometimes they provide a set of empirical case studies that give added insight into the role of the EU as a security actor. There are also volumes such as those that the present author has contributed to that explore the added value of the EU in specific dimensions of policy. But little material was found covering the entire scope of the relationship between the EU and security: no entire volumes were found that describe a more organic link between the different paradigms analysed here.

# Introduction

Ever since the end of the Second World War, most Europeans have felt fortunate to have lived through the longest period of relative peace ever experienced on the continent. Some now take this for granted.

Is their sense of security realistic? Other people have led completely different lives in very different circumstances. Millions have little or no hope for a peaceful, let alone prosperous, future. Is there cause to hope for more security in places like Syria, Afghanistan, and Somalia? Or are these countries and their regions simply going to remain arenas where conflicts can be contained and managed but without any prospects for real solutions?

The answers to these questions must also take into account that security is increasingly perceived not only as the absence of war. It now also includes development, freedom, and justice, all part of a comprehensive concept of security.

## What role does the European Union play in this context?

This is a question that often came to mind during the writing of this book, in the three years 2012 to 2014. When the work started, most people in Central and Northern Europe saw security as a remote issue, but with the Ukraine crisis of 2013–14 it has become much more real. At this point probably few would challenge the notion that the European Union is an important security actor. However, whether the EU can be called effective in the realm of

24                                                    INTRODUCTION

security, as proposed by the EU member states in the EU Council is still debated:

> *From the EU member states' Council Conclusions on the*
> *Comprehensive Approach 2014:*
> The European Union and its Member States can bring to the
> international stage the unique ability to combine, in a coher-
> ent and consistent manner, policies and tools ranging from
> diplomacy, security and defence to finance, trade, development
> and justice.[20]

Further destabilization in the European Neighbourhood – countries to the east and south of the EU territory – not least after the
Arab Spring protests that broke out in the end of 2010, has been
an important subject of discourse. However, it was the events in
Ukraine that really brought the issues to life, as the 9/11 attacks on
the United States did in 2001. Crises make us see things in a new
light. But of course, the crux of the matter is the response to crisis
in the short, medium, and long term.

A decade ago the European Security Strategy (ESS) eloquently
defined the challenges ahead for Europe, again optimistically as
regards the future role of the European Union:

> *From the European Security Strategy 2003:* In contrast to the mas-
> sive visible threat in the Cold War, none of the new threats
> is purely military; nor can any be tackled by purely military
> means. Each requires a mixture of instruments. Proliferation
> may be contained through export controls and attacked
> through political, economic and other pressures while the
> underlying political causes are also tackled. Dealing with ter-
> rorism may require a mixture of intelligence, police, judicial,
> military and other means. In failed states, military instruments
> may be needed to restore order, humanitarian means to tackle
> the immediate crisis. Regional conflicts need political solutions
> but military assets and effective policing may be needed in the
> post conflict phase. Economic instruments serve reconstruc-

20   Council of the European Union, 'Council Conclusions on the EU's Compre-
     hensive Approach Foreign affairs Council meeting Brussels, 12 May 2014'.

tion, and civilian crisis management helps restore civil government. The European Union is particularly well equipped to respond to such multi-faceted situations.[21]

So there is a reason to explore the *added value in terms of security of the European Union to governments and individuals within and outside the Union. This book identifies problems encountered in creating this added value.*

## The main focus: Generic problems of impact

The focus of this book is on what can be called *generic problems of impact.* These are the problems, issues, challenges, or opportunities that can be expected to be relevant in the medium to long term. The notion is that – to the extent such issues can be dealt with – this may increase the impact of EU security-related policies. The problems may be directly and indirectly security-related. The main emphasis is on EU *external action.*

This study collects ideas in the literature and through interviews, referring to such problems of impact and recapitulates them, section by section throughout the text in order to help the reader see them from different angles. Each angle represents a key policy perspective in EU external action. The full arguments are concentrated in sections where this seemed useful to promote the flow of the text. Each section or perspective is organized in its own set of arguments with a structure deemed appropriate for the topic at hand. Sometimes several sets of arguments represent different sub-perspectives in a section. The recurrence of individual perspectives can be searched using the index at the end of the book.

A number of different individual perspectives are applied that are frequently discussed in the literature, but less often from a comprehensive perspective. And when they have been discussed from a broader perspective proposing a *comprehensive approach*, there is usually a single point of departure, such as conflicts, crises, geography, norms, or power. The EU treaties have for some time

---

21    'A secure Europe in a better world, European Security Strategy, Draft presented
      to the Thessaloniki European Council, 20 June 2003', 15708/03, 2003.

required coherence in the policy actions of the EU institutions. However, a comprehensive approach is more than that: it entails seeking real synergies between various policy areas as agreed by the EU member states:

> The Council stresses that the comprehensive approach is both a general working method and a set of concrete measures and processes to improve how the EU, based on a common strategic vision and drawing on its wide array of tools and instruments, collectively can develop and deliver more coherent and more effective policies, actions and results. The need for such a comprehensive approach is most acute in crisis and conflict situations and in fragile states, however, its fundamental principles are also relevant for the broad spectrum of EU external action.[22]

Comprehensive approaches require capacity building, not only in relation to key objectives in each specific policy context but also with a view to achieving these synergies.

Capacity building must be coherent with a comprehensive concept of security. This does not mean securitizing every policy area, but it does mean creating an awareness of the direct and indirect relevance of different policies for security in the comprehensive sense.

A real comprehensive approach needs to take into account the fact that implementation is not improved through a strict hierarchical ordering of perspectives, except in overall dramatic crises, but rather through an informed development of policy where each responsible actor in the system is aware of and tries to coordinate with others. In concrete terms this means that a truly comprehensive approach cannot only take as its point of departure conflicts or crises, but as many as possible of the policy approaches existing in EU external action and the problems of impact encountered in those approaches.

Broad ownership and respect for the competencies of others thus are key in combination with the realization that impact is achieved through the constant interaction of different actors and factors.

---

22   See the Council Conclusions on the Comprehensive approach, 2014.

The issue of generic problems of impact is the primary focus of the book rather than historical references to efforts to solve the problems. When discussing capacity building in order to achieve a security impact, they refer to shortfalls and when discussing projects and operations they refer to reasons for suboptimal impact.

There is a dual reason for the emphasis on problems of impact: the book is intended to help define a future-oriented agenda rather than evaluate the outcome of previous efforts to deal with the problems. This choice is in no way intended to underestimate the efforts that have been made throughout the years, nor to devalue the successes achieved. The choice of generic problems of impact is based on literature and interviews carried out in several stages over the two years 2012 to 2013.[23]

This study may help practitioners to orient themselves in their security analysis, using a broad scope. The issue is not delimited to the added value to the European Union. When asking what the EU can do for the security of its citizens, it is obvious that EU policies may also influence governments and individuals of the member states and be important in other contexts, such as NATO or the United Nations. Furthermore, one cannot assume that all readers are interested in the EU as such; they may identify with a region that includes both EU and non-EU countries, be it in the Nordic–Baltic context or in the Mediterranean setting or in the transatlantic relationship. Some continue to be worried about the notion of a 'Fortress Europe', while some have a global perspective and are primarily concerned about the security of people worldwide.

As work on this book progressed, a framework for the analysis of these problems of impact was generated that provides an overview of the main chapters (see figure 1). This framework is under constant development. The endeavour has been to make it intuitively reasonable for practitioners. It is thus not primarily analytically derived but rather based on decades of discussions with colleagues within and outside the European institutions.

The chapters were not written in a linear order. There was a conscious attempt to develop the analysis through a number of redrafts

23  Reported in several earlier studies by the current author referenced in the respective chapters below and in the bibliography.

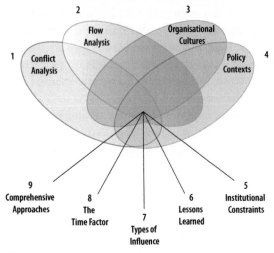

*Figure 1.*

that identified analytic links between different types of problems of impact.

## The structure of the book

The analysis is presented in each chapter based on this Venn diagram as depicted in figure 1.

The book focuses on a number of instruments and methods deployed in EU external action and to a certain extent in EU internal security-related policies of particular relevance for external action. The delimitation of the examples discussed throughout the chapters is guided mainly by the overall definition of EU external action as provided in the Treaty of Lisbon, article 21, in the context of the CFSP. This text is worth quoting in extenso:

*Article 21 Treaty on the European Union*:
1. The Union's action on the international scene shall be guided by the principles which have inspired its own creation, development and enlargement, and which it seeks to advance

in the wider world: democracy, the rule of law, the universality and indivisibility of human rights and fundamental freedoms, respect for human dignity, the principles of equality and solidarity, and respect for the principles of the United Nations Charter and international law.

The Union shall seek to develop relations and build partnerships with third countries, and international, regional or global organisations which share the principles referred to in the first subparagraph. It shall promote multilateral solutions to common problems, in particular in the framework of the United Nations.

2. The Union shall define and pursue common policies and actions, and shall work for a high degree of cooperation in all fields of international relations, in order to:

(a) safeguard its values, fundamental interests, security, independence and integrity;

(b) consolidate and support democracy, the rule of law, human rights and the principles of international law;

(c) preserve peace, prevent conflicts and strengthen international security, in accordance with the purposes and principles of the United Nations Charter, with the principles of the Helsinki Final Act and with the aims of the Charter of Paris, including those relating to external borders;

(d) foster the sustainable economic, social and environmental development of developing countries, with the primary aim of eradicating poverty;

(e) encourage the integration of all countries into the world economy, including through the progressive abolition of restrictions on international trade;

(f) help develop international measures to preserve and improve the quality of the environment and the sustainable management of global natural resources, in order to ensure sustainable development;

(g) assist populations, countries and regions confronting natural or man-made disasters; and

(h) promote an international system based on stronger multilateral cooperation and good global governance.

3. The Union shall respect the principles and pursue the objectives set out in paragraphs 1 and 2 in the development and implementation of the different areas of the Union's external action covered by this Title and by Part Five of the Treaty on the Functioning of the European Union, and of the external aspects of its other policies.

The Union shall ensure consistency between the different areas of its external action and between these and its other policies. The Council and the Commission, assisted by the High Representative of the Union for Foreign Affairs and Security Policy, shall ensure that consistency and shall cooperate to that effect.

As seen from the treaty, the scope of action for the EU is wide and there are many approaches.

Some of these approaches are aimed at capacity building, which can be seen as an intermediate measurement of success aiming at ultimate impact through the EU or in other contexts. This is important since it often entails building capacity in member states or through other actors, including international organizations, recipient countries, non-governmental organizations (NGOs), etc.

Each chapter as mentioned contains a more or less explicit chronological perspective – not simply in order to describe the interplay of the other perspectives but also to allow for the possibility that time itself may be a factor influencing impact. For instance, there is a significant time lag between when decisions to acquire defence capability are made and when they are realized. The setting up of organizational structures requires time to be effective. So sometimes, even if there is political will and the resources are at hand, it is impossible to be effective in the short term. Alternatively, in the opposite direction, the political will to make a difference may be negatively affected by time itself. As an example, the 'CNN effect' may for a certain time bring political attention to a crisis-related issue, which in turn may catalyse important decisions. Then, as these decisions are translated into programmes, projects, or missions, attention may diminish and the original political will may be translated into something else. The chronological perspective also brings out the links to different trends and megatrends, such as globalization, environmental change, and demographic developments further discussed in chapter 8.

✣❈❀

*Chapter 1* of the study opens with a discussion of security from the military perspective. The point of departure is the most well known generic problems of impact discussed in the Common European Security and Defence Policy (CSDP). First is the issue of defence as an objective in CSDP and capacity building for this purpose. Second is 1.2 crisis management, which has become a format for the use of these resources in the EU, mainly in the context of military but later also civilian crisis management. Third is 1.3 conflict prevention, illustrating generic problems of impact in preventing conflicts and crises, dealing with their aftermath, and coping with the fact that in practice CSDP operations often intervene in conflict prevention or post-conflict rehabilitation situations with the main objective to stabilize.

After having dealt on a relatively general level with these issues, which are already familiar to those interested in CSDP, the book proceeds to a second discourse in *chapter 2*, which much less often is seen as a part of overall European security and defence analysis. This discourse is not systematically integrated into CSDP but is often seen as a part of the wider CFSP. Several of the key aspects of this discourse have, however, been described by the EU member states as fundamentally important for security. They are grouped together because of the linkages between them. The issue here is flow security, where problems of impact are seen from four overlapping perspectives. The first (2.1) is closely linked to globalization as a process over time and refers to the protection and promotion of flows, such as trade, finance, energy, movement of people, etc. At the same time it highlights threats against such flows that may be due to environmental changes over time, natural or man-made hazards, etc. More or less hidden in the enormous volume of this material and virtual communication within and between states, there are also bad flows, sometimes referred to as transnational threats, beyond man-made problems of an environmental or some other nature. These may be primarily motivated by financial gains and thus take the form of organized crime[24] (2.2), including different types of trafficking. On the other hand they may have political

---

24  Sometimes in the literature described as transnational organized crime.

motives illustrated in terms of terrorism, (2.3). In a fourth section the perspective of non-proliferation of weapons of mass destruction is applied (2.4). Such a process may be state-sponsored as a part of defence policy; it can also be the object of organized crime, such as smuggling, or a part of terrorist activities. All generic problems of impact relating to good and bad flows may be overlapping and interlinked in different ways. Organized crime can be used to finance terrorism, and good flows can be exploited for criminal and terrorist purposes.

*Chapter 3* introduces a third perspective, looking at problems of impact through the lens of four organizational cultures that may be considered predominant in the EU structures. They are all familiar to students of European Union external action. The first culture, (3.1), a predominant organizing principle for the EU External Action Service (EEAS), is geography. The second (3.2) is the thematic organizing principle dominating the differentiation of European Commission structures into several dozen major policy areas. The third culture (3.3) is the multilateral organizing principle in a broader than traditional sense, basically including the negotiation of international documents between more than two parties, the representation in international organizations, and the interaction with several other states and non-state actors at the same time in various informal and formal contexts, on the international level or within specific countries. Finally, (3.4) returns to the crisis perspective, with an emphasis on the generic interface between normal bureaucratic routines, including contingency planning and crisis prevention efforts, and crisis itself, which may affect every area of EU action within and outside the Union. All of these organizational cultures, with the addition of those dealing specifically with legal, budget, and staff issues (see chapter 5), overlap, also in a bureaucratic sense since a geographic department may have thematic sub-entities and vice versa. Multilateral and crisis response departments also exist in the EEAS and several Commission Directorates-General (DGs). Again, there is a need to cross-reference the context for the CSDP in chapter 1 with that defining flow-relevant policies in chapter 2. For instance, the Central Asian regional strategy cannot be properly understood without taking into account the proximity to Afghanistan and the various problems of impact existing there that are relevant to CSDP.

The three perspectives outlined above do not apply solely to the European Union. They are equally applicable on the level of the EU member states and other actors outside the Union. But there is a fourth, more general paradigm, discussed in *chapter 4,* that is much more specific to the EU itself as a *sui generis* case of international cooperation. This fourth set of overlapping ovals addresses generic problems of impact, starting (4.1) with the dichotomy of intergovernmental and Community policies, with reference to the more general context in which they are produced. For instance, it is noteworthy that CFSP, with its integral part the CSDP, are both intergovernmental policies. They are (4.2) also fundamentally external to the Union. They are to a large extent (4.3) explicit security policies, although the scope of CFSP goes beyond security in a strict sense, including human rights, etc. As any student of the EU knows, much of the debate on EU external action and security is about getting these various policy contexts to function in synergy. One way to do that is through the double-hatting of the roles of the High Representative for foreign and security policy on the one hand and as vice-president of the European Commission on the other, through a High Representative of the Union for Foreign Affairs and Security Policy/Vice-President of the European Commission (HR/VP), as set out in the Lisbon Treaty.

In the fifth paradigm, discussed in *chapter 5,* the focus is on the interplay between the (5.1) legal, (5.2) budgetary/staff, and (5.3) structural problems of impact in EU security-related policies. The legal basis for everything that is being done in the European Union is defined with a point of departure in the treaties. Problems are linked to financial and staff resources at the disposal of the institutions for their administrative and, as regards the Commission, operational budgets. The financing of military CSDP takes place through direct financial contributions by member states. The way static and dynamic structures are set up bring additional problems.

*Chapter 6* discusses difficulties encountered in the process from the definition of problems to be addressed and the measurements of success (6.1), to impact assessment *ex ante* (6.2) and ex post (6.3) in the European Union. The acronym SMARTER (indicating that policies should be Specific, Measurable, Attainable, Relevant, Time bound and subject to Evaluation and Reevaluation) helps to structure this discussion.

In *chapter 7*, a step back is taken in a brief overview that examines the overall picture from the perspective of power and influence. This makes it clear that the EU's actions and non-actions can affect security in both planned and unplanned ways. First, the traditional discourse on power and influence (7.1) is referred to. The chapter then proceeds to discuss problems relating to 7.2 assistance, which of course is a major tool of the European Union both in terms of enabling recipients to do what they otherwise could not achieve, with or without conditionality.[25] This second discourse is closely linked to a third, the EU as a normative power (7.3), with explicit values linked to interests but also to internationally agreed commitments. The fourth section refers to the importance of perceptions (7.4). The perceptions of objects of influence is a central part of the soft power discourse where the proof of the pudding is not what the European Union does but what it is perceived as doing and what it is perceived to stand for in terms of intentions, values, etc. This fourth section, of course, raises a wide range of questions relating to impact for discussion, including how the power of attraction of the European Union has been influenced by its internal integration processes, its perceived democratic legitimacy, and hopes and expectations for the future.

*Chapter 8* contains a discussion of timelines.

*Chapter 9* contains a concluding personal reflection on the overall issue of the EU and security.

The wide scope of the book in terms of substance means of course that not all problems of impact can be identified and discussed. The choice in each section was made through enumeration rather than classification. Obviously, many issues could not be covered.

✦⁘✦

The reader will note the inclusion of quite a number of explicit quotations from EU official documents, starting with Article 21 of the Lisbon Treaty on the European Union and continuing with a number of explicit and detailed references to agreements among the EU Member States in the EU. As EU practitioners will know a detailed

---

25  Conditionality is commonly defined as the use of conditions attached to the provision of benefits such as a loan, debt relief or bilateral aid.

analysis of such texts is essential to understand the declared level of agreement in the EU on key issues discussed in this book.

The present book seeks to raise awareness. Readers will find many questions – and they may or may not agree with some statements. The study is intended to help those, notably practitioners, who are seeking a broader overview in an area under constant development, with very wide and overlapping concepts, structures, and activities.

The premise when defining the target audience is that many people play a role in security beyond simply being affected by security problems themselves. This is true if they are working on the national or international level, in civil society organizations, in business or in government. Indeed, many people have to take security issues into account in their work even if their work objectives are not explicitly security-related.

❧❦

The book takes a medium-term outlook. This means several things. First, it has to avoid excessive detail and focus on generic problems. Had it been written five years ago it would have been largely irrelevant today if it had contained a detailed description of the structure of the European security institutions before the entry into force of the Lisbon Treaty, in 2009.

This study is designed to avoid some of these pitfalls. Empirical examples are used rather than attempting to create a handbook of facts and figures, focusing on perspectives that may be of more general relevance for the future. The ambition is to be thought-provoking rather than a source of facts.

There are many time perspectives in the book that refer to developments over the past few decades and show that history is still relevant. This refers to the period until more or less the end of the 1990s with the entry into force of the Amsterdam Treaty, the birth of the CSDP, and the end of the pre-9/11 period with regard to terrorism. Then there is the period until the entry into force of the Lisbon Treaty. Finally, there is the period from the entry into force of the Lisbon Treaty and the setting up of the European External Action Service (EEAS) in 2010 with a future perspective.

This division into periods is not always applicable, however. For instance, in the area of development there is another, perhaps more

important chronological set of milestones. As always when discussing security, an area requiring extensive investments in structures
and equipment, one has to be aware of the fact that investments in
capacity building that will be made in the coming decade need to
be relevant for at least 10–20 years. This book therefore needs to
refer to some discussions that may seem theoretical or unrealistic,
but this is necessary for any discussion of a long period. Finally,
trends are important and the spectrum of uncertainty in this regard
needs to be taken into account. Some recent trend-related studies
are referred to.

Opening minds to possible future trends is not easy. When
the author started as a young research assistant with the task
of interviewing Swedish security elites in the early 1970s about
their perceptions of security, the appetite for speculation among
respondents was limited: the world was nuclear and bipolar, and
the cold war entirely dominated security perceptions. The name
of the potentially deadly game was military. But in fact it would
have been useful to be more receptive to change. Very soon other
factors entered the security equation, starting with the energy crisis
in 1973. It is also important to keep in mind that a situation which
at any point in time may be perceived as almost static is a snap-
shot of a process of change, which may be visible only in a longer
perspective. The cold war ended not so long ago. One does not
have to work with a 40 to 50 year perspective in order to observe
fundamental changes in the international system. As regards the
European Union and its role in security policy it is enough to go
back 10–15 years to see a completely different situation. The ESDP
did not exist before 1999. At the same time this is an area with
an uncertain future in many ways as regards both the role of the
European Union and the overall security challenges ahead.

The EU is undergoing constant change, so there is great uncertainty about how things will develop. For instance, for a large part
of the first decade of this millennium there was a fundamental
uncertainty about whether what became the Lisbon Treaty would
ever enter into force. The second decade started with a period of
uncertainty about the future of the euro, the UK's membership of
the EU, and the prospects for further enlargement of the Union,
not least in view of the serious financial crisis then. But work had
to continue. People working at higher or even lower levels cannot

stop and wait for things to become more clear. It is important to learn to function well under uncertainty and stress in a system such as the European Union.

The EU deals primarily with problems in a normalcy mode – crises are reacted to when they happen. At the same time crises also occur that require efforts over longer periods. A major example is the financial crisis, which has required enormous effort and crisis management capability on the part of the European Council and the European Commission for many years. The current crisis in EU relations with Russia will no doubt pose a longer-term problem. At the same time Europe has so far not been hit by a multi-sector crisis such as the one Japan faced in 2011, but it cannot be excluded as a future possibility.

❧❧❧

This book operates on two levels.

First, it appears in early 2015, when a new set of leaders in the EU institutions in Brussels will commence their work for a five-year period, importantly the newly elected European Parliament. Hopefully, many are looking for ideas, strategies, and material to underpin a new plan of action for giving the EU added security value in a broad sense, which requires an overall identification of generic problems of impact. This book is intended to contribute to that debate, to that brainstorming exercise, which is so important for the coming years.

Second, on a deeper level, the book should inspire some soul-searching on the part of readers who, like the present author, may have reason to re-evaluate their assessments of security and more specifically the role of the European Union in the context of security. It should be recognized that this is an extremely contaminated area in terms of cognitive biases not only with regard to the European Union.

Deliberation about European security is to an important extent about the United States, that is, positive and negative assessments of how Americans affected security in Europe and worldwide. It is also about the Russian Federation and the need to situate thinking in the post-post-cold war setting, when Russia is re-establishing itself as a regional and possibly a global power, even using methods of the Soviet past. It is about the EU Neighborhood Policy (ENP) and the Neighborhood of the Neighborhood – about trying to understand and view these areas with more respect for these states' problems as well as their culture and history, above all with a less Eurocentric perspective.

Underestimating generic problems of impact is an overarching fallacy in any foreign policy context focusing on the power and influence of major players. A second fallacy relates to the choice of instruments and the way in which people try to exert influence. There are many examples of questionable measurements of success, misunderstandings of situations, and a glaring lack of lessons learned. But many hopeful signs for the future seen from the perspective of soft power will also appear, finding common ground, focusing on interaction between civil societies, etc. In this sense this book is not cynical or deterministic: things can change, but change will often require agonizing reappraisals of policies that have been pursued over long periods of time.[26]

26   Kuhn, T S, *The Structure of Scientific Revolutions*, 2 ed., University of Chicago Press, 1970.

# 1. The Conflict Cycle

*Chapter 1* of the study opens with a discussion of security from the military perspective. The point of departure is the most well known generic problems of impact discussed in the Common European Security and Defence Policy (CSDP). First is the issue of defence as an objective in CSDP and capacity building for this purpose. Second is 1.2 crisis management, which has become a format for the use of these resources in the EU, mainly in the context of military but later also civilian crisis management. Third is 1.3 conflict prevention, illustrating generic problems of impact in preventing conflicts and crises, dealing with their aftermath, and coping with the fact that in practice CSDP operations often intervene in conflict prevention or post-conflict rehabilitation situations with the main objective to stabilize.

## 1.1 Defence

*From the European Security Strategy 2003:* A more capable Europe is within our grasp, though it will take time to realise our full potential. Actions underway – notably the establishment of a defence agency – take us in the right direction.

To transform our militaries into more flexible, mobile forces, and to enable them to address the new threats, more resources for defence and more effective use of resources are necessary.

Should European integration include defence? Many would say no: this is a task for NATO in the transatlantic format. There is no EU agreement to set up a European army or to deal with territorial defence in a traditional sense.

The operational side of European defence policy is situated in the context of crisis management, which is dealt with in the next section as a sub-paradigm under the conflicts heading.

Nonetheless, the issue of defence is explicitly referred to in the context of the European Common Security and Defence Policy (CSDP). There is also an intergovernmental European Defence Agency (EDA) that focuses on defence capabilities.[1] The possibility of a European Defence Community was discussed as early as in the 1950s: the Western European Union (WEU) included a defence commitment and some of the legacy of WEU efforts has been transferred to the legal framework of the European Union.[2]

Indeed, the European Security Strategy (ESS) sets an ambitious goal not only for EU action but also for the transformation of member states' defence systems.

A number of member states insist on retaining the intergovernmental nature of this cooperation in the EU, with full respect for state sovereignty. The Article 5 defence commitment is solidly anchored in NATO even if a solidarity clause[3] with unclear implica-

1    EEAS Website: "The European Defence Agency's mission is to develop defence
     capabilities; promote defence research and technology (R&T); foster arma-
     ments co-operation; and to create a competitive European Defence Equipment
     Market as well as to strengthen the European Defence, Technological and
     Industrial Base. The Agency is funded by its members in proportion to their
     GNP. This budget covers the Agency's operating costs; individual projects
     are funded separately. The EDA is governed by its Steering Board, which
     meets at the level of defence ministers. The Head of the Agency is the High
     Representative of the Union for Foreign Affairs and Security Policy."

2    Article 4 of the 1948 WEU Treaty of Brussels stipulated that "if any of the High
     Contracting Parties should be the object of an armed attack in Europe, the
     other High Contracting Parties will, in accordance with the provisions of article
     51 of the Charter of the United Nations, afford the party so attacked all the
     military and other aid and assistance in their power." This clause has its succes-
     sion in the EU's Treaty of Lisbon.

3    http://europa.eu/legislation_summaries/glossary/solidarity_clause_en.htm
     http://www.lisbon-treaty.org/wcm/the-lisbon-treaty/treaty-on-the-function-
     ing-of-the-european-union-and-comments/part-5-external-action-by-the-
     union/title-7-solidarity-clause/510-article-222.html.
     From the EEAS Website: "The (Lisbon) Treaty introduces solidarity and mutu-

tions in terms of defence was introduced into the Lisbon Treaty. CSDP remains an intergovernmental policy area in the context of the Common Foreign and Security Policy (CFSP).

## Evolution of the key objective: Military capacity building

The literature on the development of the CSDP often takes as a point of departure the British-French St Malo Declaration of 1998:

*From the St Malo UK-France summit declaration 1998:*
The Heads of State and Government of France and the United Kingdom are agreed that:
1. The European Union needs to be in a position to play its full role on the international stage. This means making a reality of the Treaty of Amsterdam, which will provide the essential basis for action by the Union.

It will be important to achieve full and rapid implementation of the Amsterdam provisions on CFSP. This includes the responsibility of the European Council to decide on the progressive framing of a common defence policy in the framework of CFSP. The Council must be able to take decisions on an intergovernmental basis, covering the whole range of activity set out in Title V of the Treaty of European Union.
2. To this end, the Union must have the capacity for autonomous action, backed up by credible military forces, the means to decide to use them, and a readiness to do so, in order to respond to international crises. In pursuing our objective, the

---

al assistance clauses. The former states that 'the Union and its Member States shall act jointly in a spirit of solidarity if an EU Member State is the object of a terrorist attack or the victim of a natural or man-made disaster' (TFEU Art. 222). The mutual assistance clause, inspired by Article V of the WEU Treaty, states that 'if a Member State is the victim of armed aggression on its territory, the other Member States shall have towards it an obligation of aid and assistance by all the means in their power, in accordance with Article 51 [the right to self-defence] of the United Nations Charter. This shall not prejudice the specific character of the security and defence policy of certain Member States' (TEU Art. 42.7). The clause, however, includes a caveat that 'commitments and cooperation in this area shall be consistent with commitments under the North Atlantic Treaty Organisation, which, for those States which are members of it, remains the foundation of their collective defence and the forum for its implementation'."

collective defence commitments to which member states sub-
scribe (set out in Article 5 of the Washington Treaty, Article v
of the Brussels Treaty) must be maintained.[4]

So how did the St Malo Declaration[5] pave the way for subsequent
EU agreements towards the end of the 1990s and what did this
imply in terms of defence? The commonly agreed minimum objective in terms of impact can be summarized in one term: *capacity
building*.

It was believed from the start that EU efforts to promote military
capacity building could boost the effectiveness and support the
defence efforts of member states. It was recognized that member states could decide to use this capacity in their own national
defence, in NATO, and thus as a contribution to burden sharing
with the United States[6] in the United Nations or the Organization
for Security and Co-operation in Europe (OSCE) – in addition to
European Union crisis management operations proper. But also
here, the added value to be provided by EU efforts referred mainly
to capacity building, and measurements of success were clearly
related to a number of benchmarks defined in the 1999 Military
Helsinki Headline Goals (HLG) and subsequent commitments
undertaken in the framework of the ESDP (after the entry into
force of the Lisbon Treaty called the CSDP).

The first goal was quite quantitative in character:

*From the EEAS Website:*
[EU member states] will be able to deploy rapidly and then
sustain forces capable of the full range of Petersberg tasks as
set out in the Amsterdam Treaty [Petersberg tasks], including
the most demanding, in operations up to corps level (up to 15
brigades or 50,000–60,000 persons). These forces should be
militarily self-sustaining with the necessary command, control

---

4   Joint Declaration issued at the British-French Summit (Saint-Malo, 4
    December 1998).

5   http://www.atlanticCommunity.org/Saint-Malo%20Declaration%20Text.html.

6   Howorth, J, *European integration and defence: The ultimate challenge?*, Institute
    for Security Studies, Western European Union, 2000; Lindstrom, G, 'EU-US
    burdensharing: who does what? *Chaillot Paper* No. 82', IISS, http://www. iss-
    eu.org/chaillot/chai82.pdf (13.12.2005) 2005.

and intelligence capabilities, logistics, other combat support services and additionally, as appropriate, air and naval elements. Member States should be able to deploy in full at this level within 60 days, and within this to provide smaller rapid response elements available and deployable at very high readiness. They must be able to sustain such a deployment for at least one year.

Later in the next decade more qualitative requirements were developed.

Which have been some of the most obvious problems of impact in relation to these capacity-building goals? The present study does not dwell on technicalities but rather focuses on the more generally discussed issues of relevance.

### Fundamental problems of impact

First, not all EU member states were members of NATO, which posed a problem in terms of interoperability[7] of defence equipment. Even if they had been members of both the EU and NATO, their national defence systems still had different configurations depending on their specific threat perceptions. For instance, Greece has a very different type of defence system from Belgium's. It was therefore a problem of impact that capacity building on the EU level meant very different things to different member states. The agreed benchmarks required the definition of a lowest common denominator for capacity building across all the member states, in itself a significant problem of impact. This introduced the need to discuss and try to harmonize threat perceptions.

Furthermore, not all the EU member states were producing defence equipment[8] and some, if not all, were heavily dependent on the procurement of weapon systems from outside Europe, primarily from the United States.[9] It was therefore a struggle to define at least the minimum level of ambition to make such production in

---

7   Ashton, C, 'Preparing the December 2013 European Council on Security and Defence Interim Report by the High Representative', 2013.

8   http://ec.europa.eu/enterprise/sectors/defence/index_en.htm

9   http://students.washington.edu/nupsa/Docs/Volume4/Wes_Steinbach_European_Military-Industrial_Complex.pdf

the EU more cost-effective. The point of departure was a protec-
tionist system where even the most basic form of division of labour
between member states' industries was made difficult at national
borders. Just the cost of processing the transfer of defence equipment parts across borders could be measured in hundreds of millions of euros per year.[10] This was then one of the first issues to be
discussed in a Council working party towards the end of the 1990s,
as it had already been discussed – but not resolved – by the Western
European Union. Alleviating these problems has required a long-
term process of dialogue and cooperation in the European Union
where one aspect of the way ahead was outlined by EU member states
in the Council in a December 2013 session dedicated to defence:

*From the European Council conclusions on defence, December 2013:*
To ensure the long-term competitiveness of the European
defence industry and secure the modern capabilities needed,
it is essential to retain defence Research & Technology (R&T)
expertise, especially in critical defence technologies. The
European Council invites the Member States to increase
investment in cooperative research programmes, in particular
collaborative investments, and to maximise synergies between
national and EU research.
   Civilian and defence research reinforce each other, including
in key enabling technologies and on energy efficiency technology.

Third, in member states, defence production was usually an
integral part of general industrial research and development. The
defence sector was important in terms of both employment and
technological progress for the economy of a number of these states.
The issue of indigenous defence production was therefore a significant domestic problem. In the EU context, the discourse had to be
broadened beyond the otherwise well-defined intergovernmental
context. This was clearly shown in several studies of the industry
and the EU institutions carried out during the first years of this
millennium. Key areas included the future of the aircraft and space
industries as well as research.

10   Finally resolved through an EU directive see http://ec.europa.eu/enterprise/sec-
     tors/defence/legislation/transfers/index_en.htm

The issue of capacity building thus requires the involvement of actors in a large number of Community policy areas in order to boost defence industry productivity, ranging from trade to industry to research, including thematic sectors such as informatics, transport (including air traffic controls), etc. By 2013 EU leaders had come a long way towards acknowledging this:

> *From the European Council conclusions on defence, December 2013:*
> A well-functioning defence market based on openness,
> equal treatment and opportunities, and transparency for all
> European suppliers is crucial. The European Council welcomes
> the Commission communication "Towards a more competitive
> and efficient defence and security sector". It notes the inten-
> tion of the Commission to develop, in close cooperation with
> the High Representative and the European Defence Agency,
> a roadmap for implementation. It stresses the importance of
> ensuring the full and correct implementation and application
> of the two defence Directives of 2009, inter alia with a view
> to opening up the market for subcontractors from all over
> Europe, ensuring economies of scale and allowing a better cir-
> culation of defence products.

Discussions of capacity building were also intimately linked to the fact that the industrial format in which this development took place was truly multinational. Even if the final product assembly was domestic, it was typically dependent on key parts from the United States.[11] The companies had to be able to participate in the global market in a level playing field with US companies and others, an issue of trade and bilateral relations with the United States.[12] All this indicated a series of problems of impact that could be addressed mainly by the EU in the Community context. This in turn required a process of both domestic and EU-level debate on joint EU efforts to improve what is called the defence technology industrial base (DTIB),[13] which is also a very long-term process.

---

11  http://ec.europa.eu/enterprise/sectors/defence/files/final_report_trans_en.pdf
12  http://ec.europa.eu/enterprise/sectors/aerospace/files/report_star21_screen_en.pdf
13  http://www.eda.europa.eu/Aboutus/Whatwedo/strategies/technologicalandin-
    dustrialbase

### *Focus so far on intergovernmental cooperation – but potential for significant progress on the Community side*

Work has so far been incremental, rather focussing on identifying a few areas of potential cooperation between member states, with emphasis on issues of particular importance in terms of capability shortfalls identified when evaluating progress towards the Helsinki Headline Goals. EDA is an intergovernmental agency that has had to be built up from scratch and depend on the mobilization of non-existent budgets in the EU context.

Although some progress was achieved over the years, even a dedicated European Council in December 2013 could not achieve more than point-by-point agreement on cooperative efforts in a few specific impact areas. The improvement of the conditions for the EDA's effectiveness is a process that has been going on for over a decade.

On the side of the Community, the political conditions for significant progress were not promising. General provisions promoting more effective defence production in the entire EU space were effectively counteracted by a number of member states' concerns about the effects on their own defence production. This concern was of course exacerbated by the financial crisis from 2008. Countries such as the UK, focusing on very close cooperation with the United States in the defence sector, remained ambivalent. The hostility against a Community approach was fuelled by the debate before and after ratification of the Lisbon Treaty.

Still, after a slow start in the early years of the millennium, a decade later the European Commission had defined a number of issues that needed to be dealt with in the Community framework. At the time of writing, it remains to be seen whether recent conflict-related crises in the European Neighbourhood would strengthen support for more European efforts in capacity building using the Community potential.

For reasons also related to bilateral relations with the US a number of EU member states developed an ambition to acquire a capacity to participate in international military operations more actively from the 1990s, within and outside the EU framework. In the EU context this meant creating new concepts, including the *EU battle group*, which involved a readiness to engage based on cooperation between groups of member states.[14] However, several problems negatively affected this capacity-building process. First, there was increased domestic concern over the lack of progress in the military operations in which some member states were engaged, notably in Iraq and Afghanistan. Already in the period 2005–2010 this led to acrimonious debates in countries such as the Netherlands about participation in such perilous operations.[15] It also started to dawn not least on finance ministers that participation in international operations depleted resources; equipment had to be replaced and new equipment had to be bought that better corresponded to field conditions that often were not the same as those in Europe.

Indicators of military capability continue to reveal the increasing gap between US and European efforts.[16] European defence spending in relation to US spending has in recent decades continued to decline in percentage terms, and output in terms of deployability has been further decimated. Then, real alarm signals about contradictions between territorial defence objectives and objectives in capacity building for international operations started to be registered. The fragility of the Middle East and North Africa hit the south European member states and then a similar, perhaps even stronger effect was created by the Ukraine crisis. Europe found itself with fundamental shortfalls and low deployability. The technological evolution did not make defence equipment cheaper; on the contrary, the cost of protectionism, domestic interest groups, and differing threat perceptions multiplied over the years.

The issue of the relative utility of conventional defence also surfaced from time to time. For many, among the lessons they learned

---

14 EEAS website: "The Battle Group Concept, endorsed at the informal meeting of defence ministers in Brussels in April 2004 became a central part of the Headline Goal 2010. Battle Groups are high-readiness forces consisting of 1,500 personnel who can be deployed within 10 days after an EU decision to launch an operation and that can be sustained for up to 30 days (extendable to 120 days with rotation). At the 2004 Military Capability Commitment Conference, Member States made an initial commitment to the formation of 13 EU Battle Groups, with the aim of always having two Battle Groups on standby. On 1 January 2007, the EU Battle Group Concept reached full operational capacity. To date, the EU Battle Groups have yet to be deployed."

15 http://www.worldpoliticsreview.com/articles/7669/the-netherlands-and-afghanistan-nato-solidarity-vs-war-wariness

16 http://strategicstudiesinstitute.army.mil/pubs/parameters/Articlesautumn/coonen.pdf

from the cold war was the notion that what mattered for real safety and security in Europe was nuclear deterrence. It was believed that in the early phases of an East-West war battlefield nuclear weapons were likely to be used.[17] All these factors taken together constituted a major set of problems. Together they can lead to the perception that European conventional defence efforts have an uncertain added value.

These overall questions became a serious subject of debate when Russia started to engage in actual post-cold war military operations in Europe, as was the case in Georgia in 2008 and in Ukraine from 2014. The latter is a conflict which at the time of writing can be seen as a precursor to a new period when the relevance of European territorial defence is again considered urgent and issues related to readiness levels are again being put on the table in EU member states. Here the spotlight is on NATO, and in NATO primarily on the early mobilization of US capabilities to demonstrate limits to what is acceptable for the Western world in terms of Russian use of military resources.

But in parallel a debate has already started about what is possible for the EU to do through more cost-effective defence production. For the first time for many decades this debate may focus not on burden sharing with the United States in an abstract sense but on identifiable European threat perceptions.

### A broader perspective on problems of impact in the area of defence

Chapter 2 discusses flows and the security of flows. This has been a major issue in the development of US defence doctrines for obvious reasons relating to energy, trade, etc. The European Union and its member states have long relied on the US contribution to the safety of the seas and on the unhindered availability of essential raw materials from outside Europe.

However, piracy around the Horn of Africa has contributed to introduce a new defence-related discourse in the EU debate. The Western European Union had been discussing Mediterranean security since the 1990s[18] and started to look at needs in terms of

17   https://www.fas.org/sgp/crs/nuke/RL32572.pdf
18   http://www.geetha.mil.gr/index.asp?a_id=3704

naval cooperation. But the threat perceptions were never as concrete as those related to the piracy developing around the imploding societies on the Horn of Africa. So far many have been taken for granted that there is a shared US-European interest in containing this threat worldwide and that as a consequence US taxpayers will have to be willing to pay for the cost of maintaining readiness.

Several factors, however, contradict the notion that the US' willingness to contribute to European defence will stay at the same level over the coming decades, a fundamental problem of impact for Europe in terms of security. First, there is the US pivot towards Asia in general. Second, there is a potentially reduced US dependence on energy from abroad due to the development of shale gas technology. Third, there is the issue of the weakness of the US economy which already has led to the Obama Administration's sharper focus on the domestic agenda and decisions on important cuts in defence expenditure.

A second feature related to flows is the link to cyber security[19] and indirectly to the protection of critical infrastructure, finance, etc. The awareness of the security problems related to these issues was clearly upgraded in the EU some years after the ESS, in 2003:

*From the Review of the implementation of the European Security Strategy 2008:*
Modern economies are heavily reliant on critical infrastructure including transport, communication and power supplies, but also the internet.

One of the notable decisions taken at the European Council on defence in 2013 was to include cyber security as an objective in the cooperative framework of European defence. This is probably only the beginning of a discourse that will increase in intensity and priority over the coming decades, given the rapidly increasing vulnerability of modern societies, creating new problems in terms of securing business continuity in many critical societal systems. This problem was taken up by the Clinton Administration in the 1990s

---

19   Clarke, R 'War From cyberspace', National Interest 2009, Tehan, R, 'Cyber
     security: Authoritative reports and resources', Congressional Research Service,
     2012.

in the context of counterterrorism[20] but it later become a much broader issue. It is now a part of not only the defence discourse but also the issue of organized crime. A number of EU Community endeavours are already reaching a critical mass in terms of relevance to cyber security. A crisis response capability in the EU will perhaps not be military in the first instance because these virtual flows cannot be defined in terms of internal or external action.

Developments in flow-related technologies are highly demanding for defence since European defence efforts traditionally, with the exception of certain flagship units in the air force, etc., did not build on state-of-play technology. Even if they did, at the time of production the technologies soon became outdated by the very rapid technological developments. In terms of cyber security this is measured in months rather than years. In a sector where technological superiority is of fundamental importance, addressing cyber technology issues in defence is likely to be a major problem related to globalization.

It is, however, also a major defence problem for other actors, not least the Russian Federation. The difficulties to acquire the latest technology were already a major problem for the Soviet Union, and since then globalization in terms of technological development has accelerated enormously.

An additional factor limiting the willingness to invest in European defence capabilities through the European Union has of course been the limited willingness to accept casualties in conflicts. The casualties in Afghanistan and other wars have in recent decades had a dramatic impact on domestic public opinion not only in Europe but also in other developed societies around the world. Also here the issue of where technological developments might lead has already started to be more openly discussed.[21] The degree to which drone technology is accepted for use in conflicts will have a major impact on the European defence debate. Many ethical and international legal aspects are involved. The argument used to promote the use of drones is that they open up new possibilities for states to contribute to international military operations without incurring significant casualties. Depending on where the European discus-

---

20   https://www.fas.org/irp/offdocs/pdd/pdd-63.htm
21   http://www.jamesigoewalsh.com/drone.pdf

sions on these issues land, not least in the European Parliament, this may become a factor in the debate on how to reduce problems of impact in demanding cases of conflict.

However, this will not solve problems that are now increasingly encountered in fragile countries where EU civilian personnel need to be present for humanitarian and development assistance tasks. The increased frequency of hostage taking for not only terrorist but also criminal purposes can bring potentially frightening implications for the capabilities of the European Union to promote post-conflict rehabilitation and be effective in conflict prevention and development. This may deter member states from developing capabilities for defence in international operations overall.[22] The idea that all development workers need to be integrated in provincial reconstruction teams,[23] as was the case in Afghanistan, is not likely to be generally supported through allocations in European defence budgets.

## *Will current crises reanimate the European defence debate?*

In summary, the perceived need to safeguard the sovereignty of EU member states through defence measures and to protect national industrial interests as well as the financial crisis and other threats felt particularly acutely by European citizens have for a long time hampered the EU contribution to member states' defence capabilities. The initial but limited enthusiasm to deploy in EU-specific military crisis management operations (see further below) has been replaced by a widespread scepticism about the relative value of such operations, which in turn arguably has had a negative effect on the willingness to invest in capacity building.

A number of trends outlined in this section point to an almost indistinguishable link between defence and civilian technology, between civilian and military threats, and between globalization and national security. These developments arguably point in the direction of an increased relevance of efforts through the European Community rather than only through intergovernmental efforts.

---

22   http://privatewww.essex.ac.uk/~ksg/esrcjsps/Hinkkainen.pdf

23   McArthur, S, 'Provincial Reconstruction Teams', http://atlismta.org/online-journals/0607-journal-development.-challenges/provincial-reconstruction-teams/.

The impact of crisis has been and is likely to continue to be fundamental for the analysis of EU security policies as a catalyst for a greater willingness to address generic problems of impact. The literature frequently makes the observation that the absence of crisis leads to an unwillingness to invest in defence capabilities. What is more, as long as the United States and NATO take a primary role this is also argued to negatively affect the willingness to develop the CSDP. The crisis in and around Ukraine has in early 2014 animated the European security policy debate in a way not seen since 9/11 and perhaps not even since the end of the cold war. The impact on EU contributions to capacity building in defence, however, is still difficult to predict.

## 1.2 Crisis Management

*Evolution of the key objective: To deploy crisis management operations*
EU crisis management efforts are often described as a series of ad hoc events in response to specific situations, where the measurement of success typically is the number of operations. Neither the end state at the time of the withdrawal of the operation nor its sustainable impact is systematically made the focus of success.

As was the case after the First World War, the United States and the European states quickly cashed in on what they believed to be the new situation and the new requirements after the cold war. The United States, which had deployed a quarter of a million troops in West Germany alone, rapidly started to redeploy out of Europe.[24] At the same time most EU member states started to restructure their armed forces and downsize them drastically, in some cases much further than was required by the Treaty on Conventional Armed Forces in Europe (CFE), signed between NATO and the Warsaw Pact in 1990.

In contrast, rather than entering the new phase colourfully described by Francis Fukuyama as the end of history and the

---

24  http://www.heritage.org/research/reports/2004/10/global-us-troop-deployment-1950-2003

prospect of a democratic future,[25] the United Nations found itself overwhelmed by requirements for peacekeeping intervention after the cold war. The number of UN peacekeepers increased worldwide from around 10,000 to 100,000 in just a few years' time. Genocides committed in Africa in the mid-1990s revived memories of the Biafra war in the late 1960s but there was little international response and strong criticism against several European governments as well as the USA. The implosion of fragile countries progressed, not least in the Horn of Africa.

Individual EU member states were called on to respond to the genocides in Central Africa. However, even more obvious was the responsibility to do something about the situation in the Western Balkans after the cold war where there was a return to conflict situations experienced even before the First World War. The rotating presidency of the European Union Council, in the person of the Luxembourg Foreign Minister Jacques Poos, took on the challenge, declaring that this was the 'Hour of Europe'.[26] For the first time a serious expectation was created for the European Union to do something about a major crisis, also in military terms.

But there was little to substantiate the claim that the EU could make a serious impact. There was no agreement on the conceptual basis, there was an insufficient legal basis, and there was no real institutional foundation for an EU role.

The focus of this section is therefore on the dual discussion of capacity-building aspects of crisis management undertaken by the EU itself and the problems of impact met in the implementation of crisis management policies of the EU in CSDP.

A conceptual discussion started in the 1990s in parallel in the Western European Union and the European Union in the context of a more general debate about peacekeeping, taking place on different levels. There was the Agenda for Peace in the United Nations, a debate about peacekeeping in the OSCE, focusing not least on potential so-called third-party peacekeeping in the area of the former Soviet Union. There was a broadened dialogue initiated by US President Clinton and hosted by NATO in the context of

25  Fukuyama, F, *The End of the History and the Last Man*, Reprint ed., Penguin
    Books, 1992
26  Guicherd, C, 'The Hour of Europe: Lessons from the Yugoslav Conflict',
    *Fletcher Forum of World Affairs*, 1993

its outreach for the Partnership for Peace, involving many of the same states as the membership of the OSCE. The discourse was to a large extent also multilateral between the international organizations, highlighting major problems in terms of duplication and bad coordination. For a short while, discussion of the issues who should do what, in what type of situations, and in what areas was genuinely open. Some, including NATO, spoke about the need for mutually reinforcing institutions, while others warned about the risk of international organizations contradicting and blocking each other.

The EU contributed a proposal put forward in the OSCE in the mid-1990s for a Platform for Cooperative Security between international organizations. This concept became a part of the European Security Charter adopted by heads of state and government in the OSCE at the Istanbul summit in 1999. Participants witnessed the appearances of two outgoing presidents, Yeltsin and Clinton, and the start of another new period in international relations that would be characterized by the 9/11 attacks, much less interest in multilateral solutions by the US government, and a rather different and less cooperative Russian posture under Vladimir Putin.

It was already clear from the peacekeeping operations deployed in Bosnia and elsewhere in the Western Balkans that this was not just a discussion of operations taking place based on chapter 6 of the United Nations Charter requiring consent between the parties.[27] It was not always clear who the parties were. Whereas the number of interstate conflicts started to decline after the cold war, the opposite was the case for intrastate conflicts with sometimes very diffuse lines of contact. Increasingly, peacekeepers found themselves involved in operations to protect human lives against elusive entities. Somewhat more robust rules of engagement would be necessary and now, if mandated by the United Nations, based on its chapter 7.[28] In NATO, this led to the adoption of another, broader concept: peace support operations.[29]

What could and should the WEU and later the EU do? A proposed definition of what came to be called the Petersberg Tasks

---

27  http://www.un.org/en/documents/charter/chapter6.shtml
28  http://www.un.org/en/documents/charter/chapter7.shtml
29  http://www.nato.int/docu/sec-partnership/html_en/nato_secur06.html

had been developed in the debate, including contributions from non-EU and non-WEU members Finland and Sweden[30] both acceding to the EU only in 1995. This enumeration of potential tasks was first elaborated in the former framework of the Western European Union and then transferred into the European Union after the St Malo Declaration in 1998:

*From the EEAS Website:*
The Petersberg tasks were first agreed upon at the June 1992 Western European Union (WEU) Council of Ministers near Bonn, Germany. Article 11.4 of the subsequent ministerial declaration outlined the following three purposes for which military units could be deployed:
- humanitarian and rescue tasks;
- peacekeeping tasks;
- tasks of combat forces in crisis management, including peacemaking.

The term 'peacemaking' was adopted as a consensual solution and as a synonym for 'peace-enforcement'. The Petersberg tasks were subsequently incorporated into Article 17 of the Treaty of the European Union (TEU) through the Treaty of Amsterdam. The 2009 Treaty of Lisbon (TEU Art. 42) then further expanded these tasks to include:
- humanitarian and rescue tasks;
- conflict prevention and peace-keeping tasks;
- tasks of combat forces in crisis management, including peacemaking;
- joint disarmament operations;
- military advice and assistance tasks;
- post-conflict stabilisation tasks.

For member states the added value of participating in EU crisis management operations differed according to their defence policies. International military operations had traditionally a low standing in terms of perceived added value of defence for many

---

30 A joint article by the Finnish and Swedish Foreign Ministers Halonen and Hjelm Wallén in *Dagens Nyheter* and *Helsinki Sanomat* 1996.

member states – but not for all. The latter included France, which even in peacetime in Europe expected to be engaged in military operations, notably in Africa. The United Kingdom saw value in training interoperability with NATO. One major operation with the USA had been undertaken in Iraq in 1991 and it revealed major deficiencies.

In Europe, NATO effectively set the stage for the definition and actual deployment of peace support operations of a new kind, not necessarily based on approval in UN Security Council resolutions but directly based on the principles of international law. In Kosovo in 1999, NATO intervened against Serbian aggression in what its Secretary-General Javier Solana called a humanitarian intervention. At that point there was, as mentioned above, an agreement in principle on an EU role in crisis management between the UK and France at St Malo. The Kosovo operation illustrated the level of capabilities that would be necessary in order to make a real difference in an escalated situation. For most EU member states, it became obvious not only that capacity building in CSDP required interoperability with NATO in a general sense. It also seemed natural that if the European Union deployed a crisis management operation it would for some time need to cover up some of its major shortfalls in cooperation with NATO and reach agreement on being able to use NATO as the operational line of command. This meant that the emergence of an EU military staff was limited to define the strategic concept for an operation. The link to the field would go through NATO where EU-led forces would operate.

### Initial focus on military crisis management in cooperation with NATO

This was the model chosen for the first two EU military operations in the Former Yugoslav Republic of Macedonia (FYROM) and Bosnia, taking over and rebranding earlier NATO operations in those two countries, providing an important opportunity to exercise, and enhancing interoperability with NATO. The operations were important but not so challenging that significant attention could not be given to the parallel development of a series of modalities and procedures, including cooperation with NATO.

This brief historical background is important in order to understand the emergence of crisis management policies in the

European Union. The cooperation with NATO and adaptation to NATO thinking and rules introduced a whole set of opportunities but also serious difficulties for the European Union. These problems to a large extent still exist. Some are discussed *in context* in the chapters below. Suffice it here to summarize some of the most obvious issues. NATO is a predominantly politico-military organization with very limited civilian staff. Its doctrines typically take as a point of departure military requirements where civilian aspects are often seen as complementing what is being done by the military. Its mandate is much less multifaceted than that of the EU and is based on intergovernmental principles. The political level defines mandates and the military level implements them under strict security rules, allowing for limited openness and interaction with civil society and other organizations.[31]

The EU institutions realized that they needed to comply with NATO security procedures and use some of the alliance's doctrinal thinking and terminology in order to cooperate effectively with NATO. In so doing, they were automatically constraining the possibilities to deploy at the same time and in a flexible way civilian capabilities also for conflict prevention purposes. This became a major problem since the mainstream EU crisis management-related activities over time developed a different profile from that of typical NATO operations. First of all, the EU crisis management operations involved many non-military actors in active cooperation and consultation. In particular it was not foreseen from the start that these operations could be purely civilian and might not even be deploying in real crisis situations but more in a stabilizing context. It was also not envisaged that such operations would require extensive, open cooperation and coordination with the European Commission, by and large operating outside secure areas in terms of information. They also required extensive outreach to NGOs and to civil society at large.

More concretely, whereas the French presidency in the autumn of 2000 had been almost totally focused on military crisis management, in the spring of 2001 the Swedish presidency[32] had already

---

31  For an analysis of the way ahead for NATO see Aybet, G, & R R Moore, *NATO: in search of a vision*, Georgetown University Press, 2010.

32  Animated not least by the energetic efforts by late foreign minister Anna Lindh

started to focus on civil-military cooperation and the possibility of civilian crisis management operations. The initial rationale for civilian elements in crisis management operations had been developed in NATO, focusing on winning the hearts and minds of the population in the field with small civilian projects, mainly implemented by the military itself.[33] But very soon the EU objective started to broaden, while mainly remaining in the intergovernmental framework of the European Security and Defence Policy (ESDP). Separate objectives were developed from the objectives of the military operation itself, focusing on the rule of law, etc. More efforts were deployed in the areas of civilian capabilities, conflict prevention and a broader link to justice and home affairs and international cooperation. The complexity of these objectives itself constituted a generic problem of impact, laying the foundation for the later emergence of a comprehensive approach for external crises and conflicts in the EU.

## Broadening towards civilian crisis management

At the June 2000 Feira European Council civilian targets were established corresponding to the Helsinki Headline Goals in the military area. It was decided that the ESDP thus created should become operational in 2003. In late 2002, the first civilian operation, the European Union Police Mission in Bosnia and Herzegovina (EUPM) was deployed. The implementation of this capacity-building objective would require a strong sense of ownership on the part of justice and interior ministers in the EU. This was problematic since they were not politically responsible for the EU crisis management operations and had much closer relations with the Commission than with this intergovernmental part of the Council.

*From the EEAS Website:*
The first Civilian Headline Goal was set in 2000 at the meeting of the European Council in Santa Maria da Feira, Portugal. It identified policing, the rule of law, civil administration and civil protection as four priority areas for the EU. In the area of

---

33   The concept of CIMIC.

policing, the 2000 Feira Council set concrete targets whereby EU member states could collectively provide up to 5,000 police officers for crisis management operations, with 1,000 officers on high readiness (able to be deployed within 30 days). EU member states also identified a number of key tasks for civilian policing which included: monitoring, advising and training local police, preventing or mitigating internal crises and conflicts, restoring law and order in immediate post-conflict situations, and supporting local police in safeguarding human rights.

The 2001 Gothenburg Council subsequently set concrete goals for the other three priority areas. By 2003, the EU set out to be able to: have 200 judges and prosecutors prepared for crisis management operations in the field of rule of law that could be deployed within 30 days, establish a pool of experts in the area of civilian administration (including general administrative, social and infrastructure functions) and provide civil protection teams of up to 2,000 people, all deployable at very short notice. These teams included 2–3 assessment/coordination teams consisting of 10 experts that could be dispatched within 3–7 hours.

The CHG 2008 added two new priorities to those identified at Feira: monitoring missions and support for EU Special Representatives. The CHG 2008 also emphasised the need for the Union to conduct simultaneous missions and highlighted two further focus areas for the EU: security sector reform (SSR) and disarmament, demobilisation, and reintegration (DDR).

EU member states then set an additional goal, the Civilian Headline Goal 2010 (CHG 2010), to continue the capability-development process and to synchronise it with the Military Headline Goal 2010. The CHG 2010 goal drew on the now extensive experience in civilian crisis management of the EU, and placed greater emphasis on civil-military cooperation in addition to a continued focus on improving readiness and deployability. It also identified other capabilities to be developed, such as making available 285 additional experts on transitional justice, dialogue, and conflict analysis. The CHG 2010 also focused on the creation of Civilian Response Teams

(CRT), a 100-person strong pool of experts prepared for rapid deployment.

## Dependent – but in other ways

Another set of difficulties was identified when the EU contemplated new theatres of operation, outside Europe. The EU not only faced a large number of shortfalls in terms of military and civilian capabilities. It also came to discuss operations in even less permissive areas than Bosnia. This problem hit the EU particularly when discussing operations in Africa, where the EU was seen as a small actor in terms of capabilities, in particular compared to the UN. The EU was also a weak actor in terms of logistics where there were huge distances, weak societal infrastructure, etc. It was dependent on good cooperation with regional organizations. It was a vulnerable actor given the increasing frequency of hostage taking with links to both organized crime and terrorism.

In the Western Balkans and later even more so in Africa, the United Nations was an important actor on the ground and had an overall leading role in post-conflict rehabilitation situations, such as in Kosovo. The EU needed to coordinate better with the UN on crisis management and later also with regional organizations, as already envisaged with the OSCE in the 1999 Istanbul Summit document. Of primary importance in this regard was the African Union (AU), and later subregional African organizations such as the Economic Community of West African States (ECOWAS). In 2003 the EU developed an agreement in principle on crisis management cooperation with the UN. The fact that the EU might even be dependent on the strength of regional organizations in the areas where it was operating became a serious issue, primarily with the AU. Here the intergovernmental framework of the EU with its very limited budgetary and institutional resources did not offer a way out. A way had to be found to permit the use of EU funds to support the build-up of an African peacekeeping capability. An innovative solution was found through the Africa Peace Facility, financed by EU development funds.

NATO had its own priorities; these were limited to specific operational areas and were highly dependent on the priorities and threat perceptions of the US president, from 2001 George W.

Bush. NATO support could thus not be expected for less than vital US interests. The United States did not routinely react to threats related to genocide.[34]

This was also what French and other proponents of an autonomous EU capability in CSDP had foreseen. They wanted to open up the possibility to use available EU member state setups for the operational chain of command. Thus it would be possible to share more broadly the responsibility for operations that otherwise would have been purely national interventions into African situations.

The first opportunity to do this appeared in 2003 when a genocide was threatening in the eastern province of Bunya in the Democratic Republic of the Congo (DRC). The wider perspective of EU action was also illustrated here: the European Community Humanitarian Office (ECHO) was responsible for the situation in Bunya on behalf of the United Nations. It was not least ECHO that warned about a situation that risked escalating in the immediate neighbourhood to the earlier genocides in Rwanda and Burundi. In the face of this situation it was agreed that France would provide the operational command for the Artemis operation, which came to include robust special forces from both NATO and non-NATO countries including Sweden. No doubt, the perceived success of this operation stimulated the further development of the CSDP as a whole.[35]

### Facing increasing external difficulties

During these years, the discourse on numerous traumatic security situations started to gain increasing prominence also on the EU level. There were many points of reference in this debate: serious situations had occurred involving EU member states in the Western Balkans, notably the Netherlands in Srebrenica;[36] Kosovo was described as humanitarian intervention as was the DRC. The 9/11

34 Power, S, *A Problem from Hell: America and the Age of Genocide*, Harper Perennial, New York, 2003.

35 http://www.eeas.europa.eu/csdp/missions-and-operations/artemis-drc/index_en.htm

36 See Supreme court case in the Netherlands http://www.rechtspraak.nl/Organisatie/Hoge-Raad/Supreme-court/Summaries-of-some-important-rulings-of-the-Supreme-Court/Pages/Ruling-Dutch-Supreme-Court-Mothers-of-Srebrenica.aspx

attacks contributed to direct the spotlight on the security of the individual. A norm called the Responsibility to Protect started to be developed at the initiative of Canada and evolved into a human security doctrine in Europe.

The 2003 European Security Strategy warned about emerging regional crises and possible failing states.

It was increasingly a source of concern in Europe that international actors such as China were supporting regimes in Sudan and elsewhere that were presiding over several serious humanitarian situations in their own vast countries. How could the EU have a meaningful and sustainable impact in such situations? The answer offered by a number of EU member states was instinctively: in most situations not.

It would have to be the United Nations and to an increasing extent the regional organizations of Africa that would have to take the main responsibility. For some time this led to a tendency to look for operations that could be seen as at least useful contributions, case in point being the EU support for holding elections in the DRC in 2006, a contingency operation aimed at filling a temporary gap in the UN presence.

One more well-defined deployment objective was a flow-related threat to EU interests, piracy. The EU was not alone in reacting to piracy off the Horn of Africa. This was an international concern also involving US, Russian, Chinese, and other naval assets. But again this was a limited intervention, which at the same time linked up to a situation on land where the EU was trying to make a difference in a fragile, even imploding setting. It was a limited option for an EU military operation, which partly explains what later became the perceived way forward for EU external action in terms of crisis management. However, it also illustrates the enormous capability requirements for more than punctual effort in securing international trade on the high seas.

Otherwise, the door for significant EU military operations remained half closed for a number of additional reasons. As noted above, the EU member states had started to drastically reduce their armed forces after the cold war and the result was in general much less deployability. This led to a much stricter prioritization where the first victim was participation in UN operations, where EU member states started to be largely absent.

The challenges faced in theatres such as Iraq and Afghanistan led to an escalation of costs to protect the deployments there and find ways to have an impact.

The proponents of further military crisis management missions through the EU found that the burden of proof was increasingly on their side. A brief attempt in 2006 to propose an EU-Russian joint peacekeeping intervention in Moldova was also thwarted, partly because there was no agreement with Russia on principles for peacekeeping in the area of the former Soviet Union.[37] With the financial crisis from 2008, resistance to actual deployment of battle groups increased in member states' governments. There was a constant fear of opening a Pandora's box in several national parliaments: of entering into commitments that could lead to an escalation of defence requirements in peacetime in Europe. Those in favour of further developing EU military operations in dangerous theatres found that such operations had to be credible in the face of a possible escalation. This meant that very serious situations that risked defining the EU as a party to a conflict were not even under discussion. This was a role for NATO.

In its military crisis management discourse the EU enveloped itself in many procedures and instructions reducing the possibility for the Union to improvise and be able to intervene quickly in difficult situations. Not least the security rules and the lack of resources, procurement procedures, etc. contributed to this. Micromanagement of ongoing and planned operations characterized much of the work of the Political and Security Committee (PSC), the role of which was supposed to remain strategic – a problem referred to in the *EEAS Review*. This meant losing many of the positive characteristics that had characterized the OSCE missions in terms of flexibility.[38]

In bureaucratic terms the CSDP is at the time of writing locked into isolation, physically illustrated by the Cortenberg building

---

37 Huff, A, 'The role of EU defence policy in the Eastern neighbourhood', IISSS, 2011

38 The OSCE had started to develop detailed mechanisms for how it should operate in the field during the early summits and ministerial in 1992-93. But this was soon replaced by a very flexible format. The decision latitude of the OSCE Chairman in Office was considerable. OSCE lacked substantial resources, multiannual planning but this was also the case for EU crisis management operations. The OSCE lacked the EU power of attraction, but this power of attraction was in any case less visible outside the Western Balkans.

where the CSDP part of EEAS is located, separated from other parts of the service.[39] It is thus not only isolated from the geographic parts of the EEAS but also from the many flow-related and thematic departments of the Commission. It is constrained in its interaction with NGOs and civil society. It is governed by an information security regime that emphasizes the protection of information more than the protection of people. Its integration in overall crisis management and crisis response systems is deficient, partly because of the decoupling of links with the Commission but also because of the fact that there is no consistent deployment ambition for the CSDP over time.

To some extent the policies adopted by the incoming High Representative after the entry into force of the Lisbon Treaty can be interpreted as a fatigue with the EU political and administrative restrictions. Faced with demanding situations in Haiti and elsewhere she appointed special trouble-shooters outside the earlier established line of command including a new managing director for crisis response working in parallel with other crisis management structures. The contributions to crisis management for which she has been more widely credited over the first five years (Iran, Belgrade-Pristina) had little to do with crisis management in the sense of the St Malo Declaration. It typically involved only a few people. Even when developing what later would be described as a comprehensive approach, this primarily used another paradigm than that developed for crisis management, namely, the geographic paradigm.

The EU ran into further serious difficulties when the issues to be dealt with required more political and strategic multitasking concepts. The real test started to appear with the Arab Spring[40] and its subsequent proliferation into a series of existential crisis management situations from Maghreb to Iran. A second front was opened up in Ukraine in early 2014, six years after the war in Georgia. The accumulation of simultaneous crises made the EU increasingly adopt a reactive mode, which brings the discussion to the issue of conflict prevention.

---

39   Interviews with several senior officials in CSDP.
40   Schumacher, T, 'The EU and the Arab Spring: between spectatorship and actorness', *Insight Turk.* 13, no. 3, 2011, pp. 107–119.

# 1.3 Conflict Prevention

Different people often perceive the need for conflict prevention in widely different ways over time. Memory is short and the tendency to be optimistic about the future varies. People are vaguely aware of the overwhelming statistics speaking in favour of conflict prevention: the cost of conflict in terms of suffering and destruction is often tremendous. Already the step from civilian efforts to military crisis management can represent a major increase in costs.

## *Moving beyond the normal-curve paradigm in* CSDP

This section discusses the issue of conflict prevention in the civilian context as well as the role of defence to prevent conflict as a Petersberg Task. Exploring the problems of impact of conflict prevention is not new in the EU. It was a topic seriously analysed and discussed in the European Commission from the mid-1990s, in the context of development. Conflict prevention was to be mainstreamed into all relevant Community programmes from 2001.[41]

ESDP, however, introduced a more specific paradigm, influenced by the NATO perspective on crisis management. This perspective was not seldom built on a normal-curve paradigm, moving into crisis management mode if and when civilian efforts to prevent conflict would fail. A military operation[42] would then take over responsibility for the situation on a much higher level of engagement of the international community than was the case before the conflict. The military would typically be supported by targeted and relatively limited civilian efforts to make the military presence more acceptable to the local population. Once the military efforts had led to prospects for peace, it would be time for negotiations to start and civilian efforts to resume. Major civilian post-conflict rehabilitation contributions of a civilian nature in such a stereotype scenario would come as a part of a negotiated settlement.

When testing this paradigm in EU ESDP exercises during the first years of the millennium[43] it was thus natural that civilian

---

41   http://ec.europa.eu/europeaid/how/evaluation/evaluation_reports/
     reports/2010/1277_vol1_en.pdf
42   Council of the Union, 'Civil Military Co-ordination', 12307/02, 2002,
43   For an overview of exercises see http://eeas.europa.eu/csdp/structures-instru-
     ments-agencies/exercises/index_en.htm

efforts were not seen as a major part of the exercise. But with experience gained over the years, several things were recognized: First, military resources in the crisis management context were often deployed with conflict prevention or stabilizing objectives even if the situation on the ground did not fulfil the criteria for a UN Charter chapter 6 operation: consent of the conflicting parties. Even if there already was a conflict, it could always get worse. The notion that EU military crisis management did not have to plan for broad-based organic cooperation with civilian efforts soon proved untenable. Indeed, in most conflict situations where the EU was involved, the civilian part of the efforts came to dominate the EU contribution. This was a natural consequence of the fact that the number and size of military crisis management operations were reduced over the years. But it also had something to do with the analysis of the conflict situation and the fact that the EU distanced itself from the initial NATO-influenced paradigm and started to adapt to its own comparative advantages.

Very soon and certainly already in the Western Balkans, EU operations in the intergovernmental domain entered into a post-conflict rehabilitation mode. The EU identified a major police task where European Union member states already had experience from the region in the context of the WEU in Albania. The Albanian operation had been a semi-military operation using gendarmerie, a police corps predominantly organized according to military principles.[44] Following initial efforts by the OSCE in Kosovo in the framework of the United Nations Mission in Kosovo (UNMIK), the EU built up a major police operation first in Bosnia and later in Kosovo. These did not have executive police mandates but were organized according to semi-military principles; a military officer, as noted above, initially commanded the Kosovo operation.

Measurements of success in this work were strongly related to benchmarks-based progress in building up local police units and making them more effective in their work. The idea was that the operation could be drawn down and discontinued when the situation in this regard improved. The focus on the rule of law and secu-

---

44   Marcio, R, 'Operation Alba": a european approach to peace support operations in the balkans', US Army War College, 2000.

rity sector reform in EU crisis management operations then became an almost permanent feature. Capacity building thus became not only an issue for defence.

## Towards more conflict prevention efforts in the Community sphere – synergies and frictions

According to an early Commission decision from 2001, conflict prevention should be mainstreamed into all relevant Commission programmes. This issue was initially discussed in the development context towards the end of the 1990s. The European Union developed several parallel types of programmes that were important for conflict prevention. In addition to crisis management-related operations in the intergovernmental context, there were also important external programmes related to enlargement and Neighbourhood policy in the Community sphere, which in a few cases were very similar to rule-of-law crisis management missions. The coordination of these efforts in the intergovernmental versus Community spheres – also with internal DGs in the Commission focusing on justice and home affairs – became a significant issue. On the Community side, a conflict prevention network of academic institutions and think tanks in Europe was first built up with strong support from the European Parliament, but it was soon discontinued.[45]

A new Community methodology was developed, first in the context of enlargement and then in a wider European and even Central Asian framework based on existing intra-Community cooperation. This methodology was related to the process of accession to the European Union and was first applied in the candidate countries to be admitted into the Union. The objective was to harmonize legislation but also administrative best practices in areas such as justice and home affairs. For this reason a so-called twinning instrument was developed whereby experts from EU member states were implanted into ministries and agencies of the candidate countries in question. They were expected to help in

---

45 Rummel, R, 'Die Europäische Union lernt Konfliktprävention', Konflikt-prävention zwischen Anspruch und Wirklichkeit, Wien 2007, pp. 39–59.

the transformation of those structures from the inside, using their own professional expertise and building upon strict conditionality. Progress was continuously measured in specific reports that detailed how harmonization improved.

Comparing the evolution of civilian crisis management operations with Community efforts in the concerned countries, which also included countries not yet candidate EU members, the following observation can be made. In some areas, both geographic and thematic, there was a convergence of purpose and even methods. The most visible and most heavily debated examples were perhaps the second-pillar rule of law mission in Georgia, which for a short time implanted legal experts into Georgian ministries to help amend practices and legislation in order to improve governance.[46] In parallel the European Commission set up a politically highly visible customs assistance mission at the border between Moldova and Ukraine, an operation that was in some ways difficult to distinguish from some of the civilian crisis management missions in the Western Balkans. The mission was deployed in the area of a protracted conflict involving the Transnistrian region of Moldova.[47]

These two operations soon illustrated two more specific problems of impact.

First, as regards sequencing, the Georgia intergovernmental operation was funded from the CFSP budget and thus had to compete with many other requirements in a very limited budget frame. It was therefore contemplated as a short-term operation but when it came to an end the problems addressed were not solved and there was no automaticity on the Community side to continue the work.

Then there was the issue of political coordination and visibility: the Community Moldova programme was highly sensitive due to the unresolved conflict situation and needed to be closely coordinated with other political efforts to contain and resolve the conflict. The programme was therefore exceptionally put under the political auspices of the EU Special Representative for Moldova.

Both these cases also highlighted a legal problem: it was not obvious who, according to the treaties, were competent to do the

46   http://www.eeas.europa.eu/csdp/missions-and-operations/eujust-themis-georgia/index_en.htm
47   http://www.eubam.org/

work. In these two situations the issue was resolved after extensive discussions without the matter being referred to court. In another area, mine action, it was possible to find a pragmatic solution just after the year 2000.[48] It was agreed among member states, against the advice of the Council legal service, that mine action was a necessary condition for development and thus could be pursued with Community funding.

In another area, the illicit spread of small arms (a bad flow in the sense of chapter 2), the European Union entered into a protracted competence dispute. There were examples already from the 1990s of international efforts to strengthen the capacity of police to fight the illicit spread of small arms and light weapons (SALW) and thus to contribute to preventing conflict. The problem was enormous and was further aggravated at the end of the cold war due to fragility and implosion in a number of countries and regions close to the European Union. Albania was a spectacular case in point in 1997, when hundreds of thousands of SALW were taken out of arms depots and spread throughout the region, fuelling conflicts, terrorism, and organized crime. Due to political sensitivities in both Europe and the transatlantic setting (the SALW issue was of course a major domestic political controversy in the United States), several member states insisted that this was a problem to be dealt with by the second intergovernmental pillar of the European Union. NATO also made an effort through a dedicated military operation in FYROM to deploy a mission aptly called Essential Harvest[49] also in order to see if weapons could be found and recuperated. This effort largely failed: only a few thousand weapons of low quality were found. There were also proposals for joint actions, including second-pillar financing of projects of the UN Development Programme (UNDP) to offer development assistance in exchange for handing in weapons. This logic soon encountered serious opposition since it risked attributing the weapons value in terms of money.[50] Real contradictions between Community and second-pillar ambitions in this area then arose in West Africa and the issue was brought to the European Court of Justice for a legal

48  http://eeas.europa.eu/anti_landmines/index_en.htm
49  http://www.nato.int/fyrom/tfh/home.htm
50  http://www.isn.ethz.ch/Digital-Library/Publications/Detail/?id=15132

settlement, a damaging process given the seriousness and urgency of the problem.

On both the Community and intergovernmental sides this illustrates a related issue: seeking to guarantee that once a European institution has recognized competence in a specific area this does not necessarily mean that the institution will take responsibility for dealing with the problem. The battles for the competencies were to a large extent fought by the legal services of the institutions, whereas decisions on appropriations were taken by other parts of the same institutions.

*Both the intergovernmental and Community frameworks are necessary*

So, then, which is the most appropriate EU framework for conflict prevention efforts, the intergovernmental framework or the Community framework? The answer is probably: both. Both have distinctive comparative advantages but also distinctive drawbacks. Both may be necessary in order to fully exploit the comparative advantages of EU cooperation as a whole. The language agreed on this by EU member states is important:

> *From the EU member states' Council conclusions on the*
> *Comprehensive Approach, 2014:*
> The Council stresses the key importance of early warning and
> conflict prevention to reduce the risk of outbreak or recur-
> rence of violent conflict and human suffering, also recalling
> the EU Programme for the Prevention of Violent Conflicts
> and the 2011 Council Conclusions on Conflict Prevention.
> The Council welcomes the progress achieved so far to better
> integrate the EU's early warning capacities, inter alia through
> the development of an Early Warning System and looks for-
> ward to a global roll-out of this process before the end of 2014
> and encourages the use of the early warning system reporting
> across the institutions. The step from early warning to early
> action should then be fast and decisive. The Council also
> recalls the 2009 "Concept on Strengthening EU Mediation
> and Dialogue Capacities" and welcomes the work undertaken
> by the institutions and Member States in the area of media-
> tion as well as other recent initiatives to strengthen capac-
> ity or take forward the EU's engagement in these areas. In

this regard, the Council welcomes the establishment of the European Institute for Peace and the opportunities it offers as an independent and flexible partner to the EU. The Council also encourages closer cooperation and coordination of the various situation and emergency management centres of the Union and Member States.

First, when discussing the intergovernmental framework it is important to recognize that most efforts that are relevant to conflict prevention are undertaken by the member states themselves, in cooperation between groups of states or in other international organizations. It is of course vital that there is a continuous harmonization of goals and assessments in the consultation between member states in the various Council formations as well as in the field whenever representatives of EU member states meet locally or in multilateral contexts. Such coordination can be organized through Community efforts, such as typically in the cooperation between the European Commission and the World Bank when hosting donor conferences and other financing events. But they can also be organized in other ways and it is important that these formats for coordination are harmonized.

Implementation of conflict prevention efforts through the European Community normal programme cycle is sometimes adequate if problems are not entering decisive political phases. In such situations, it may be necessary to have a continuous deliberation among member states and with the EU institutions on the way ahead. It is for this reason the Council's PSC was created. The new capabilities in the form of the High Representative also being vice-president of the Commission, the EEAS, and the EU delegations coordinating the work of member states in the field are helpful additions made in the Treaty of Lisbon. The way these different tools are harmonized and optimized illustrates another problem of impact: political visibility. This is important for at least two reasons. Political visibility towards EU citizens is important to prepare the political ground for early action to prevent conflict through efforts that may require significant resources,[51] a current case in point being Ukraine.

---

51 General question for all the protracted conflicts is that the value of absence of war is underestimated and leads to complacency.

Political visibility is also key in order to catalyse more action on the ground as a complement to EU material support or restrictive measures.

## Significant shortfalls

Only one person on the political level is legally[52] and politically fully empowered to represent both the EU intergovernmental and the Community spheres: the High Representative/Vice-President of the Commission. The multitasking capability required in order to prevent and manage conflicts worldwide is difficult to create under the current treaty. Second best solutions are being tried, such as deploying Commissioners, ministers from member states, or senior officials. Still,[53] it can be argued that the creation of the European External Action Service (EEAS) has offered a promising way to combine the Community and intergovernmental frameworks in order to ensure that political messaging and visibility efforts are being harmonized with the way in which programmes and missions are being implemented. Officials from the EEAS are now being used in explicit troubleshooting and other missions to an extent that was not the case before.

When a conflict prevention effort enters an intensive stage, requiring high-level mediation logistics, other problems pose challenges to the EU and other potential mediating factors that are seldom overcome. The example of Georgia in 2008 showed that only the top level was engaged after the conflict had broken out. The President of France could then perform shuttle diplomacy, but there was no generic, full-scope institutional capability in the EU to do the same, and not on that level. Even reaching a decision on a decisive conflict prevention effort required a trigger, a Problems of impact sometimes described as the CNN effect; the example of Biafra in 1968 showed that low media presence undercut necessary attention to this enormous human tragedy.[54] Atrocities had to cross new thresholds in relation to what the media had previously reported, a problem widely discussed not least in the context of the Bosnia war.[55]

52  Notably in the European Parliament
53  EEAS, *EEAS Review* 2013 p. 13
54  Case study from the Swedish press by the author in unpublished essay from 1969.
55  http://www.e-ir.info/2013/09/17/media-as-a-driving-force-in-international-politics-the-cnn-effect-and-related-debates/

The CFSP budget, which is the only operational budget available to the intergovernmental framework beyond the direct contributions to military crisis management operations, is very limited and under heavy competition from acute crisis management needs. It is not intended to finance long-term conflict prevention efforts. Indeed, over time ways have been discussed and are likely to be discussed even more in the future for transferring responsibility for the financing of such operations to the Community pillar. As long as the implementation of almost all Community programmes are under the direction of Commissioners not subordinate to the HR/ VP, this is likely to remain a difficult problem. A helpful development has been the creation in the European Commission's DG for Development Cooperation (DEVCO) of a capacity to focus on fragility and thus conflict prevention but with more of an African paradigm than the European neighbourhood perspective.

A real time control over Community programmes from a member state political perspective is likely to remain a major challenge for other reasons as well and is contradicted by the Community notion that, once a mandate for an action is issued by the Council, it is up to the Commission to implement it. Community programmes typically have a long project cycle, up to a decade or more. They are implemented through tenders delegating implementation to external organizations, such as the UNDP.[56] They are in most cases based on long negotiations with host countries where the ownership principle is very important. Principles related to sound financial management, procurement, etc. that are generic to the financial regulation of the EU as a whole put a high premium on acting in secure conditions. Risk-taking is not encouraged, and sometimes an official will do better not approving a contract than taking a calculated risk in going forward.

It is also important to note that conflict prevention often has to be weighed against other goals in the EU. Thinking carefully about whether to go forward with a project or a programme can be warranted in view of rampant corruption in many key countries. Sometimes the need to promote international human rights, democracy, and rule-of-law principles may be perceived as more important for the EU than a mediating position. In particular the

56  http://eeas.europa.eu/organisations/un/index_en.htm

link between corruption and conflict is very complicated and not always easily solved. In many countries preventing conflict between factions, including warlords as in Afghanistan, has included a certain level of corruption accepted not least by intelligence services[57] trying to avoid unnecessary bloodshed by satisfying the personal wishes of different factions. How different objectives should be harmonized with the need to fight corruption requires a strategic and difficult analysis and has been discussed in a number evaluations of EU programmes.[58]

### Goals of conflict prevention and the perceptions of EU intentions

In general terms it is recognized that the most important historic comparative advantage of EU efforts in support of conflict prevention is the European Union idea itself, promoting interdependence intended to make war impossible between mutually dependent countries. As the European Union has proceeded towards enlargement to include countries in conflict and with significant problems related to minorities, etc., the power of attraction of the European Union has clearly been an important factor in support of conflict resolution. Former EU Enlargement Commissioner Olli Rehn wrote in 2008:

> [...] the EU has relied primarily on soft power, pursuing its objectives by influence rather than by force. Enlargement policy is the EU's most important soft power tool. The power of attraction exerted by the EU has acted as an incentive for stability and democracy in Central and Eastern Europe.

Many of the countries now members of the European Union have resolved some of their differences either during their accession process or when they became members of the Union, supported by various regional and other financing instruments.

However, this power of attraction is a perception from the outside. Hopes for a better future can be dashed if optimism within

---

57   http://www.csmonitor.com/USA/Military/2014/0430/How-deluge-of-US-
     military-spending-fed-corruption-in-Afghanistan-video
58   As also discussed by the European Parliament: http://www.europarl.europa.eu/
     sides/getDoc.do?type=REPORT&reference=A7-2013-0250&language=EN

the EU itself is dwindling, as has been the case during the financial crisis on the one hand and due to political battles over the future of the European Union on the other. The strength of the attraction is often difficult to determine and is an important problem of impact precisely because it is an issue of perceptions and may be quickly affected by the mobilization of political will on both the governmental and non-governmental level, facilitated in the modern world by social media. The Ukraine case is interesting from this perspective: in the United States and elsewhere the European factor was initially not deemed very important, but it turned out that the issue of a Trade and Association Agreement with the EU catalysed intensive grassroots mobilization on the Maidan Square of Kiev.

If EU enlargement or EU neighbourhood policies aiming at closer integration with the EU is perceived as a way for the Union to extend its sphere of influence, this may exacerbate rather than prevent conflict. This in turn is closely connected to the issue of whether sufficient efforts have been deployed through political dialogue to ensure that such EU policies are not seen as part of a zero-sum game.[59] Already in the 1970s, peace researchers debated the 'Fortress Europe' concept,[60] analysing the situation of those outside the European Union as EU integration progressed and the greater risk of increasing the gap between developing and developed countries. This was seen as a factor relating to the negotiating power of a large European Union in relation to small and poor states, dependent on the delivery of raw materials to the European Union's increasingly more sophisticated industries.

From the perspective of the current Russian leadership, EU enlargement, as NATO enlargement, is clearly defined as a zero-sum game in relation to the Russian sphere of influence. A Trade and Association Agreement with Moldova, if it can include Transdnjestr in some way, is likely to solve some of the economic and other problems hindering reconciliation across the river. But in the declared view of Russia this is not seen as a promising perspective. As long as Russia has a decisive say over the policies of Transdnjestr, such efforts are unlikely to succeed if the wider problems with Russia

59   Ury, W, & R Fisher, *Getting to yes*, Harvard Negotiating Project, 1981.
60   Notably Johan Galtung.

are not addressed on the strategic level. To a certain extent this also applies to US efforts to promote reconciliation between Turkey and Armenia or international efforts to alleviate discord in Georgia. The Russian leadership currently seems to believe that continuation of the protracted conflicts is preferred if this leads to a lower level of Western influence in its neighbourhood.

### Conflict prevention and defence

This brings us back to the issue of conflict prevention through military means, as foreseen in the Petersberg Tasks. In order to see the picture in a more strategic perspective it may be useful to revisit the relationship between the United States and the Soviet Union during the cold war. Military doctrines were developed not least on the Soviet side in order to define which conflicts were acceptable and which were unacceptable because of the risk of nuclear escalation. From the Soviet side, particularly after the demise in the 1962 Cuban missile crisis, it was important to characterize certain conflicts as dangerous in this respect. But the distinction was never clear. The notion of limited wars in Soviet military doctrine should normally have applied to the Arab-Israeli October War of 1973.[61] It led to additional precautions being taken by the superpowers to prevent nuclear war by mistake. The war by proxy pursued by the United States in Afghanistan, after the Soviet invasion of that country in 1979, is also an interesting case in point: both sides were aware that they were at war with each other but through a US client, the Mujahedin.

The role of NATO in the Ukraine crisis until this point, strongly supported by the United States, has been to create a demarcation line for the spread of the conflict to the borders of NATO.[62] This is a very significant conflict prevention effort since the three Baltic States were a part of the former Soviet Union and include a large Russian-speaking population, especially in Latvia. Russia has over the years repeatedly tried to incite unrest in this population with

---

61   Lundin, L-E, *Påverkan genom militärt stöd: sovjetisk militär resursöverföringspolitik visavi Vietnam och Egypten*=[Influence through military support: Soviet arms transfer policy towards Vietnam and Egypt: four case studies] Doctoral dissertation, Statskunskap, UI, 1980.

62   http://www.nato.int/cps/en/natolive/opinions_109231.htm

limited success; as members of the European Union, the citizens of Latvia enjoy benefits that far exceed those of their neighbours on the other side of the border. Still, it cannot be excluded that the propaganda war could also escalate here with unforeseen consequences. Russia has also used other methods to seek to project power in the Baltic region: buying Baltic assets, using its leverage on the basis of energy dependence, etc. So far the EU has only limited importance in the military conflict prevention context. It seems mainly to be a role complementary to that of NATO, helping to promote capacity building for defence.

## *Towards realistic and sustainable conflict prevention objectives*

What, then, does conflict prevention mean in the Middle East and North Africa? Again, this is a complex issue requiring strategic analysis and 'slow thinking'. Henry Kissinger:

> In my life, I have seen four wars begun with great enthusiasm and public support, all of which we did not know how to end and from three of which we withdrew unilaterally. The test of policy is how it ends, not how it begins.[63]

Such visions exist in certain contexts. They include the two-state solution with Israel and Palestine inside internationally recognized borders, a reintegrated Iran as a respected member of the international community without nuclear weapons, North African democracies based on the rule of law and limited level of corruption, a settlement in Syria bringing this historic civilization back on track after a traumatic colonial and postcolonial period, Turkey as an emerging regional power at peace with its neighbours with a reinforced democratic framework, and respecting religions but not being governed by a religion.

There are not going to be any simple solutions to finding the right way forward in terms of conflict prevention – not for the European Union nor for the United States in these theatres. The EU relationship to Turkey as such is not only about enlargement but also about managing relations with Turkey, which to a large

---

63  http://www.henryakissinger.com/articles/wp030614.html

extent is a matter of managing perceptions in Europe and in
Turkey. Keeping the EU together in this sense is a major problem
of impact since different signals from different EU member states
obviously undercut the EU credibility in this context.

The European Union member states are not yet convinced that
creating a sufficient conflict prevention capability with appropriate
staff is worth doing in the context of the work of the EEAS. It will
need to work very intimately together with the diplomatic efforts
deployed by EU member states in various formats. The organization of such strategic conflict prevention capability needs to be
targeted but at the same time flexible. Sometimes the sources of
conflict are not to be found in the country in question but perhaps
in a neighbouring country or region. So there is a need to take up
defence in depth and to analyse the relevant flows carefully.

There is a need for a deep historical and cultural analysis. The
roots of the conflict in the Western Balkans goes back to before
the First World War, and some of the roots of the problems in the
Middle East have historic foundations. There is a need for intelligence in the real sense of the word. Ukraine, as was the case with
the Western Balkans, is full of deception in terms of information
aimed at influencing perceptions and provoking reactions. There is
the need to go back to study the lessons learned from negotiations
during the cold war.

Finally, there is a need to use international organizations in an
intelligent way. In addition, consensus-based organizations such
as the OSCE have a decision of latitude in their actions to send
fact-finding missions, etc. The United Nations executive branches
are not wholly dependent on agreement between the permanent
members of the Security Council. The tendency inside the EU to
consider only what the European Union can do through its own
resources remains a significant constraint.

# 2. Flow Security

The issue in this chapter is flow security, where problems of impact are seen from four overlapping perspectives. The first (2.1) is closely linked to globalization as a process over time and refers to the protection and promotion of flows, such as trade, finance, energy, movement of people, etc. At the same time it highlights threats against such flows that may be due to environmental changes over time, natural or man-made hazards, etc. More or less hidden in the enormous volume of this material and virtual communication within and between states, there are also bad flows, sometimes referred to as transnational threats, beyond man-made problems of an environmental or some other nature. These may be primarily motivated by financial gains and thus take the form of organized crime[1] (2.2), including different types of trafficking. On the other hand they may have political motives illustrated in terms of terrorism, (2.3). In a fourth section the perspective of non-proliferation of weapons of mass destruction is applied (2.4).

1   Sometimes in the literature described as transnational organized crime.

## 2.1 Flow Security

*Protecting the good flows*

*From the Review of Implementation of the European Security Strategy 2008:*
Globalisation has brought new opportunities. High growth in the developing world, led by China, has lifted millions out of poverty. However, globalisation has also made threats more complex and interconnected. The arteries of our society – such as information systems and energy supplies – are more vulnerable. Global warming and environmental degradation is altering the face of our planet. Moreover, globalisation is accelerating shifts in power and is exposing differences in values. Recent financial turmoil has shaken developed and developing economies alike.

The focus of the previous chapter was capacity building for defence, crisis management, and conflict prevention.

None of these perspectives highlights the consequences of globalization: the increased interdependence between states and peoples due to flows. The European Union has developed a number of thematic responses to problems relating to the security of flows. They are discussed in this section with examples from the energy, environment, cyber, and migration sectors.

As a first topical illustration, a major debate is developing in Europe on the dependence on energy resources from Russia where the discourse until recently has concentrated on mutual economic benefit, on more interdependence as a good thing in itself. Events in and around Ukraine have revived another longstanding debate on how to reduce dependence through an Energy Security Strategy in combination with a dedicated effort to reach energy saving goals in the period up until 2030. Methods have already been under discussion for decades how to circumvent Russia through pipelines going through its neighbouring states. Now an overall decrease of energy supply from the East is being contemplated. A reduced dependence on Russia is already seen as a goal in itself for a number of EU member states. Russia is dramatically increasing is diversification efforts, including through new agreements with China.

Good flows are vulnerable in times of crisis and conflict. However, after the Second World War security attention was primarily directed to the military dimension, with emphasis on nuclear deterrence. In 1973, OPEC (Organization of the Petroleum-Exporting Countries) used another type of power base, oil, as a political instrument, provoking a global energy crisis.

In the following decades, quite a number of other references to scarce resources as a source of influence appeared in the literature.[2] Common to many of them is the notion that dependence can be used as a tool to influence the policies of other nations and seriously impact on the functioning of societies, including critical infrastructure and financial stability.

This has become – and perhaps has for a very long time been – a geopolitical factor argued to influence defence, including the deployment and use of military resources around the world. It is seen as a motive explicitly or implicitly influencing decisions to go to war and sometimes even to delay the resolution of conflicts.

Flow security is therefore a useful complement to the analysis in the previous chapter. It may help to promote an understanding of the roots of problems and thereby increase the impact of security policies.

Flow security is an area where the European Union has a major comparative advantage in being able to coordinate policy within the Union and to exercise leverage for change outside its borders. This may be a potential major growth sector for Union competences in the future.

## Technical vs political approaches

The study of flows is increasingly specialized and complicated in technical terms. The European Union's approach to flows is strongly linked to Community objectives, notably to trade and development. The preferred way to deal with problems in institu-

2   Mildner, S-A, G Lauster, W Wodni, & G Mounier, 'Scarcity and abundance revisited: A literature Review on Natural Resources and Conflict', *International Journal of Conflict and Violence* 5 (1) 2011, no. 1, pp. 155–172.

tionalizing these policies is often technical, based on negotiations between the EU and the most concerned countries, involving expertise from the member states.

There is strong resistance against politicizing disputes; the legal settlement procedures are often prioritized. Much energy is spent to develop standards, best practices and cooperative methodologies and then to get them agreed in legally binding documents on the bilateral or international level. Wherever there are strong and possibly asymmetric dependencies, the technical solutions involve diversification of dependence through networking and alternative transport routes.

Dependence can be seen from the perspective of both the producer and the consumer. Producers have the power to deliver or not to deliver. Consumers, to the extent they are well organized and work together with each other, have the power to buy or not to buy. Both producers and consumers have reason to diversify their dependence.

Still, after long periods of non-crisis, higher levels of dependence have often been accepted for commercial reasons. This has made some societies very vulnerable. Germany, for instance, has had an interest in delivering pipeline equipment and knowledge to Russia, further increasing the willingness to compromise on diversification of gas imports from Russia.[3]

In the European Union the issue of how to handle such situations was particularly highlighted in relation to the gas crisis that affected Ukraine starting in early 2006.

From the Community side there was a preference to deal with the gas crisis in a low-key way by sending experts to analyse delivery data and come up with technical solutions.

From the intergovernmental side a number of countries that were particularly affected by the crisis felt the need to bring the issue up on a political level and to use other tools of influence to manage the situation.

The jury is out on how these methods can be combined in order to make the best impact, as could be seen in the revived Ukraine crisis in 2014.

3   Case in point being the German RMA firm, which now also builds pipeline production plants in Russia: http://www.rma-armaturen.de/seiten/index.php?id=2&sprach=1

## Dependence on information and other flows

An additional problem related to flows is the increased technical capability of state and non-state actors to disrupt flows in an
anonymous way, particularly using cyber technology. Initially, this
was probably seen as a rather marginal problem that could be dealt
with by limited technical precautions.

Nevertheless, most countries that were fully integrated in the
world economy soon found themselves in a situation where their
dependence on the functioning of information systems, promi-
nently the Internet, was decisive for their societies as a whole.

> *Examples*: When the threat of the so-called millennium bug
> was discussed just before the year 2000 it was still possible to
> find engineers who knew how to operate nuclear power plants
> without computers. Most aircraft systems had an inherent
> aerodynamic stability. Ships could navigate without global
> positioning systems. Air traffic could be controlled without
> computers. However, in the new world, global positioning
> systems have become essential not only for civilian life but
> also as a tool in conflict situations. Aircraft are nowadays often
> constructed with a stability provided by computers. The previ-
> ous redundancy in terms of communication with alternatives
> to use radio, radar, fixed telephone lines etc. has been reduced
> and more and more people have only the option to use the
> Internet. Here there is already a major shift in comparison
> with the situation at the time of 9/11, when the main link
> from the EU headquarters in Brussels to its delegations was
> through using the fax machine – and the telephone was the
> main method of communication in crisis.

In a fierce competition between countries and companies in the
globalized economy, the proposition again is that redundancy is not
going to be a priority, unless there is a high level of security awareness.

Staying out of this global interactive system is no longer seen
as an option, not in Washington, Brussels, Moscow, or Beijing.
Dependence may be asymmetric in certain limited thematic or
geographic contexts, but there is a fundamental interdependence
where the escalation of any one conflict risks crippling many other
societies in the developed world.

Given the enormous investments made by Russians and Chinese in Western economies, the financial crisis first affecting the United States was also a problem for these countries.

## Flow security brings a new perspective to power and conflict

Flow security has brought a new dimension to the analysis of conflicts and crises. Today it is clear that conflicts can escalate to very high levels without the use of military means, in fact even through non-decisions.

This is not what might be called a 'soft security threat'. It is very real; it costs human lives and even in extreme cases can bring down entire economies. Also, from the EU's point of view this brings a new dimension to conflict prevention, one that is not necessarily geographically limited to the intrastate conflicts now dominating the global map.[4]

It requires a new form of strategic analysis, which will have to include the military dimension of flow security. Notably, it will have to combine the perspectives of the EU as a mediator[5] and as an actor in potential conflicts.

Perceptions are key in determining whether the discourse needs to be both technical and political. Whereas from the European point of view integration should bring peace and well-being, this may not always be the view of other countries. When the European Union develops the Energy Community concept, linking up energy markets and transport routes near the EU area, this may be perceived by others, in particular by Russia, as a way to extend a European sphere of influence. How to deal with this problem is of course a political issue and cannot be dealt with only on the technical level.

*A typical historical illustration*: the different railway track widths in the East and the West. This type of problem caused many debates over the decades concerning the pros and cons of interconnecting, for instance, electricity networks in Europe.

---

4   http://www.pcr.uu.se/research
5   http://www.pcr.uu.se/digitalAssets/112/112149_ucdp_paper_7.pdf

Standardization can thus also be seen as a tool for exerting influence not only as a technical discourse. Even more limited standard-setting formats can produce political controversy, such as the GPS system versus the Galileo project for navigation.[6]

Building coalitions is another key aspect. As a case in point, no single EU member state can pursue efforts to constrain climate change on its own. The main problems of impact here are arguably both internal and external: the extent to which the member states can reach agreement between themselves and with the United States on climate change policy determines a large part of their effectiveness in external negotiations.

This was recognized in the second Barroso Commission when a dedicated climate change Commission portfolio was created for the first time.

In the face of the combined opposition from major players in Asia, European leverage so far has proven insufficient.

This remains a generic problem of impact, which links to the issue of effective multilateralism through the European Union in line with the principles set out in the 2003 European Security Strategy. The strategy is relevant not only for climate change but also for other key flow areas, such as trade, nuclear security, etc.

In order to achieve maximum impact there is a need to focus on opportunities, threats, and future challenges using a very broad concept of security. Such a conceptual effort must take into account the intimate link between domestic and foreign policy in many of the areas discussed above.

Decisions and non-decisions of member states are strongly influenced by crises in various areas relating to flows. In many cases these postures have not been forward looking. There is a need not only to determine what needs to be prevented but also to find positive solutions for the future.

In such a process, the perceived democratic legitimacy of the EU decision-making process is a key factor. If it is perceived by external partners as low, this will make the European posture less credible and thus less effective.

✳︎✳︎✳︎

6   http://news.bbc.co.uk/2/hi/science/nature/4555276.stm

This discourse relates not only to states. Globalization has brought with it a complex network of multinational commercial and other entities with economic and other resources that sometimes even exceed those of states. These entities operate in order to reduce dependence on any one country, thus increasing the need for international regulations. The European Union has a strong comparative advantage in regulating otherwise very elusive multinational activities, as illustrated in recent years by for example Microsoft, Google, and recently Gazprom.

Again, there is a link to broader security questions and even crisis. Microsoft and Google are not independent from the US government, as shown by the National Security Agency (NSA) debate over personal privacy vs national security concerns, and Gazprom is certainly not independent from the Russian government. Multinational companies and commercial strategies can also be used as tools of influence by governments.

In the conflict analysis pursued by the EU in specific geographic situations it is also important that it takes into account the longer-term ambitions of major players in terms of infrastructure and networks. And today such an analysis must include Chinese as well as Indian interests, for instance in Central Asia, Afghanistan, Africa and the Middle East, and in other fragile and conflict-ridden regions.

In addition, for the United States such considerations play a major role in the debate about US interests relating to energy in various parts of the world. Conflicts in Africa cannot be properly analysed without an understanding of the situation as regards production and trade in scarce minerals, including notably so-called conflict diamonds.[7]

This illustrates the urgent need for a horizontal coordination of thematic policies in the EU, both internally and externally, with an eye to security policy considerations.

## Migration

An increasingly prominent part of the debate on flows relates to people. There are many indications that the attention to migration has increased in the process of drafting recent strategic EU

---

7   http://www.kimberleyprocess.com/

documents.[8] Migration is historically of central importance for the development of Western societies and thus arguably a good flow.

The United States has literally been built on the influx of trained and motivated immigrants, not least those coming from Europe. The industrial development of many European countries has been dependent on the arrival of skilled workers on all levels, and from near and far. Millions of families in the developing countries have one or several family members abroad who send remittances that help the family to survive. Tourism and industrial investments abroad have led to an increased flow of people also from countries such as Russia and China, where free movement was prohibited only a few decades ago.

An enormous brain drain has, however, taken place from the underdeveloped world to the industrialized countries over the past century.

Conflicts and crises produce refugees, strengthening the case for the benefits of effective conflict prevention.

Migration is closely linked to trafficking and smuggling as forms of organized crime.

The freedom to move and to own property in other countries has become a major opportunity for reinsurance for corrupt elites in many countries around the globe.

Here again, it is essential to focus on both opportunities and threats. Furthermore, there needs to be a seamless integration between internal and external policies. Regulation of these flows has developed in stages prompted by occasional crises over the years. The Schengen system was set up already in 1985 to include most of the EU member states. The 9/11 attacks on the USA provoked enhanced security restrictions around the world and more investments into controlling security at ports, airports, and border crossings.

Against this background, negotiations on visa liberalization and rules regulating work permits are not technical but rather highly political issues. They are a major tool of political influence.

There are several pitfalls in the migration debate. On the one hand the risk is that the discourse is becoming too securitized, fuelling the domestic political debates in EU member states in a way that breeds reactionary tendencies.

---

8    Case in point being the Comprehensive Approach.

On the other hand the discourse must also not only be focused on positive aspects but also take into account future risks of negative flows, including those discussed below in the sections on organized crime and terrorism.

## Comparative advantages and weaknesses of the EU

In conclusion, the European Union is arguably uniquely equipped to deal with most if not all of these flow-related issues, with its strong expertise in a large number of complex thematic policy areas and with an extensive outreach in terms of geography and multilateral presence.

The European Union is also in theory able to set up a conflict prevention and crisis management framework on a level that would be impossible to construct even in the larger member states of the Union.

It can develop a strategic political framework for negotiations with the major players in the world, and participate with the most important countries in the world in the negotiations on how to continuously prevent and manage crisis.

The proposition of this study is, however, that the European Union is only at the beginning of a very long process of capacity building in order to respond to challenges to flow security. This may have to be the next major generation of the EU's security-building efforts.

The next chapter takes up the discussion of the various organizational cultures that need to be interconnected in order to reach this goal, through comprehensive approaches. It shows that the interface between several of these organizational cultures in terms of the security of flows is currently weak. The priority paradigm in the setup of the European External Action Service (EEAS) is geographic, with very few experts both at headquarters level and in the field who are able to deal with specialized flows

The departments of the European Commission, on the other hand, are often not well connected to the broader security contexts in which various thematic issues play out. Decisions on which tools to use in which conflict prevention and crisis management situations are often delimited to the competences of the respective Commissioner. Horizontal coordination procedures involving not only geographic but also thematic expertise, pre-crisis and during crisis, are not yet well established between the Commission and the EEAS. Case in point was the handling of the Fukushima nuclear catastrophe in 2011.[9] For more on this see section 3.4.

## 2.2 Organized Crime

*From the European Security Strategy 2003:*
Europe is a prime target for organised crime. This internal threat to our security has an important external dimension: cross-border trafficking in drugs, women, illegal migrants, and weapons accounts for a large part of the activities of criminal gangs. It can have links with terrorism. Such criminal activities are often associated with weak or failing states.

### Fighting organized crime as a bad flow

This section examines a major set of what can be called 'bad flows', through organized crime.[10] Fighting transnational organized crime with its close link to corruption arguably brings with it some very difficult security problems, notably in a post-conflict rehabilitation situation. Organized crime also involves violence, sometimes on the level of military conflicts.[11]

In democratic societies, it is police and other civilian authorities who deal with crime; in most countries organized crime is not a task for the military and thus not seen as an integrated part of the defence discourse – which, as argued below, is not entirely appropriate.

Before the 9/11 attacks in 2001, it was also widely believed that organized crime was not really linked to terrorism. Therefore it was not expected to be a major target in what the G. W. Bush administration later called the war on terrorism, or in EU terminology the

9  Findley, T, *Unleashing the Nuclear Watchdog. Strengthening and Reform of the IAEA*, The Center for International Governance Innovation, 2012.
10  Defined as criminal activities for financial motives carried out by three or more individuals.
11  Central America.

fight against terrorism, discussed in the next section.

This analysis soon changed after 9/11, when it was more widely recognized that terrorists finance their activities through organized crime. Using financial intelligence as a tool also made it possible to trace terrorists.[12] But this raised the problem of how to pursue this work and at the same time to respect the need for data protection and civil liberties.

## Organized crime and corruption[13]

There is often an underlying assumption that a certain level of organized crime, including notably corruption, is unavoidable in conflict societies. Corruption among warring factions is even seen as an instrument to keep the peace between them. Harmonizing these different goals has evidently proven difficult in several military theatres.

Corruption can to a certain extent be counteracted through sanctions targeted at ruling elites. The effectiveness of sanctions is, however, closely related to the political approaches deployed and how these restrictive measures are perceived in the general population.

EU assistance and accession policies that are dependent on conditionality are also fundamentally complicated by corruption. Conditionality typically refers to the perceived interests of a country as a whole and its population. If the ruling elites have another calculus of interests, the conditionality may fail and the power of attraction of the European Union may more or less disappear as a tool of influence.[14]

---

12  The international Intergovernmental cooperation, notably through the Financial Action Task Force (FATF) set up by the G7 already in 1989, decided in October 2001 to expand its mandate in corporate efforts to combat terrorist financing in addition to money laundering. The European Commission is one of the two regional organizations members of the organization. For a manual on this work see https://www.unodc.org/tldb/pdf/Asian-bank-guide.pdf

13  For further reading see the bibliography.

14  Example of a case study: Glüpker, G, 'Effectiveness of EU Conditionality in the Western Balkans: Minority Rights and the Fight Against Corruption in Croatia and Macedonia', Journal of Contemporary European Research 9, Issue 2, 2013,

## Organized Crime and Conflict Analysis

When seeking to identify the root of the problem in conflict prevention strategies, the limelight is often directed towards ethnic and other divisions within societies – towards potential clashes of civilizations, to use the term coined by Samuel Huntington.[15]

However, there are also empirical cases where corruption and organized crime sponsored by elites result in revolt on the part of an impoverished and unemployed population.[16]

This has led to the realization that organized crime needs to be an integral part of conflict analysis[17] and needs to be properly factored into the mandates of crisis management missions and operations with a strong conflict prevention ingredient.

Organized crime thus threatens to complicate conflict analysis in a serious way. Crime infiltrates the leadership of countries through corruption, which may reduce their willingness to deal with security threats.

Corruption also affects Europe and its willingness to act, linking European economic, including commercial, interests with those of corrupt elites, be they oligarchs investing in the United Kingdom or African leaders with second homes in France, Italy, or Spain. A case in point is of course the corruptive links between European elites and the former Libyan dictator Muammar Gaddafi that arguably affected the willingness of the Europeans to effectively counteract Libya's support to armed groups and terrorists.

## Organized crime and defence

There are also links to defence. One is of course the vulnerability of defence and security forces to corruption and organized crime. This became a major issue during the post-cold war efforts to improve democratic control over armed forces. Important steps in this direction were made in the OSCE region followed by the development of security sector reform work. In Africa, the

---

15   Huntington, S P, *The Clash of Civilizations and the Remaking of World Order*, Simon & Schuster, 2011.

16   Often quoted cases are the so-called colour revolutions and the crisis in Bosnia from 2013.

17   As currently animated by the Security Policy Directorate in the EEAS.

European Commission also pursued this type of work.[18]

However, organized crime in combination with support to terrorist groups may also be a state-sponsored activity, a part of wider defence-related strategies.

Yet another link to defence is the illicit trafficking in arms, defence-related materials, and knowledge. A case in point was the Khan network in Pakistan, which proliferated various elements of nuclear capabilities to a number of countries.[19] As regards nuclear security, this touches upon a very sensitive discourse pursued in the intergovernmental framework. (See further 2.4)

In addition, the enormous illicit trafficking in small arms and light weapons (SALW), fuelling conflicts throughout the world, is a major problem. This trade is also delicate for several other reasons. It is brought up in calls for domestic support for the right of individuals to bear arms, a consideration that has led to an ambivalent US policy over the years but has also affected licensing policies in European countries.

There are also many European traders in SALW, both licit and illicit, and arms are provided not only by the US but also European countries to various recipients around the world as part of the global arms trade.

Problems related to organized crime through trafficking in small arms, ammunition, explosives, mines etc. deserve comprehensive efforts combining many different methods, but many political problems undermine this effort.[20]

The fight against organized crime is often pursued with military means, cases in point being eradication campaigns carried out by US and Russian[21] forces in Afghanistan and the Iranian operations directed against drugs trafficking at the border with Afghanistan. The problems here include the fact that such efforts risk recruiting more terrorists and make it even less possible for alternative development strategies to work.

---

18   For further reading see references to security sector reform in the bibliography.

19   Levi, M A, *On Nuclear Terrorism*, Harvard University Press, 2007.

20   For further reading Saferworld, 'Turning the page: Small arms and light weapons in Albania'; C Hillion, & RA Wessel, 'Competence Distribution in EU External Relations after ECOWAS: Clarification or Continued Fuzziness?', *Common Market Law Review* vol. 46, no. 2, 2009, pp. 551–586.

21   Wheaton, JK, J Sperling, & J Hallenberg, *The Soviet War in Afghanistan*, Golgotha Press, 2010.

## Organized Crime in a Geographic Context

The discourse on issues of organized crime links up with the discussion in chapter 3 on organisational cultures. It illustrates an at least initial weakness of the geographic paradigm that is predominant in the EEAS. Many EU assistance programmes focusing on governance started up after the cold war with mandates restricted to one country. Soon it was realized that programmes needed to be able to bridge several countries and have a cross-border nature. Regional horizontal programmes were defined. By 2006, the next step was taken through the realization that entire departments of the external relations DG of the Commission did not fully cover certain key types of transnational threat. It was also understood that the fight against trafficking in drugs on the one hand from Afghanistan and on the other from Latin and Central America needed to be tackled in transregional coordination. This became particularly important for the European Union when it was realized that drugs travelled a route not only through Iran and the Western Balkans but also through Africa, and they emanated from both Afghanistan and the states in the Western Hemisphere.[22]

## Organized crime seen as a transnational threat

Seen again from the perspective of flows, organized crime can therefore often be described as a transnational threat. In the European Union, for the administrative purpose mentioned above, such crime is often described as a transregional threat.

The question is then, if there is a decision to take up defence against organized crime, where should this be done? Law-enforcement resources are stretched and many crimes in European countries today are left uninvestigated. First, this introduces a question of subsidiarity, which already in European countries is a major issue of debate: how should police forces be organized in order to most effectively counter organized crime?

What resources and mandates are the European countries ready and willing to set aside for international cooperative endeavours

---

22 European Commission, 'Report from the Commission to the European Parliament, The Council, The European Economic and Social Committee and The Committee Of The Regions 2012 Annual Report on the Instrument for Stability', COM (2013) 563 final, 2013,

such as Interpol or the EU Europol? The fight against organized crime is very much a question of defence in depth. The European Union has in many cases determined in its justice and home affairs analysis that there are international roots to the problems as well as domestic. However, the bulk of the efforts are made in the Union and a certain lack of coherence arises when dealing with complex situations at the borders of the European Union when organized crime meets problems of refugees and forced migration. (See further the section on institutionalization in chapter 5)

*Organized crime as part of a comprehensive approach*

Then there is the problem of creating the necessary and sufficient conditions in the fight against organized crime, including through policing and other rule of law efforts.

There is of course not much use in arresting the perpetrators of minor crimes if the main culprits cannot be identified and if court and prison systems are corrupt. This is a problem that has undermined the effectiveness of a series of international crisis management operations and Community programmes over recent decades. It has no doubt been further aggravated by the fact that a large share of the police forces in these countries were themselves involved in the armed conflict, with still existing loyalties to the one or the other side and experience in using violence to solve conflicts.

Such problems have also been highlighted in the fight against piracy on the Horn of Africa, where it has been found incredibly difficult to identify appropriate prison facilities to host so far more than 1000 pirates inside or outside Somalia for fear that further acts of terrorism or organized crime would be directed against those taking care of the prisoners.

The European Union has been engaged in several efforts to prevent conflict and terrorism by promoting police reform. One case was the early assistance – already before 9/11 – in the development domain to assist the Palestinian police in respecting human rights provisions when treating prisoners and detainees.[23] Another

---

23   European foreign policy unit, Chronology: European Union Foreign Policy –
     Policy Developments (partial), <http://www.lse.ac.uk/internationalRelations/
     centresandunits/EFPU/EFPUpdfs/chronologyEuforpol.pdf>.

was the deployment of European experts to police stations in Osh, Kyrgyzstan, through the so-called Community Security Initiative, sponsored by the OSCE.[24] In this way, it was hoped that a presence in order to discourage the police from mishandling minorities who were detained for various crimes would in 2010 prevent the conflict from flaring up again.

The problem of dealing with the rule of law is not specific to this approach but it is an overarching issue in post-conflict rehabilitation. One key example is of course Iraq, where the initially successful military operation leading to regime change was immediately followed by a de-Baathification campaign eradicating the foundation for law and order in that country.[25] This made it almost impossible for international donors, including the United Nations and the European Union,[26] to work effectively in the country and forced the EU to work mainly from assistance offices outside Iraq or heavily protected in the green zone in Baghdad with very restricted freedom of movement.[27]

## Organized crime as a multinational corporate activity

Organized crime is today an industry with its own research and development branches and with technologies and a focus on growth much like any industrial or commercial activity. The literature claims that it is one step ahead of law enforcement methods, organized in divisions of activity, and ready to commit widely different crimes. Organized crime is increasingly a global phenomenon for profit where significant efforts are deployed to prevent detection of the top hierarchies, not least within Europe itself. Organized crime is strongly differentiated, including financial crime, use of the Internet and cybercrime, and trafficking in arms, sensitive technologies, scarce resources, human beings, drugs, intellectual property etc. The development of organized crime is likely to be facilitated through the further technological evolution in a number

24  http://www.osce.org/bishkek/89477
25  Bremer III, L P, 'with Malcolm McConnell', *My Year in Iraq: The Struggle to Build a Future of Hope*, 2006.
26  As symbolized by the tragic death of Sergio Vieira de Mello, head of the UN office in Baghdad, in a terrorist attack in 2003.
27  As witnessed by the author during a visit to Baghdad in 2006.

of areas, including miniaturization of delivery vehicles, development of real-time surveillance techniques, etc.[28]

For law enforcement it remains a constant struggle with often fewer resources and a slower decision-making system to respond to this threat, closely related to globalization itself.

### Organized crime and multilateral and thematic approaches

All these considerations have successively led to more holistic multilateral approaches, as illustrated on the level of the United Nations and its Office on Drugs and Crime (UNODC), the OSCE etc. but where the division of labour remains a problem. It has also led to the rule of law becoming a central objective not only in security-related programmes but also in development work as well as in other important thematic areas including EU enlargement.

Manifestly, the ambition for current responses on the international level are extremely limited. To start with, the main UN body responsible for combatting organized crime and terrorism including *e.g.* human trafficking, the UNODC, has a very limited regular budget. It is highly dependent on extra-budgetary contributions for specific projects. Its strategic overview and possibility to provide a strategic basis for international coordination have been extremely reduced. Some of the UN member states clearly do not wish the UNODC to take a leading role, and the governance of that institution does not even allow it.

Similarly, international police intelligence cooperation through Interpol also needs significant extra-budgetary funding.

Setups such as the G7/G8 Roma-LYON group, with its combined discussions of organized crime and terrorism, are very useful forums for comparing notes but include only a few countries and have no permanent coordination mechanism. If Russia will have to stay outside this framework, this will reduce the relevance of this format considerably.

28   Naim, M, *Illicit: How Smugglers, Traffickers, and Copycats are Hijacking the Global Economy*, Anchor, 2006.

*The Need for Broader Strategies and Coordination Formats*

In conclusion, the present study favours the proposition that this set of generic problems of impact has faced the European Union with the need to create broader strategies and coordination formats. The following chapters provide further examples of this need, including notably when discussing more generic formats for coordination, such as border management.[29]

## 2.3 Terrorism

*From the European Security Strategy 2003:*
Terrorism puts lives at risk; it imposes large costs; it seeks to undermine the openness and tolerance of our societies, and it poses a growing strategic threat to the whole of Europe. Increasingly, terrorist movements are well-resourced, connected by electronic networks, and are willing to use unlimited violence to cause massive casualties.

The most recent wave of terrorism is global in its scope and is linked to violent religious extremism. It arises out of complex causes. These include the pressures of modernisation, cultural, social and political crises, and the alienation of young people living in foreign societies. This phenomenon is also a part of our own society.

Europe is both a target and a base for such terrorism: European countries are targets and have been attacked.

*Fighting terrorism as a bad flow*

This section focuses on the 9/11 attacks in the United States as a milestone in the EU's fight against terrorism, the ways in which the EU has proceeded in this struggle, and the most widely discussed generic problem of impacts encountered.

Before 9/11[30] the European Union Council body working on counterterrorism issues, (COTER), was not in high gear. This

---

29 eeas.europa.eu/.../fs_integrated_border_management_canciani_en.pdf
30 Personal notes of the author from the period in question.

intergovernmental working body was relatively alone among the EU structures discussing terrorist threats. Most member states described this as a thoroughly intergovernmental area, highly sensitive, and difficult to discuss in multilateral settings. No real link was established to organized crime and there was no perceived legal basis to conduct counterterrorism projects outside the CFSP budget.

The G8 had formed a dedicated working group on organized crime in 1995 in Lyon but it would last until October 2001 before it was complemented by a counterterrorism group (the Roma group). The European Commission was represented on high level from the emerging DG on justice and home affairs in the Lyon group dealing with organized crime. In contrast, the counterterrorism Roma group soon merged with the Lyon group and initially had only a single working-level representative from the European Commission external relations DG.[31]

There were more than a dozen international antiterrorism conventions in the UN system, including the International Convention for the Suppression of the Financing of Terrorism and the International Convention on the suppression of Terrorist Bombings.[32] However, there was no UN committee dedicated to dealing with these issues, and the level of adherence to these conventions was low. The UN Office on Drugs and Crime in Vienna began slowly to focus on promoting the ratification of these conventions from 1999, but this work started to accelerate only in 2002.

In the United States, the Clinton Administration had initiated work on issues related to the protection of critical infrastructure, but these discussions found no real counterpart in the European Union before 9/11.[33]

---

31  The so-called Roma group representative was initially David Spence and thereafter the current author in cooperation with Patricia Holland.

32  Keohane, D, 'The Absent Friend: EU Foreign Policy and Counter-Terrorism', *JCMS: Journal of Common Market Studies* 46, no. 1, 2008, pp. 125–146. The link was also established with the FATF recommendations and to national law in the member states. There was also an Indian proposal on a draft UN global conventional terrorism.

33  USA, President of the, 'Presidential decision directive Critical infrastructure protection', NSC-63, 1998.; European Commission, Communication from the Commission on a European Programme for Critical Infrastructure Protection', COM(2006) 786 final, 2006.

Against this background the 9/11 terrorist attacks became a milestone for the European Union in the fight against terrorism.

The EU did not go as far as the United States did. There, the entire homeland security system was oriented to fit the concept of the war against terrorism, while the approaches chosen in the EU were predominantly only indirectly related to counterterrorism and were mainly internal to the Union. From the US perspective it soon became clear where the interest should be focused as regards European contributions: it was to a large extent about the fight against terrorism within the European Union. This required harmonized legislation among the member states in a number of specific areas.

Here the EU was better prepared. There was already a project in place to produce a common definition of terrorism as well as a harmonized system for arrest warrants.[34] Both initiatives received the highest priority in the post-9/11 action plan.

The link between internal and external action was important, although this was not always openly discussed.

On the external side the EU's role was less interesting from the US point of view and progress was very slow. As could be expected, each rotating presidency of the Council sought to define a visible priority for its work in the area of counterterrorism. It often took the form of selecting a few priority countries for intensified counterterrorism cooperation. However, the resources available for such work in the intergovernmental pillar turned out to be insufficient.[35]

Whenever attempts were made to start serious discussions with major interlocutors on the topic, for instance with Pakistan, it became obvious how small and insignificant EU activities in this area were perceived to be, already in relation to what was being done by member states bilaterally and in particular by the United States. This made the European Union a rather uninteresting partner in cooperation on counterterrorism.[36]

---

34  Wouters, & Naert, *Of Arrest Warrants, Terrorist Offences and Extradition Deals* *An Appraisal of the EU's Main Criminal Law Measures against Terrorism after '11 September'.*

35  Personal notes of the author.

36  Personal impressions of the author.

*Harmonizing Counterterrorism with Rule of Law Objectives*

This remained a serious problem also after the entry into force of the Lisbon Treaty in 2009. When efforts were made to define projects with objectives connected to counterterrorism the EU soon ran into serious internal difficulties. Strong resistance was quickly mobilized in the European Parliament against using generic development aid to promote counterterrorism objectives.[37] The critical discourse continued to broaden over the years to include important issues related to human rights and protection of data. Several measures that the US wanted to introduce in order to pre-identify potential terrorists resulted in drawn-out negotiations, particularly in the European Parliament.

Balancing rule of law interests with counterterrorism objectives continued to be a significant problem.

The legal basis for external counterterrorism projects remained difficult to establish. It was also counteracted by other high-priority objectives in both the Council and the European Parliament.

Many of the leaderships in key fragile countries where counterterrorism was a major national objective were also dictatorships with very corrupt elites. In some countries, such as Uzbekistan, counterterrorism was also seen as an opportunity for the regime to legitimize more or less brutal activities directed against the opposition, including free media and NGOs.[38]

For the EU institutions it became extremely important not to become a party to such activities. This meant that the EU had to refrain from taking action in many areas where such counterterrorism action was warranted, even if it could have been implemented without difficulty.

*The tendency to underestimate the EU contribution*

By and large, however, the EU contribution to counterterrorism is underestimated because of its largely implicit nature: most of what the EU and its member states do in order to counter terrorism is

---

37  Wennerholm, Brattberg, & Rhinard, *The EU as a counter-terrorism actor abroad: finding opportunities, overcoming constraints,* EPC Issue Paper 60, 2010.
38  A Pyati, & N Hicks, 'Karimov's War,Human Rights Defenders and Counterterrorism in Uzbekistan', *Human Rights Defenders and Counterterrorism Series* ,Series 3, 2005,

solidly embedded in policies with other strategic objectives.

Partly, this can be seen as a tactical posture intended not to make it too difficult to implement such programmes in terms of political support and legal basis within the Union. It may also in some cases be difficult to get agreement with external partners on counterterrorism objectives in external assistance. The way forward thus has not become more secrecy but rather more generic policies.

### The importance of generic policies

The EU is pursuing a number of generic and thematic policies that are highly relevant to counterterrorism without including counterterrorism in their legal basis. Examples include border management and counteracting radicalization and recruitment of terrorists through development policies. Generic ways have been found in order to promote programmes that indirectly would counter terrorism, beyond more general rule of law programmes. The added value of making these policies more explicit is now discussed in the context of the Millennium Development Goals.

### Counterterrorism as an explicit objective

The second major priority in the 2003 European Security Strategy was counterterrorism. This overall priority was not replicated in the following decade in any strategic document approved by the EU. In the website presentation of different policy areas followed by the EEAS, counterterrorism is currently listed as one of many global challenges and not as a specific policy area. It is symptomatic that the link from this website does not, at the time of writing, direct access to an internal part of the EEAS but rather to the counterterrorism coordinator in the Council Secretariat.

This means that a conscious, constant effort is required not to lose the link to counterterrorism in the external presentation of EU policy. This has proven to be very difficult to achieve.

### Counterterrorism and flow security

The implementation of efforts to link counterterrorism with flow security analysis at large is uneven throughout the EU policies.

However, in some areas, notably nuclear security, a systematic approach has been developed.[39]

More generic discussions related to flows, including the protection of critical infrastructure, are gradually developing.

The previous section noted the proliferation of activities of organized crime into areas where law enforcement is less developed. The fact that proficient knowledge in the use of the Internet is widespread around the world and does not require important financial resources is also an aspect of this proliferation and allows the development of increasingly more sophisticated methods that can also support terrorist objectives.

## Counterterrorism and the link to defence

This discourse may have a strong link to defence since several state actors involved in serious conflicts around the globe have also been known to support terrorist groups.

The fact that terrorism is often supported by religious leaders has also made it possible to recruit a large number of suicide candidates, which is very difficult to counteract. The infiltration of suicide candidates into law enforcement structures and even military structures has proven very problematic in countries such as Afghanistan and Iraq. It also has proven possible to implement terrorist acts using very simple methods such as so-called improvised explosive devices (IEDs). The countermeasure to this very simple technology has cost the US Defense Department several tens of billions of dollars due to the need to acquire new armoured vehicles that can protect at least to a certain extent ground transportation in sensitive areas.

## Counterterrorism in a comprehensive approach

There is also a strong link to fragility and to the comprehensive geographic and crisis management approach that has been promoted for some years in the Horn of Africa.

The multilateral discourse on counterterrorism has started to be mainstreamed into a broader set of issues often referred to as transnational threats, including organized crime and different forms of

39   Levi, MA, *On Nuclear Terrorism*, Harvard University Press, 2007.

trafficking. This has been the case for UNODC and the OSCE[40] and is a major issue related to the rule of law.

### Terrorism as an internal threat

Otherwise, counterterrorism can in the first place be seen as an internal discourse for the EU.

And there is a solidarity clause in the Treaty of Lisbon referring to this threat in terms of crisis response and more controversially as a defence perspective.[41]

Terrorist objectives can be pursued without major means. This has made it extremely difficult to prevent for example lone terrorists such as the young man who perpetrated a horrific crime in Norway.

It remains very difficult for large countries such as Russia to protect their entire territories against terrorist acts.[42] As a case in point, it was possible for the Russian Federation through enormous investments in security to protect the highly visible Sochi Winter Olympics in 2014. However, it was not possible to prevent individual terrorist attacks such as the ones that took place in Volgograd just before the Olympics.

At the time of writing, increasing attention is being given to the fact that many Europeans are fighting on the rebel side in Syria, and some may return to Europe with terrorist ambitions. This issue that is likely to be followed quite closely by European intelligence services but at the same time it is difficult to deal with on the European level through explicit policies.

### Setting priorities

Counterterrorism work has to be prioritized in time and space and according to the level of threat posed by individual terrorist

40  Lundin, L-E, 'OSCE and Transnational Threats', OSCE Focus Seminar October 2012, 2013,

41  Ekengren M, 'New security challenges and the need for new forms of EU cooperation: the solidarity declaration against terrorism and the open method of coordination', *European Security* vol. 15, no. 1, 2006, pp. 89–111.

42  Orttung, R, & A Latta, *Russia's Battle with Crime, Corruption and Terrorism (Routledge Transnational Crime and Corruption*, Routledge, 2012.

acts. It is only natural that the greatest attention to counterterrorism objectives has been given to the issue of the proliferation of weapons of mass destruction for terrorism purposes, discussed in the next section.

## 2.4 WMD Proliferation

*From the European Security Strategy 2003:*
Proliferation of Weapons of Mass Destruction is potentially the greatest threat to our security.

### Combating the proliferation of WMD

This section focuses on WMD non-proliferation policies in the EU and their generic problems of impact. A large part of this story is directly linked to the implementation of the WMD non-proliferation strategy adopted by the EU in 2003 in the intergovernmental context.

The issue of the inclusion of Community policies in this strategic framework is a second major challenge.

The balancing act of non-proliferation and other strategic security-related objectives is a third challenge.

Fourth, the issue of multilateral leverage is briefly discussed.

The issue of crisis response is further discussed in section 3.4.

In the previous sections referring to defence, crisis management, and counterterrorism, strategic breakthroughs in policy development are observed, sometimes catalysed by major crises.

The conflict prevention, flow security, and organized crime sections describe a more gradual process of policy development.

### The WMD strategy in the CFSP context

In this respect, WMD non-proliferation in the European Union shows more similarities with the first group of sections than the second. Decisive steps towards an EU policy in this area were taken during the traumatic year 2003, with its debate on Iraqi nuclear capabilities and the promulgation by the European Council of the

European Security Strategy in parallel with the Strategy Against the Proliferation of Weapons of Mass Destruction.[43]

The latter document became an overall external WMD strategy situated mainly in the intergovernmental CFSP framework. It had a clear link to geography. It was often seen as a part of the response to the US National Security Strategy[44] and thus a part of the strategic partnership with the USA.[45] It had a clear reference to the multilateral vector with the emphasis on international law, and in particular on the nuclear Non-Proliferation Treaty (NPT) and its associated legal documents.

The objective of the strategy was to support the work of the International Atomic Energy Agency (IAEA), not least in the area of nuclear security. At the same time, it was intended to influence potential future nuclear powers not to pursue nuclear weapon programmes.

It was in the intergovernmental domain mainly dependent on the resources that could be liberated within the Common Foreign and Security Policy (CFSP) budget, but in strong competition with other demands. The political coordination around these goals resulted, however, in a possibility also for member states to orient their own political and material efforts in the same direction.

### Little initial emphasis on the community side

Initially, the WMD strategy did not explicitly address much of the relevant work underway in the Community sphere. Notably, Euratom was not mentioned in the strategy itself. Also conceptually, non-proliferation was in the work of the Council closely linked to the legal basis established in the framework of the CFSP. What the European Commission did was initially seen more as associated measures that could be useful in supporting non-proliferation efforts in a general and indirect way.

This meant that at least initially there was no attempt to include

---

43  'Fight against the proliferation of weapons of mass destruction – EU strategy against proliferation of Weapons of Mass Destruction', 2003,

44  Bush, G W, *The national security strategy of the United States of America*, 2002,

45  The thinktank Fride maintains an observatory collecting papers on EU strategic partnerships http://www.fride.org/project/28/european-strategic-partnerships-observatory

in the strategy more than what could be described as explicit, security-related WMD issues. Broader considerations of what other issues could be relevant was not at this stage a major priority, which was natural given the initially very limited staffing levels in the Council Secretariat dealing with these issues. The main interested Council formation was the second-pillar CONOP non-proliferation working group as well as the Political and Security Committee (PSC) itself.

The first-pillar Atomic Questions group devoted little time to broader non-proliferation issues.

In order to support Council efforts, a few exceptional decisions had been made in 2000 to use expertise from the European Commission to not only support but also implement joint actions decided in the CFSP.[46]

But later efforts to create inter-pillar coordination through the development of an informal WMD Monitoring Centre were slow in becoming effective and were largely discontinued in the first years after the entry into force of the Lisbon Treaty.[47]

The question to what extent Community policies really need to be integrated into sensitive nuclear programmes is discussed extensively in the literature and is often linked to the notion of mainstreaming.[48]

*Nuclear security as a form of layered defence*
*requires broad mainstreaming*

It is noteworthy that nuclear security, to take a prominent example, can be seen as one of the most sophisticated models for border management. It is built on the concept of *layered defence*, mean-

---

46  A part of the unit headed by the author from 1 September 2000

47  Council of the European Union, 'EU Strategy against the proliferation of WMD: Monitoring and enhancing consistent implementation', 16694/06, 2006. Interview with EEAS official.

48  Grip, L, 'Mapping the European Union's Institutional Actors related to WMD Nonproliferation', SIPRI, 2011; Grip, L, 'Assessing Selected European Union External Assistance and Cooperation Projects on WMD Non-Proliferation', EU Non-Proliferation Consortium Non-Proliferation Papers 6, 2011; Anthony, A, & L Grip, *Strengthening the European Union's future approach to WMD*, Sipri Policy paper 37, 2013..

ing that every step along the way to making violations of existing national and international legislation more difficult adds to the probability that the criminal or terrorist will fail in his endeavour.

The European Union has also given higher priority to the area of nuclear security in the past decade. The Pakistani Khan network that helped to proliferate knowledge and equipment to several countries in the beginning of the millennium was shown to have used many links to Europe. This[49] required enhanced cooperation not least in the area of nuclear security in order to beef up border management export controls and other activities such as the Proliferation Security Initiative.[50]

The way the European Union approached transnational threats through geographically defined border management programmes was very different from the initial US approach. For some time after the creation of the internal Homeland Security system, the United States promoted a host of specialized programmes deploying border management equipment in order to detect WMD and other sensitive materials, etc. The EU chose primarily a mainstreaming approach, region by region.

It is understood that the more contributions that could be given from the Community side to this layered defence, the more effective it will be.

## *Other relevant Community programmes: From regional to global*

The Community has over many decades developed considerable expertise and activities relevant to the nuclear domain. The European Commission set up extensive external programmes parallel to the CFSP on nuclear issues. These were initially concentrated in the area of enlargement, the EU Neighbourhood and Russia, notably dealing with existing or possible future civilian nuclear energy installations, including Chernobyl, in several cases in countries with a legacy of WMDs.[51]

---

49  *Ibid.*
50  Nikitin, M B, 'Proliferation Security Initiative (PSI)', *Congressional Research Service*, 2012.
51  Council of the European Union, 'Council Regulation (Euratom) No 300/2007 of 19 February 2007 establishing an Instrument for Nuclear Safety Cooperation', 2007.

A task after the cold war and the combination of unilateral disarmament decisions with multilateral and bilateral arms control agreements was to finance important programmes to destroy excess material and reorient and re-employ excess staff, including scientists who had been involved in developing WMD technologies.

Through the Commission the EU developed into a major international donor. This was notably exploited by the G8 countries when developing support for the Global Partnership Against WMD Proliferation in 2002.[52] At that time the European Commission pledged €1 billion for a period of a decade, including the considerable funds devoted to the post-Chernobyl nuclear safety agenda.

With the adoption of the Instrument for Stability[53] in 2006, efforts to combat WMD proliferation received a global mandate in the Community framework. The geographic scope was broadened and now encompassed almost all parts of the world. The relevant multilateral and thematic contexts also increased in number.

In terms of flows, there has been a partial integration of different nuclear concerns into an overall chemical, biological, radiological and nuclear framework[54] through the establishment of so-called CBRN centres of excellence. This has enabled the use of Community funds in many areas and opened up possibilities to mainstream with other both internal and external policies, including notably through the Internal Security Strategy from 2010.[55]

*Euratom and the Lisbon Treaty: Coexistence but limited synergy*

The opportunity, sadly, was not taken to integrate the Euratom Treaty into the Lisbon Treaty. Instead, the Euratom Treaty – one of the three communities set up in the 1950s – was kept intact.[56] This was of course very strange logic as nuclear safeguards are a key element of security in the European Union and the rest of the world. However, the domestic political hesitation to renegotiate

52   http://www.nti.org/treaties-and-regimes/global-partnership-against-spread-
      weapons-and-materials-mass-destruction-10-plus-10-over-10-program/
53   *Ibid.*
54   *Ibid.*
55   Council of the European Union, 'Internal Security Strategy of the EU', 2010.
56   Piris, J-C, *The Lisbon Treaty: a legal and political analysis*, Cambridge University
      Press, 2010.

this very sensitive treaty as regards the use of nuclear energy was seen by many as 'a bridge too far'.

The literature includes extensive mapping of the potential of different Community policies in support of non-proliferation. This is also continuously discussed in the academic network set up by the EU in support of the NPT. At the time of writing, this discourse is however not a priority item on the agenda of EU leaders.

### *Difficulties to develop a principled approach to non-proliferation*

Implementation of non-proliferation principles over time developed into a very difficult task, contrasting values and principles with the interests of EU member states in other related areas.

The EU made a point in the European Security Strategy of declaring its allegiance to the international legal framework set out in the Non-Proliferation Treaty. Partly, this could be seen as a message to the Bush Administration regarding its unilateralist policies focusing on rogue states rather than on the NPT regime as a whole.[57]

Already before decisions were taken on the overall strategies of late 2003, non-proliferation clauses had been introduced which were supposed to be mainstreamed into all mixed agreements between the EU and external partners. This legally excluded the Euratom agreements from being covered, but still meant a potential constraint on EU trade and other policies.[58]

The implementation of these clauses soon ran into difficulties.

The first significant compromise made in this regard was related to the policy vis-à-vis Israel as a non-party to the NPT and the decision to try to protect the Middle East peace process from destabilizing effects. This meant an agreement on the part of the European Union together with the United States and a number of other like-minded countries not to focus on Israel as a non-declared nuclear power. The first priority when discussing a nuclear weapon-free zone in the Middle East therefore became to focus on peace in the Middle East at large and only thereafter to discuss the specific nuclear issues.[59]

---

57  Personal notes of the author.
58  *Ibid.*
59  Council of the European Union, 'Council Decision 2010/799/ CFSP of 13 December 2010 in support of a process of confidence-building leading to the

A second problem appeared in 2005 when the United States made a major concession to India, paving the way for their cooperation in the field of civilian nuclear energy, an industrial sector under considerable development in India.[60] This concession was soon followed by a change in policy also by Canada and several European countries. India, also not a party to the Non-Proliferation Treaty, would normally not have been eligible for such cooperation. This led to acrimonious discussion between the parties to the Nuclear Suppliers Group, leading to a compromise that made an overall application of a principled approach to the NPT more difficult for the future.

To this was added the problem of prestige in the bilateral negotiation of clauses with like-minded countries such as Canada and the Republic of Korea: it was difficult for these important countries to accept that the EU imposed language on them that had not been drafted through common effort. All of this meant that a systematic application of clauses in EU external agreements became essentially non-effective.

Against this background, the EU's dealing with problematic proliferation cases became largely a case-by-case policy affected by extraneous considerations.

### Progress on Iran

At the time of writing, significant progress is being made in the negotiations with Iran after many years of frustration. An initial effort to engage with Iran in a win-win negotiation format, including the prospect of a trade and cooperation agreement, became essentially impossible during the first George W. Bush Administration.

Instead, under UN auspices the international community introduced significant restrictive measures which over the years imposed enormous suffering on the Iranian people.

---

establishment of a zone free of weapons of mass destruction and their means of delivery in the Middle East in support of the implementation of the EU Strategy against proliferation of weapons of mass destruction', *Official Journal of the European Union* L341, 2010.

60   Kerr, P K, 'U.S. Nuclear Cooperation with India: Issues for Congress', Congressional Research Service, 2012.

At the same time, High Representative Javier Solana, with his personal expertise in physics, took on a leadership role for contacts and negotiations with Iran. This was made possible not least due to the absence of high-level US-Iranian contacts for many years. The new High Representative, Catherine Ashton, continued in this role after the entry into force of the Lisbon Treaty. The presidential elections in Iran in 2013 paved the way for progress in these negotiations.

So there is a combination of problems of impact ranging from the internal situation in Iran to the coherence of the international community in its policies towards Iran.

### Preventing further horizontal proliferation

Several potential nuclear weapon powers have over the years taken the decision to abstain from acquiring nuclear weapons. Others, notably countries in the former Soviet Union, have forsaken their nuclear weapon arsenals in exchange for security guarantees. A third category includes notably Libya, where a nuclear capability has been counteracted through intensive efforts to interdict trafficking in WMD materials and knowledge, not least from Pakistan.[61]

North Korea remains a special case where the survival of the regime seems closely linked to a nuclear weapon capability in the eyes of the leadership of the country. Extensive offers to create a viable negotiating framework through the Six Party talks has been made more difficult due to internal transitions in the country, including power struggles and changes in the leadership.[62]

### The multilateral level

The EU has also been active on the multilateral level in support of non-proliferation objectives, in particular as regards the NPT regime. Experience over the years, not least from the IAEA, shows that for the EU to win in multilateral diplomacy it is necessary to engage in very broad political consultations and demarches with

---

61   Levi, MA, *On Nuclear Terrorism*, Harvard University Press, 2007.
62   One of the first examples of the use of the term 'comprehensive approach' in the literature: Armitage, RL, *A Comprehensive Approach to North Korea*, DTIC Document,1999.

a large number of countries, which may or may not be focusing on non-proliferation. In such political dialogue, it is essential for the EU representatives to be able to build on the full range of EU relations with the country in question, including on Community matters. This became easier to do after the entry into force of the Lisbon Treaty but is still problematic due to the continued existence of the Euratom Treaty.

## Crisis response: Experiences from Fukushima

Occasionally, the nuclear area has entered into crisis mode and was associated with actual or potential conflicts.

For instance and perhaps mainly, this was the case in Iraq, where the WMD issue became a part of a wider spectrum of issues relating to the Middle East, to oil as a flow issue, and to a certain extent also to terrorism.

Initially, the EU could not contribute much to this discourse except by adapting its CFSP tools to the general situation. This set of tools included sanctions decided by the United Nations Security Council. But it also involved geography in the sense that it shaped EU bilateral policies on the relevant countries and also involved decisions and non-decisions in important thematic areas such as trade.

When discussing crises with implications in terms of violence and human physical suffering, at the time of writing the European Union has not yet come to a situation that can be described as a multisector major crisis response situation. This is obvious when one considers the level of suffering and destruction encountered by Japan during the combined catastrophe of a devastating tsunami followed by a nuclear catastrophe in 2011.

In external crisis situations affecting thematic areas, the instinctive reaction from the EU is rather natural: when the Fukushima nuclear disaster occurred in 2011 the main actor in the follow-up was the European Commissioner responsible for energy. He sought to ensure that the European public did not see the catastrophe as something that could also happen on European soil.[63] For this reason stress tests were undertaken to check the viability of the nuclear

63   Personal notes of the author.

safety systems in the EU. Still, Germany and Italy took drastic decisions to end expansion of nuclear energy.

The nuclear energy renaissance in Europe as promoted not least by France was at least temporarily halted in Europe – but not in the world as a whole.[64]

### An area of untapped potential

In summary, this is an area with a lot of untapped potential for the EU to develop a more comprehensive approach. However, it is also an area fraught with risks due to insufficient preparation for potential future crises.

---

64  WN Association, *The Nuclear Renaissance.*

# 3. Organizational Cultures

This chapter introduces a third perspective, looking at problems of impact through the lens of four organizational cultures that may be considered predominant in the EU structures. They are all familiar to students of European Union external action. The first culture, (3.1), a predominant organizing principle for the EU External Action Service (EEAS), is geography. The second (3.2) is the thematic organizing principle dominating the differentiation of European Commission structures into several dozen major policy areas. The third culture (3.3) is the multilateral organizing principle in a broader than traditional sense. Finally, (3.4) returns to the crisis perspective, with an emphasis on the generic interface between normal bureaucratic routines, including contingency planning and crisis prevention efforts, and crisis itself, which may affect every area of EU action within and outside the Union. All of these organizational cultures, with the addition of those dealing specifically with legal, budget, and staff issues (see chapter 5), overlap, also in a bureaucratic sense since a geographic department may have thematic sub-entities and vice versa.

## 3.1 Geography

*From the EU member states' Council conclusions on the Comprehensive approach 2014:*
The point of departure for EU policy and action must always be the country or regional context and the political reali-

ties and needs on the ground. This is where we face and deal with security threats, crisis situations, and development challenges. EU Delegations together with EU member states Representations have a key role to play in supporting a coordinated, comprehensive and effective EU approach, in particular on issues relating to joint analysis, coordinated programme implementation, and the preparation and sharing of political reporting. Co-location of EU actors in the field should also be considered wherever feasible. The substantial progress made in taking forward joint programming in the EU's development cooperation provides a good model for how to link up the efforts of EU institutions and Member States in a comprehensive approach at the country-level.

### *Developing EU external action towards specific countries and regions, including strategic partners*

The point of departure for this section is the conception that geography[1] is a key organizing principle for foreign ministers and their main counterpart in the EU, the High Representative of the Union for Foreign Affairs and Security Policy (High Representative, HR). It was not unusual in the past for foreign ministries to have a constitutional prerogative to deal with correspondence with foreign states. For a very long time, states and state borders constituted and perhaps still constitute the predominant cognitive map of the world.

For the purpose of this study, it is therefore natural to see EU relations with its strategic partners,[2] other key actors, and most significantly neighbouring regions as a fundamental approach that has an important bearing on security. This is also the approach taken by the EU both before and after the entry into force of the Lisbon Treaty. The literature is replete with discussions about the need for a holistic EU posture in such relationships and their bearing on security over time.

---

1    On geography as a paradigm see: Kaplan, R D *The Revenge of Geography: What the Map Tells us about Coming Conflicts and the Battle Against Fate,* Random House, 2012.

2    On strategic partnerships see http://strategicpartnerships.eu

## The United States, Russia and China

The first case in point is the EU's relationship with the United States.

> *From the European Security Strategy 2003:*
> The United States has played a critical role in European inte-
> gration and European security, in particular through NATO.
> The end of the Cold War has left the United States in a domi-
> nant position as a military actor. However, no single country
> is able to tackle today's complex problems on its own.

Taking into account that since the Second World War the United States has taken overall responsibility not only for global but also to a large extent European security, for good and for bad, this becomes entirely obvious. Anything that makes it more difficult for the US government and citizens to perceive Europe as important for US development and security is thus a problem for European security policy.

There are several factors frequently discussed in the literature. One is the degree to which US foreign policy is determined by domestic factors.[3] Another is the discourse relating to the US pivot towards Asia. When seeking to counterbalance trends that are making Europe less important for the USA, a wide range of EU policies become relevant, such as trade negotiations, cultural policies, etc.

At the time of writing, enormous attention is being devoted to defining the long- and short-term EU relationship with Russia. The strategic partnership is questioned. The historic contribution of the Russian people to security in Europe during the Second World War is still widely recognized. At the same time, what is perceived as increased unpredictability and aggressiveness of Russian policies is met with strong criticism.

What Russia does as a regional power and not least its role as a global nuclear-weapon power continue to be vital for Europe. The focus has, however, at least temporarily shifted away from creating a strategic interdependence between the EU and Russia, promoting common ground. The emphasis has recently shifted to diversifying

3    See for example: Moore, WH, & DJ Lanoue, 'Domestic Politics and US Foreign
     Policy: A Study of Cold War Conflict Behavior', *The Journal of Politics* 2003,

European dependence on Russia, notably in the field of energy. Russian reactions to increased European integration with its neighbours in the post-Soviet space are met with restrictive measures. The literature often links this to problems of internal cohesion in Russia itself, which thus is seen as a problem of impact for the EU. The same applies to perceptions of EU intentions in Russia and its neighbourhood. Economic and social, including demographic, conditions arguably push the Russian leadership to focus domestic political attention on external problems.

A wide range of EU actions have been discussed over the past decade ranging from multilateral cooperation towards a security community in the Eurasian space,[4] to policies intended to isolate Russia and restrictive measures affecting freedom of movement, capital etc., and a more assertive Western defence posture.

The importance of China for the EU and its member States is sometimes and perhaps most often related to assumptions about a continued success story for China as an economic and later also military power. A significant role of China in Africa and elsewhere has already been developed, including an interest-based cooperation with a number of undemocratic regimes around the world. A more assertive military posture has also emerged, not least at sea and a more complicated relationship with Japan with references back to the traumatic experiences during the Second World War. Several factors could make things worse from an EU point of view. The Chinese military-industrial complex could start more actively to look for theatres where the Chinese military could gain operational experience. An arms race related to the American Air-sea battle doctrine could escalate.

But the trend projections of Chinese growth could also turn out to be false, possibly due to environmental problems (air and water), or due to internal corruption.

A lack of success for Chinese power ambitions does, however, not necessarily mean less of a problem for Europe. In such scenarios internal destabilisation could lead to increased projection of threats externally.

In such situations security of supply may become even more of a real issue for Europe.

---

4   Carnegie Endowment, *Towards a Euro-Atlantic Security Community*, 2012;
    Zellner, W 'Towards a Euro-Atlantic and Eurasian Security Community From
    Vision to Reality', 2012.

❋❀❋

These key examples illustrate the wide scope of security-relevant policies in the geographic paradigm. It should be obvious that a security policy based only on conflict analysis, as discussed in chapter 1, or even flow security, in chapter 2, is not sufficient. The examples above illustrate the overall importance of European internal and external integration.

This study returns to these issues in chapter 4, in the discussion of the overall leverage of the EU, significantly based on the Community framework, notably access to the internal market of the European Union for both goods and people.

## Overlapping regional subdivisions

The picture may not seem to be too complicated, but the next question, from the geographic perspective – how should the world be subdivided in terms of external action and security-related policies? – raises more difficult conceptual issues.

These issues can be tackled either by recalling the historical evolution of geographically defined EU policies or through a more analytical approach. Even a superficial look at EU security-relevant geographic policies shows that the map of the world continents does not shed light on how EU policies are shaped. For instance, there has been no holistic document on an EU strategy for Asia for more than a decade.[5]

If the post-cold war frame of reference for external relations is taken as a point of departure, the special emphasis in the literature on the format defined by the Organization for Security and Co-operation in Europe (OSCE) deserves mention. The OSCE membership includes the United States and Canada and the entire post-Soviet space, and recently also Mongolia. This format has influenced not only the configuration of regional multilateral units in the Commission before entry into force of the Lisbon Treaty, but also the geographic subdivision in the EEAS, which treats Central Asia as a part of Europe rather than Asia. It is a subdivision that reflects expectations based on joint political com-

5    Lundin, LE 'From a European Security Strategy to a European Global
     Strategy: Take II: Policy options', UI Occasional Papers 13, 2013,

mitments related to higher standards of democracy, human rights, and fundamental freedoms as well as the rule of law. Importantly, these commitments are not only politically agreed on the level of the osce but also to a large extent legally binding for the members of the Council of Europe and enshrined in a number of partnership and cooperation agreements between the eu and non-eu countries. Theoretically, this is a discourse very much related to the works of Fukuyama,[6] with his hope for a democratic future of the world after the cold war.[7]

A second subdivision of considerable importance for the organization of the eu geographic approach refers to problems related to economic development and more specifically to the Millennium Development Goals (mdgs).[8] This is a sub-paradigm that has emerged from an initial focus in eu development policies on supporting and linking the eu up with former colonial areas. Within this framework, a specific focus has recently emerged on areas, altogether around 60 countries with 1.5 billion inhabitants, where mdgs are not reached because of fragility.

A third subdivision can be said to constitute areas and countries of primary importance for European trade and access to natural resources. Here the literature typically discusses a list of economically strategic partners, including the rapidly developing brics countries[9] (Brazil, Russia, India, China and South Africa) on the one hand and on the other other countries rich in natural resources, including energy. Theoretically, this is a debate close to the discourse on great powers, geopolitics, and the realist school of politics.[10]

A fourth subdivision is based on the notion of proximity to Europe and the extent to which countries may or may not be

6   Fukuyama, F, *The End of the History and the Last Man.*, Reprint ed., Penguin
    Books, 1992.
7   *Ibid.*
8   High-Level Panel of Eminent Persons on the Post-2015 Development Agenda,
    *A New Global Partnership: Eradicate Poverty and Transform Economies through
    Sustainable Development*, 2013.
9   Keukeleire, S, & H Bruyninckx, 'The European Union, the brics, and the
    Emerging New World Order', International Relations and the European Union
    2011, pp. 380.
10  Mearsheimer, J, *The Tragedy of Great Power Politics*, Revised edition ed., W. W.
    Norton & Company, 2014.

affected by the EU's power of attraction. This geographic paradigm encompasses both problems and opportunities: potential accession to the EU, and problems in terms of various transnational and other threats including the proliferation of conflict and uncontrolled migration. Just as development policies initially focused on earlier colonies, different neighbourhood policies have also attracted different levels of attention over time depending on the balance of interests in the EU itself, resulting in policies for the eastern, southern, and lately also northern and Arctic dimensions, as well as attention to the Western Balkans.[11]

A fifth, very controversial discourse relates to the clash of civilizations fault line put forth by Samuel Huntington.[12] Here the cognitive map of the world is more complex and a debate has raged for the past two decades about the viability of this concept., This debate is largely about the importance of religions and the conflict between religions, including different strands of Christianity. Geographically, it is reminiscent of the fault line of conflicts inside the former Yugoslavia, on Cyprus, between the eastern and western parts of Ukraine, between Moslem and Western states, etc. Debates about the way ahead for more or less secular societies, with Turkey as a central focus, have been underway for decades, and the 9/11 attacks no doubt revived the debate.[13]

It should be obvious already at this point that the extent to which all these policies effectively take into account EU security interests is not only related to security issues but also to the way in which coherent policies are created across countries and regions. One can observe a trend from the early 1990s away from in-country programmes to cross-border measures, to regional horizontal efforts, and finally from 2006 to transregional coordination frameworks. In some cases, such as the European neighbourhood, it has also been vital to coordinate internal EU programmes with external programmes.

11   On the neighborhood and enlargement policies – see further the bibliography.
12   Huntington, SP, *The Clash of Civilizations and the Remaking of World Order*, Simon & Schuster, 2011, Rose, G, *The Clash of Civilizations?: The Debate*, Council on Foreign Relations 2013.
13   See Betts in Rose, *The Clash of Civilizations?: The Debate*.

Central Asia is an example of different overlaps: It is part of
the first OSCE subdivision, despite high levels of corruption
and lack of democracy. It is, secondly, a poor and fragile region.
Third, it is energy rich and has been important for Western
logistics to Afghanistan. Fourth, it has been described as part of
the strategic neighbourhood of the EU. Coordination with the
region is implemented through a regional strategy. At the same
time, the region is included in a number of transregional coordinating formats, for instance countering transnational threats
and promoting energy flows.[14] Finally, the role of Islam in relation to Orthodox Christianity has replaced the earlier debate
about the viability of a secular Communist society in this part
of the former Soviet Union.

## Generic problems of impact in cooperative and conflictual relationships

This section recapitulates references to such problems in the previous chapters. Chapter 1 discusses defence and the US interest
in contributing to European defence. The issue of the European
defence industries' ability to compete on a level playing field with
US companies was mentioned, an issue that is very relevant in the
trade context. When discussing crisis management some problematic actors such as China[15] were mentioned as well as the absence
of agreement with Russia on principles for peacekeeping in the
post-Soviet space. An overload of crisis management challenges in
the European neighbourhood was discussed. As for conflict prevention, difficulties encountered in developing a European political
dialogue with other actors, avoiding a zero-sum game, was also
mentioned.

Chapter 2 discusses flow security. The disconnect between geographic departments and thematic perspectives dealing with flows
was noted as well as the difficulties in taking up defence against
transnational threats emanating notably from Afghanistan.[16]
This problem includes the wider issue of how to mainstream a

14   On Central Asia see the bibliography.
15   See Shambaugh, *China Goes Global: The Partial Power,* Oxford University Press,
     2013.
16   For further reading on Afghanistan see the bibliography.

series of thematic concerns into geographic programmes, ranging from conflict prevention, to counterterrorism, non-proliferation, humanitarian disarmament, etc. How to develop agreements on sensitive security-related programmes with external partners was also mentioned. The role of the Comprehensive Approach to external conflicts and crises[17] was predominantly defined geographically, starting with the Horn of Africa.

In these bilateral relationships to countries in different parts of the world, the EU in many cases has developed a posture with predominantly cooperative features featuring an assistance paradigm, whenever possible built upon local ownership and joint agreements. To this posture has, in particular when the power of attraction of the EU has been more significant, been added conditionality approaches.

However, in some bilateral geographic relationships this paradigm has had to be replaced – sometimes abruptly sometimes more gradually – with a less cooperative paradigm where for instance rampant corruption[18] affecting the overall policy of the partner has led to conflicts of interest and non-implementation of jointly undertaken commitments. In such situations cooperative endeavours have been blocked, often simply through non-decisions, and been coupled by negative reactions in the European private sector reducing the level of interaction, and sometimes combined with restrictive measures targeting, in particular, corrupt elites. The last set of measures often of course has been relevant in situations where the interest of the potential partner country as a whole might not have been deemed identical with the leadership of that country.

These shifts over time constitute a problem for EU strategic continuity and increase the resistance among member states to agree

17   Council of the European Union, 'Council Conclusions on the EU's Comprehensive Approach Foreign Affairs Council meeting Brussels, 12 May 2014', 2014, ; High Representative & European Commission, 'Joint Communication to the European Parliament and the Council. The EU's comprehensive approach to external conflict and crises', 2013,
18   For further reading on corruption see the bibliography.

to long-term definitions of EU policy with concrete references to geographic relations. This has been visible both in defining the EU's strategic partners and in defining the EU neighbourhood, which in existing strategic documents, notably the 2003 European Security Strategy, is ambivalent.[19] At times this has even affected the EU-US relationship, as could be seen particularly during the first George W. Bush Administration and the EU-Russian relationship after the war in Georgia in 2008 and then again from the Ukraine crisis that erupted in 2014.

Even more complicated of course has been the situation in regions and countries where the leadership situation was unstable and where the EU has needed to focus more on interaction with civil society and the country as a whole rather than on the local leadership at any one time. In such situations, as experienced during the Arab Spring, the EU has found it difficult to apply normal practices for instance with local ownership and joint agreements on external assistance.

It is also complicated for the EU to decide to implement support programmes for civil society in countries where at the same time restrictive measures are being contemplated or even implemented. This may require action through other organizations and NGOs.

## Coherence of EU postures

It has turned out to be extremely problematic in cases such as Turkey to define a coherent posture vis-à-vis countries which on the one hand are seen to be in the process of coming closer to the European Union, and on the other as pursuing unacceptable policies of security, human rights, etc.[20] Here the balance has had to be sought between a policy that on the one hand maintains a process towards accession, while at the same time avoiding a full EU commitment to the conclusion of the process, partly due to internal differences among EU member states.

A geographic analyst can lose a clear overview in many other

19   Compare: J Solana, 'A secure Europe in a better world', *Natos Nations and Partners for Peace* 2003, pp. 28–30; E Council, 'Report on the implementation of the European Security Strategy – providing security in a changing world', 2008; EGS, 'Towards a European Union Global Strategy', 2013,
20   Further reading on the issue of Turkey see the bibliography.

ways, too. One example relates to the situation in the group of candidate countries and countries that are considered as next in line for potential accession. In such situations more clear benchmarks are developed, a good thing in itself. Increasingly, attention may be focused on some specific accession-related benchmarks, which may, however, cloud the vision of other risks.

> As a case in point the accession process in Bosnia was for a long time focusing on moving towards a more multi-ethnic society with less divisions between Bosniaks, Croats and Serbs. But then suddenly in late 2013 another paradigm started to dominate the picture, namely the contradiction between corrupt leaders in general and an underprivileged population. So those analysing the situation and the way ahead for Bosnia suddenly had to reorient their analysis in a way which in some respects reminded of the situation during the Arab Spring and then later also in the Ukraine.

This means that strategies for countries need to be carefully considered in order for them to work properly over the longer term. This also means that the categorization of countries in groups of states – for example, strategic partners, enlargement candidates, failing states, development assistance recipients, etc. – often does not work as a basis for long-term comprehensive approaches. Governments and leaders may change; crises may influence the assessment of the country in question, etc.

All the above examples effectively support the decision taken at the establishment of the European External Action Service (EEAS) that the EU needed a single unified geographic desk for each country that is not institutionally attached to any one paradigm, be it enlargement, development, trade, or neighbourhood policy. It needed to be generic in its analysis of the situation and the way ahead for the EU relationship to each country and region.[21]

This is arguably a major improvement of the situation since the entry into force of the Lisbon Treaty. Previously, many of the desks were influenced by specific cultures such as trade, enlargement,

---

21  Laursen, F. 'The European External Action Service (EEAS): the Idea and its Implementation', The EU's Lisbon Treaty: Institutional Choices and Implementation 2012, pp. 171.

development, etc. which may have blinded their analysis in some respects.

The effectiveness of EU security-related geographic policies is closely connected with the coherence with member states' policies and the degree to which the EU can promote effective coalitions with like-minded countries. A generic problem of impact often discussed in this context is the coherence of EU political dialogue with that of its member states vis-à-vis strategic partners such as China. Sometimes one can observe that a strict normative position agreed on the EU level is undercut for trade and other reasons by individual member states, leading China to prioritize bilateral relationships with EU member states, undercutting EU leverage.[22]

# 3.2 Thematic Cultures: Development, Freedom and Justice

*From the Review of implementation of the European Security Strategy 2008:*
As the ESS and the 2005 Consensus on Development have acknowledged, there cannot be sustainable development without peace and security, and without development and poverty eradication there will be no sustainable peace. Threats to public health, particularly pandemics, further undermine development. Human rights are a fundamental part of the equation. In many conflict or post-conflict zones, we have to address the appalling use of sexual violence as a weapon of intimidation and terror.

*Developing EU external action in thematic areas relevant to security*

If the geographic paradigm is the main organizing principle for the EEAS and for foreign ministers, it is arguably also true that the thematic paradigm is the main organizing principle for the European

---

22  IFfHR, & HRi China, 'RE. Joint assessment of the EU-China Human Rights Dialogue ad Legal Expert Seminars', 2008, For a contextualized discussion of normative power see Kavalski, E, 'Partnership or Rivalry between the EU, China and India in Central Asia: The Normative Power of Regional Actors with Global Aspirations', *European Law Journal* 13, no. 6, 2007, pp. 839–856.

Commission while still important for the structuring of the EEAS, including in fields such as human rights. This section looks briefly at the relationship between a number of thematic cultures and security. What generic problems of impact does the European Union meet when thematic benchmarks are defined? This is an interesting question in several respects:

First, if it can be argued that security is a generic problem of impact for achieving these benchmarks.

Second, if it can be argued that deficient achievement of these benchmarks in turn is a generic problem of impact for security.

So there can be influence in both directions, which in the end affects EU security.

### *Focus on development, freedom, and justice*

A number of examples of relevant policy areas, in themselves form-ing the basis for organizational cultures, are described in the litera-ture. The examples below illustrate generic problems rather than outline the issues in detail in relation to security: *development*[23] (in a very wide sense including industrial development and trade aspects),[24] *freedom*,[25] and *justice/rule of law*.[26]

As shown in this and the following sections, even on this general level of analysis there is a complex set of relationships. It is impos-sible to explore all types of links. Suffice it to say that the analysis

---

23   Further reading on development – see bibliography
24   Further reading on trade-related aspects – see bibliography
25   Further reading on freedom-oriented topic – see bibliography
26   Further reading on the rule of law – see bibliography. The rule of law as an objective has been horizontally approached by European Union member states both in the context of the European Union itself and in other regional and bilateral contexts. It is thus not only in the OSCE a human dimension issue. It is also and very important priority in the economic and environmental dimension of the OSCE with a early focus on investment protection by the German chair in the beginning of the 90s. It is also as noted above a prominent objective in the security domain, not only in relation to the democratic control over Armed Forces but also in other thematic areas such as developing a legal framework to prevent human trafficking and other forms of security related organised crime and terrorism. The implementation of the rule of law thus is closely related to development but corruption remains a fundamental problem. Freedom coupled with a certain amount of lawlessness has in some countries allowed a massive transfer of public goods into private.

indicates the need for greater attention to the coordination of these thematic policies with those relating more explicitly to security.

The delimitation to the interlinkages between development, justice, freedom, and security can be said to be relevant for a number of policy areas and DGs in the European Commission as it is organized at the time of writing.

First, it is relevant for DG Development and Cooperation (DEVCO),[27] which is largely organized in support of the Millennium Development Goals with its proposed emphasis on the links between development, peace, and justice.[28]

Second, it is relevant to DG Enlargement with its benchmarks, including the freedom and rule of law criteria for candidates' accession that were adopted by the 1993 Copenhagen European Council:

- stable institutions guaranteeing democracy, the rule of law, human rights, and respect for and protection of minorities;
- a functioning market economy and the capacity to cope with competition and market forces in the EU;
- the ability to take on and implement effectively the obligations of membership, including adherence to the aims of political, economic and monetary union.[29]

Third, it is relevant to the justice, liberty, and security aspects of Commission internal policies.[30]

Fourth, it is relevant for policy areas defining the rules for eco-

27  The European Union works on the basis of general definitions and priorities established in the OSCE. In its dedicated development assistance policies, it applies the definition of official development assistance ODA that governs what types of assistance are eligible to be counted under this heading.

28  As the time for revision of the Millennium development goals came closer, it was noted that some 60 fragility countries with more than 1.5 billion inhabitants were not progressing in their MDG implementation. Specific objectives to promote the rule of law and security were therefore proposed. This increased the potential for considering security goals in development policies, but was contradicted by problems in the UN to get acceptance for this. In the OECD the definition of what is eligible official development assistance (ODA) may therefore be influenced by the Millennium development goal revision of 2015.

29  http://ec.europa.eu/enlargement/policy/conditions-membership/index_en.htm

30  With a DG Home focusing on security and the rule of law and DG Justice focusing on freedom and the rule of law.

nomic and social integration within and outside the Union. Some of these rules are also defined on the international level, notably by the World Trade Organization (WTO) involving the DGs for finance and trade.

In the European Union none of these policies is explicitly security policy in their legal base, but they are at least partially included in different security concepts, such as the internal security strategy of 2010.[31]

It is also noteworthy that in one major region of the world, the OSCE region, the comprehensive concept of security promoted by the EU links security with the rule of law, economic/environmental development, and freedom.[32] EU coordination of this work is carried out by the EEAS from a CFSP perspective.

Typically, thematic policies include most of the types of policy discussed in chapter 2 related to flow security. It is therefore significantly the coherence of these thematic cultures with the conflict analysis pursued in the defence, crisis management, and conflict prevention sections of chapter 1 which needs to be highlighted here.

## Thematic policies in fragile settings

First a note on defence: In almost all Community thematic contexts, defence-related objectives are subordinate to other objectives and due to their weak legal base are often not spelled out. Still, important studies have been carried out that show how important the defence industry is for overall industrial development and research[33] and how important industrial development and research

31   Council of the European Union, 'Internal Security Strategy of the EU', 2010.
32   As for the CSCE area, focus was during the Cold War on maintaining international peace and security while at the same time from the Western perspective to promote freedom in the area of the former Soviet Union. Development objectives played a very limited role and there was little hope for a real rule of law; judicial systems were by definition seen as corrupt instruments of the Eastern leaderships. Since the end of the Cold War, there is political commitment on the part of all countries from Vancouver to Vladivostok to build democracy. Specific agreements were also achieved in the early years of the 90s to the effect that human rights do not belong to the internal affairs of countries. These principles have also been reaffirmed relatively recently. However, the implementation of these commitments is clearly being perceived as destabilising on the part of leaders in a number of countries in the world.
33   Further reading – see bibliography

are for defence in a globalized world. European industrial development is in this context closely related to trade, particularly with the United States but also significantly within Europe, which makes protectionism a general problem. A specific issue in the trade context is the extent to which the European defence industry has a level playing field, not least with the US industry.

An overall requirement for defence capacity building is of course the availability of resources for defence. However, it can also be argued that defence is a critical issue for economic development, the rule of law, and freedom.

Formally, the HR, in her function as Vice-President of the European Commission, could be argued to have a coordinating role in order to keep attention focused on all these issues. Her constraints in terms of multi-tasking capabilities make this a generic problem of impact. This is one out of many issues relating to coordination that face the Commission and the EEAS. Section 5.3 returns to this issue.

Moving into crisis management, the incremental and ad hoc nature of EU crisis management efforts can be seen as problematic in relation to development needs, not least in fragile settings, including those related to rule of law and freedom-related benchmarks.

This lack of systematic attention to crisis management has not been compensated by a more consistent approach in other organizational contexts, neither on the level of regional organizations, including NATO, nor on the level of the United Nations.[34]

In some key areas, there is a glaring lack of agreement on crisis management with global participation, notably in the region of the former Soviet Union outside NATO.[35]

In other regions, such as the Middle East, EU capabilities for crisis management cannot make a significant impact.

Conflict prevention is a security objective which, according to a 2001 Commission decision, should be mainstreamed into all rel-

---

34   As noted above the United Nations is much overburdened in terms of peace-keeping.

35   Kemp, W, & D Sammut, 'Confidence building matters. Rethinking the OSCE European Security after Budapest', Verification Technology Information Centre,1995,

evant Commission programmes.[36] It has thus been formally accepted as an integral part of the efforts deployed in the three types of thematic policy discussed in this study related to development, rule of law, and freedom. The main generic problem of impact is thus not the formal one, but one closely related to resources and structures, which ideally should enable constant, systematic attention to this objective.

Political attention in turn is conditioned by crisis and the CNN effect on the focus of attention.

Generic problems of impact include lack of coordination between intergovernmental/Community structures, internal/external structures, and the degree to which conflict prevention is made an explicit objective in relevant strategic documents, be they holistic, geographic, thematic, or agreed in the multilateral context.

It can be argued that the conflict prevention area is one of the most convincing examples of the need for comprehensive coordination of EU external action, not least in the interface between thematic and geographic policies.

### The problem of sequencing of policies and mainstreaming comprehensive security objectives

*From the EU member states' Council Conclusions on the Comprehensive Approach 2014:*
The Council underscores the need for the EU to better, earlier and more systematically link up its political engagement, its CSDP missions and operations, its development cooperation and assistance, and other relevant domains of EU action, in particular in countries or conflict situations where the EU deploys multiple actors, instruments and interventions. The Council stresses that the strategically coherent use of the EU's instruments and policies – simultaneously or in sequence – is necessary to effectively address the root causes of a conflict or crisis.

36  Kronenberger, V, & J Wouters, *The European Union and conflict prevention*, TMC Asser Press, 2004..

A comprehensive approach should also enable rapid EU action as required. The Council also underscores the need to continue to strengthen the ties between CSDP and the areas of Freedom, Security and Justice (FSJ) and more effectively develop synergies between CSDP actions with FSJ actions as well as actions carried out in other EU domains.[37]

Seen over time in the conflict cycle, the sequencing and prioritization of different goals and instruments are arguably therefore very important for stability and security.

To give one example, in the OSCE discourse representatives of a number of countries have put the argument forward that stability and peace and even development is dependent on another set of priorities than those agreed in the OSCE in the beginning of the 90s. There may still be agreement on the need to hold elections. However, in conditions that do not allow an opposition to build popular support, in particular due to lack of freedom of media including the Internet, early elections may arguably rather destabilize than stabilize. In such not infrequent situations, EU may find it difficult to adapt its posture. Should the EU still push for early elections or not?

Another example of sequencing problems can be taken from the area of trade. If the development of a Third World country has not reached competitive levels it may be difficult to apply global standards for trade without an intermediary period of trade capacity building. Thus, arguably countries in these situations also may destabilize. This has led to the evolution of development programs by the EU aiming at preventing such situations, for example in cooperation with UNIDO in Africa. Similarly, countries outside the EU may need assistance in order to be able to export to Europe, following agreed standards for European products, for instance in the area of food safety.

---

37 Council of the European Union, 'Council Conclusions on the EU's Comprehensive Approach Foreign Affairs Council meeting Brussels, 12 May 2014', 2014.

*The need for strategic overview accentuated in*
*the interface with thematic policies*

In summary, it can be noted that not only in relation to flow security but also in relation to the conflict cycle, the sequencing and the mainstreaming of various thematic objectives require a very sophisticated and strategic analysis, which needs to be updated more or less continuously.

## 3.3 Multilateral[38]

*From the European Security Strategy 2003: An International Order Based on Effective Multilateralism*

In a world of global threats, global markets and global media, our security and prosperity increasingly depend on an effective multilateral system. The development of a stronger international society, well functioning international institutions and a rule-based international order is our objective.

*Developing effective EU multilateralism*

Continuing the identification of organizational cultures beyond the geographic and thematic paradigms, there is also a multilateral paradigm. It was referred to in earlier chapters and sections and

38  There are important points of reference in the scholarly literature produced by researchers seeking to define the role of the European Union in international relations, and in particular in multilateral contexts. A series of contributors have sought to elaborate on this; the most important works seem to have been published just before the entry into force of the Lisbon Treaty and there is still not so much literature available at the time of writing of this chapter, on how the Treaty, the EEAS and the new EU delegations can be seen in this theoretical context. To a certain extent, this literature refers to roles of the EU A useful summary of different strands in the literature has been made by Jørgensen (Jørgensen, K E, *The European Union and International Organizations*, Routledge/Garnet Series: Europe in the World, Routledge, 2009) referring to five trends from legal, institutional studies, the EU as an international actor, inter-organisational networks, the EU policy of supporting multilateral institutions, multilateral organisations as prime parts of global governance. He then adds on a sixth perspective focusing on the EU as an actor inside international organisations, precisely the perspective which earlier, before recent failures of the international system to meet global challenges, was not seen as an essential issue for EU member states in Vienna.

describes further problems that are important for effective multi-lateralism in the EU in domains of relevance to security.

In the modern world this does not just involve relations between more than two states or between international organizations. It is also very much an issue of relations between international organizations and national and non-governmental actors throughout the world.

## Generic problems of impact discussed so far

Recapitulating, the following was noted in chapter 1, the conflict cycle, with reference to the multilateral context:

Defence interoperability with NATO was difficult due to the fact that not all EU member states are members of NATO.

In the area of crisis management a major discourse, in particular during the 1990s, dealt with the overlap and duplication of efforts of international organizations in crisis management.

The extension of EU crisis management efforts to the civilian domain in the early years of this millennium led to more complex coordination requirements vis-à-vis the United Nations.

In Africa, the EU was a small, vulnerable actor in crisis management, requiring strong support from both the UN and regional organizations. This prompted an effort to find new ways to support these organizations through building an African peacekeeping capability.

An EU crisis management role in the former Soviet space was difficult to define due to Russia's resistance in the OSCE to the principles for so-called third-party peacekeeping. In this region efforts had to be limited to supporting the OSCE and the UN, as well as deploying a few civilian missions, notably those in Georgia and Moldova.

The EU's readiness to contribute to conflict prevention efforts in crises remained limited partly due to a lack of support for high-level mediation through the EU itself or through other organizations.

In some areas of the European neighbourhood, such a role was also hindered because of a perception of the EU as an actor in conflicts which undermined the EU ambitions to mediate in multilateral contexts.

When designing programmes aimed at preventing conflicts, they were often integrated into complicated donor coordination schemes requiring implementation over long periods, risking loss of consistent effort in support of desired outcomes.

Another shortfall was insufficient direct links to civil society.

As regards flows, discussed in chapter 2, the EU experienced a lack of leverage in international negotiations, for instance on climate change.

Problems were encountered when taking up defence in depth in relation to bad flows. The administrative and political difficulties in organizing programmes and projects were at times overwhelming.

Contradictory approaches were sometimes developed by other actors, which made it more difficult for the EU to reach its goals, for instance to counteract drug trafficking at its source.

A positive move towards more holistic strategies addressing drugs, organized crime, and terrorism could be seen in organizations on both the UN and the regional levels. However, the division of labour with the EU remained a problem.

The EU itself was also often weak in mobilizing geographic, thematic, and notably multilateral expertise in support of its work, as referred to in sections 3.1 and 3.2.

The problem was aggravated by the fact that the international organizations dealing with bad flows, notably the United Nations Office on Drugs and Crime (UNODC), had small regular budgets, which undercut their capabilities to provide a strategic framework for international cooperation.

The European Union arguably needed to develop multilateral efforts in organizations such as the OSCE to compensate for the difficulties to implement civil society projects in countries where the EU had less comparative advantage.

Finally, when discussing thematic organizational cultures, a key factor for further progress was agreement in the United Nations and the Organization for Economic Co-operation and Development (OECD) on security and rule of law components of the Millennium Development Goals from 2015.

Similarly, the EU's possibility to be effective on the level of the OSCE and other regional organizations was linked to the extent to which these organizations adopted and were able to maintain support for comprehensive concepts of security, including democracy and human rights.

❄❆❄

Quite a number of issues relevant to multilateral organizing cultures are discussed above. These illustrate perceptions of a need for a multilateral culture in security policy going considerably beyond the cooperation established during the cold war.

The authors experience in this regard is not least related to his role as EU representative in Vienna: Euratom cooperation was served by a Commission delegation to the international organisations in Vienna. This delegation also served as a bilateral delegation to Austria before the accession of Austria to the Union in the beginning of 1995.

At that point, a new multilateral issue had come up, symbolised by the invitation to Jacques Delors to take a seat at the table of the CSCE Summit in Paris in 1990. In the early 90s the Conference on Security and co-operation in Europe which had lived through a difficult Cold War period since the Helsinki Final Act in 1975 saw a new beginning and possibly new important tasks which would require significant EU support in order to be realised.

In a relatively short period from 1995 to 2000, this was developed into an explicit EU policy for cooperation between the EU, the newly formed organisation OSCE and other international organisations in Europe. The above-mentioned Platform for cooperative security was adopted at the OSCE summit in Istanbul in 1999 and signed by not only the rotating President of the European Council Ahtisaari but also by the President of the European Commission Prodi.

It would still take another 10 years until after of the entry into force of the Lisbon Treaty until a strong role for the EU in its own right as an actor in the OSCE was developed, most visibly seen by the fact that the President of the European Council delivered the main speech on behalf of the EU at the OSCE Summit in Astana in 2010.[39]

---

39   Lundin, L-E, 'Effective Multilateralism: the EU Delegation in Vienna' in J Bátora, & S David (eds.), *European Diplomacy post-Westphalia*, Palgrave, 2015.

*The evolution of an EU security-related multilateral perspective*

Security-related challenges relevant to multilateral frameworks have been and remain wide-ranging: in the OSCE – the transformation of Europe in the Western Balkans and the post-Soviet space after the cold war; in UNODC – the emergence of so-called soft security threats, organized crime including drugs, terrorism, and different types of trafficking, typically in transnational and even transregional settings; and in the International Atomic Energy Agency (IAEA) the challenges of the proliferation of nuclear weapons and nuclear technology at the same time as the number of new actors in the field of nuclear energy increased worldwide.

The pertinent question is the point at which the multilateral approach emerged on the level of the EU itself.

The EU has a history of slowly evolving multilateral policy. The first and most well-known example of this, which at least at the time did not have an explicit connotation in terms of security objectives, was trade, an area where the European Commission at an early stage had acquired supranational competencies. These were applied on the global stage mainly in Geneva through the European Commission delegation to the international organizations there, in particular in 1995, when the WTO came into being. Closely associated to this was the relatively strong position of the European Commission in the OECD, with its leading role in defining the setting for development policy, another area with strong Commission competences exerted through the Commission delegation to the international organizations in Paris. Another early example was full membership of the UN Food and Agriculture Organization (FAO) in Rome.

The European Commission recognized the need for a dedicated Commissioner for Climate Action from 2009 after a less successful EU role in international negotiations on this important topic.

Gradually, EU policies were also developed in the area of energy, where the European Energy Commissioner started to interact with other organizations such as the Organization of Petroleum Exporting Countries (OPEC) after decades of cooperation within the framework of Euratom with the IAEA.

The European Community became a UN observer in 1974 and established its first delegation at UN headquarters in New York in the same year. Later, other multilateral delegations were established in Geneva, Vienna, Paris, and Rome. The last EU observers to arrive came to the African Union in Addis Abeba and to the Council of Europe in Strasbourg.[40]

However, over the years the EU also took on prominent informal roles in the G8 (Group of Eight industrialized nations) and other contexts.

The EU also participated in conflict resolution formats with the UN and other regional organizations.

Notably, a specific role was acquired in the area of non-proliferation by High Representative Javier Solana and then Catherine Ashton after the entry into force of the Lisbon Treaty. Here the role was even more prominent in an informal multilateral setting, namely, to speak on behalf of the EU 3+3 (China, France, Germany, Russia, the United Kingdom and the United States) in negotiations with Iran.

The Community and later the EU also participated in the negotiation of international treaties and agreements. The EU is in different capacities party to a number of international legal instruments.[41]

### From coalition building to an EU actor capability

An actor capability of the EU itself, in particularly as regards security in international organizations, is of course bound to affect member state sovereignty.

There must therefore be strong reasons for member states to want to use the EU for multilateral purposes. Should therefore multilateral approaches not be developed by the member states themselves, since they are those mainly represented in various international organizations? Is it not ineffective to go through yet another international entity in order to achieve impact?

To a certain extent, this may be the way member state govern-

---

40 Lundin, *The* EU *as a regional organization. Effective multilateralism in conflict management*, in: P Wallensteen, & A Bjurner (eds.), *Regional Organisations and Peacemaking Challengers to the UN*, Routledge, 2014

41 A perhaps surprising example was the accession of Euratom to the NPT additional protocol in 1998 where the current author had the honour to sign on behalf of the European Communities. This signature was a necessary condition for achieving full coverage in the EU.

ments see it in the context of their daily work in international organizations. It may be that only when they find their own impact on the decisions and actions of international organizations too limited that they may turn to various forms of coalition building, including through the EU. By preference, this will of course take place in an intergovernmental approach.

Such coalition building in many international organizations will typically take place through the formation of regional groups that consult on various issues and sometimes put forward joint statements and initiatives. This is what the European Union has done for a long time. Of course there have throughout the years also been other regional forums that included some EU member states, including NATO, the preferred format for arms control negotiations in the OSCE framework from the time of the cold war. In the UN context, the EU member states are split between the group of Western and other states and the Eastern group, which still is the group used for election purposes and includes some Central European member states. Some of these groupings include the USA and some other like-minded states, while others are strictly European.

For the EU to win in multilateral diplomacy it would, however, seem necessary to engage in broad, prioritized, and substance-oriented political consultations[42] and demarches with a large number of countries on issues under negotiation, as discussed in the section on non-proliferation, 2.4.

In such a political dialogue, it is essential for the EU representatives to be able to use the full range of EU relations with the country in question. EU performance in this regard is so far suboptimal.

Globally, this failure has been discussed in the context for instance of climate negotiations, where many have wished to see more EU leverage of the type existing in the WTO.

### Benefitting from the resources of the Community

As a precursor to the discussion in chapter 4 covering the main policy contexts of the EU, the fragmentation of intergovernmental

---

42  *EEAS Review* recommendation : Review priorities and seek to streamline formal political dialogue meetings at Ministerial and senior official level. Meetings should be scheduled based on the substance to be discussed.

and Community efforts must be seen as a negative factor in terms of effective multilateralism.

The issue is not only one of the EU working within other international organizations. Member states have enabled the European Commission to become one of the largest international donors and in this capacity to become a major actor in the field through the EU delegations. In some of these contexts, EU efforts have been deployed in multilateral formats, through donor coordination setups often dominated by the Commission and the World Bank.

As a general principle, of course, taxpayers should not have to contribute to an international organization through yet another international organization. But the structural rules set up after the demise of the Santer Commission in the late 1990s for EU assistance policies, to a large extent set in stone in the generic financial regulations of the EU, changed this situation dramatically. The EU was prohibited from implementing most of its projects itself – tendering procedures needed to be implemented with the exception of certain international organizations (as well as EU member states). This led to a dramatic increase in the financial support to the United Nations system, sometimes exceeding €1 billion per year. This was made possible through extensive central negotiations between Brussels and New York on the conditions for such support, including overhead costs, EU visibility, auditing, etc.[43]

The more Commission programmes intervened in security-relevant situations, the greater the need for multilateral coordination of intergovernmental and Community efforts. In the immediate post-cold war period this need was only tentatively recognized by EU member states, for instance through the above-mentioned invitation of the Commission President Jacques Delors to the CSCE (Conference on Security and Co-operation in Europe, from 1995 renamed the OSCE) summit in Paris in the latter half of 1990. This led to a presence of Community representatives in various multilateral meetings throughout the 1990s

The role of the Community was not a major issue in the discussions pursued by the European Union and to a certain extent

43   Bjurner, A, 'On EU peacemaking – challenging or complementing the UN?'
     in P Wallensteen, & A Bjurner (eds.), *Regional Organisations and Peacemaking
     Challengers to the UN*, Routledge, 2014,Lundin, *The EU as a regional organization.
     Effective multilateralism in conflict management.*

by NATO in the mid-1990s about the future division of labour between international organizations in the area of security. The OSCE concept of a Platform for Co-operative Security among international organizations started to be discussed in the EU inter-governmental security working group in the Council. There was concern that these organizations would not be mutually reinforcing in their work, but rather 'interblocking'.[44]

However, when the European Security and Defence Policy started to be developed after 1998, the issue soon became much more relevant. First of all it was deemed necessary to include the European Commission, at least formally, in the security regulations governing cooperation between the European Union and NATO. The European Commission also was represented at the regular meetings between the PSC and the North Atlantic Council, co-chaired by the High Representative and the NATO Secretary-General.[45]

As efforts broadened into civilian missions with significant rule-of-law components, the need for a combined intergovernmental and Community format started to become more evident. On the one hand, it was important to coordinate what the EU member states themselves did in terms of bilateral support to the work of organizations such as the OSCE, where EU member states financed more than half the budget and deployed an even larger percentage of the staff to large OSCE missions, particularly in the Western Balkans.

However, in other contexts and in other theatres member states decided to set up EU missions, including in the Community context. The EU also decided to support the peacekeeping capability of other organizations through Community contributions. In some contexts, such as in the Western Balkans, it was deemed more effective to create direct EU visibility in the field rather than to depend on the visibility of other organizations. The increased visibility of an EU operation was deemed important also for domestic political reasons in a number of EU member states.

---

44  see http://core-hamburg.de//documents/yearbook/english/oo/Rotfeld.pdf
45  The current author participated on behalf of the Commission in a large number of such meetings.

## Operationalizing effective multilateralism

The above clearly shows that operationalization of the effective multilateralism objective in EU explicit and implicit security policy documents has been very difficult. This was a problem even when developing the European Security Strategy in 2003. It was deemed necessary to emphasize the importance of effective multilateralism and international rule of law in contrast to the perceived US unilateralist approach under the first George W. Bush Administration. However, this was mainly seen at the time as a message to the US Administration regarding its disregard for international legal instruments, such as the Nuclear Non-Proliferation Treaty.

## Supporting international organizations

Effective multilateralism, in the end, is dependent on strong EU support to the multilateral forums in which the EU wishes to be an actor. If the EU remains ambivalent about the role of international organizations, these forums will remain weak.

> *From the EU member states' Council conclusions on the comprehensive approach 2014:*
> The Council notes that the EU should reinforce its cooperation with others and coordinate its comprehensive approach with the efforts and engagement by key international partners such as the UN, NATO, OSCE, AU, other regional organizations and bilateral partners engaged in a given conflict or crisis situation, with a view to increase operational effectiveness, with due respect to the institutional framework and decision-making autonomy of the EU. The Council stresses the importance of local ownership and local partners. The Council also highlights the value of the knowledge and contributions of civil society, such as NGOs, think tanks and academia, as well as the private sector.

Member states can cooperate under the EU flag in international organizations.

The European Union, in particular through the European Commission, can act as a major donor in cooperation with other donors.

Then there is a third perspective: the extent to which the EU conducts an effective analysis of comparative added value of its own actions in relation to the potential contribution of other international organizations. In so doing: to what extent does it support those other international organizations to reach commonly agreed goals? This issue is taken up again in section 7.2, enabling influence.

The EU and its member states never made clear-cut decisions on these issues. The deployment of EU operations was based on ad hoc decisions. The EU member states decided on a case-by-case basis to support the UN and the OSCE and deployed military resources through NATO or through a coalition of the willing, as in Iraq and Afghanistan.

Given the number of different multilateral and bilateral settings it will probably take a long time for the EU to decide how it wants to configure its coordination and implementation of multilateral cooperation.

At the seat of international organizations, there has been very uneven willingness on the part of member states to coordinate their bilateral assistance in a multilateral framework.

Member states also for a relatively long time abstained from authorising a strong EU role in various informal political mediation and conflict settlement processes. This was discussed in the early 90s for instance as regards Nagorno-Karabakh where a slightly varying configuration of countries led the so-called Minsk group for the settlement of the conflict.[46] In this scenario the EU role was foreseen to be limited to paying some of the bill through the Community budget to reconstruct destroyed settlements.

Taking such a decision is of course easier if the organization in question or the forum for informal cooperation has adopted a comprehensive concept of security that includes freedom, justice, and development.

---

46   The current author could observe this also from his work in the Minsk Group
     in the mid-1990s.

Such organisations do exist, notably the Organisation for Security and Cooperation in Europe, OSCE. Others are less comprehensive, such as the Council of Europe, which focuses on security mainly from the point of view of the rule of law and freedom, and the OECD, which is focusing more on economy and development. Efforts have, however, been made in the Council of Europe to be more involved in conflict cycle processes for instance in Georgia.

## 3.4 Crisis[47]

*From the European Security Strategy 2003:*
In a crisis there is no substitute for unity of command.[48]

### Contingency planning for security-related crisis in external action

This section is intended to correct any impression that might have been created in the first chapter: that the crisis management performed by EU institutions are implemented by the CSDP structures alone.

Crisis management or crisis response is of course a much broader issue in the EU as a whole.[49]

Essentially, and for the purpose of this study, it is an issue of mov-

47  For further reading on the EU as a crisis manager see in particular Barnier, M, *For a European Civil Protection Force: Europe aid*, 2006. Boin, A, M Ekengren, & M Rhinard, *The European Union as Crisis Manager: Patterns and Prospects*, Cambridge University Press, 2013; Méran, F, & A Weston, 'The EEAS and Crisis Management: The Organisational Challenges of a Comprehensive Approach' in J Bátora, & S David (eds.), *European Diplomacy post-Westphalia*, Palgrave, 2015, See also: http://ec.europa.eu/health/preparedness_response/generic_preparedness/planning/argus_en.htm

48  When the chair of the US 9/11 Commission, Governor Keane visited Europe, the current author had an opportunity to participate in a small lunch meeting with him in the presence of Javier Solana and Franco Frattini. When I put the question to Keane about how to coordinate millions of pieces of intelligence in view of a possible crisis, Solana answered in his place: through a single line of command.

49  What will be referred to here is a more general discussion beyond the description of European Union crisis management capabilities ably documented in the study by Boin, Ekengren and Rhinard.

ing efficiently from a normal situation into a crisis and to plan for this eventuality.

This can happen in almost any type of activity both inside and outside the Union.

There are many alert mechanisms in place in different specific contexts in the EU, not least providing a framework for coordination between the Commission and member states.

What is focused on here are crises with wider implications, affecting different policy areas at the same time.[50]

## 9/11

The EU's first real experience of a situation that could have led to a multisector crisis in Europe was the attacks in the US in September 2001. This was a frustrating experience for the European institutions, although it soon became clear that the terrorist attacks would not hit Europe, beyond those Europeans directly affected in the attacks on the twin towers and the Pentagon.

But it was a situation in which questions were asked: whether Brussels was under threat from the air, whether major population centres in Europe were at risk, and whether European Union and member states' presences outside the EU were under attack.

For someone like the current author who was working inside one of the main European Commission buildings in Brussels at the time of the attack, this led to a number of serious questions: How to communicate with the security specialists responsible for coordination in Brussels when the telephone system was overloaded? How to communicate to the hierarchy? Who was in the lead? How to communicate to European Commission delegations abroad? What should be the message to staff: should they go home or stay in their offices? What should be the standard operating procedures for the hierarchy: should it meet and discuss the situation or stay in their offices waiting for instructions? What should be the security restrictions to be established around European institution buildings? On what basis should the lead-

50   For an analysis of the role of events and crises in international security
      see Buzan, B, & L Hansen, *The Evolution of International Security Studies*,
      Cambridge University Press, 2009..

ership of the institutions react to the media and what contacts should be taken with member states and third parties? What should be done if the Internet was down in order to continue to develop situation awareness? How should different alert mechanisms, already existing for different types of crises, be coordinated? How should questions from member states and from the public be handled? Who should take responsibility for derogations in order to undertake crisis missions to outside locations?[51]

Many, if not most, of these questions could not be answered properly that September. Contingency planning for a crisis on this level did not exist.

Still, the level of difficulty in dealing with the crisis did not even vaguely resemble the one, which occurred in the Swedish Foreign Ministry with its embassy in Bangkok on the second day of Christmas in 2005. Tens of thousands of phone calls were placed in a few hours time from relatives asking what was happening to their relatives on holiday during the Asian tsunami. Many of the questions enumerated above were put both during and after that crisis.

### Swift EU reaction to crisis

European action after 9/11 challenged the view that the EU is a slow-reacting bureaucracy, unable to respond to new requirements.

As was also proven later, during the financial crisis from 2008, the European Council swiftly adopted a cross-institutional terrorism action plan comprising 69 points. The European institutions were closely examined to see what was already going on and what could be brought forward as potential European contributions to the fight against terrorism.[52]

---

51  Personal notes of the author.
52  European Commission, 'EU Plan of Action on Combating Terrorism (revised)', 10010/3/04, 2004, ; J Wouters, & F Naert, 'Of Arrest Warrants, Terrorist Offences and Extradition Deals An Appraisal of the EU's Main Criminal Law Measures against Terrorism after '11 September'', 2004, ; de Vries, G 'The European Union's role in the fight against terrorism', *Irish studies in international affairs* 16, no. 1, 2005, pp. 3–9; Bossong, R 'The action plan on combating terrorism: a flawed instrument of EU security governance', *JCMS: Journal of Common Market Studies* 46, no. 1, 2008, pp. 27–48.

One can therefore expect that if there is another major attack in the EU area or seriously affecting the Union, the attention to these issues will rise to the top of the agenda and questions will be asked about how the 9/11, Madrid and London attacks were followed up on the EU level.

This development on the one hand illustrates the importance of crisis to catalyse European integration.

On the other hand it continues to illustrate that, very soon after or even during a crisis, senses are dulled and resistance to change starts to build up.

### The problem of contingency planning: How to move from normal to crisis mode

So the issue is not whether the EU can act in times of crisis. It is more about whether it can do so in a coordinated way in broader areas relating to security and develop truly effective contingency plans.

Issues related to contingency planning are of key importance in the context of crisis response.

At what point is the Commissioner responsible for a specific area willing to abdicate overall responsibility for crisis response and to whom? To what extent can this be set out before the event in overall contingency planning?

There is a very simple answer to this in the European Commission. At the time of writing this is expected to happen in the Commission and under the leadership of the President of the European Commission and the Secretary General of the Commission through the Argus crisis response system set up in 2005.

Even at this stage there is still no accepted crisis response platform for external crises led by the High Representative. Such a platform does in fact exist, but in parallel with another crisis response platform in the Commission coordinated by the Commissioner for Humanitarian Aid and Civil Protection. Both platforms have cross-representation, but not full synergy.

In this sense, only limited progress has been achieved after the entry into force of the Lisbon Treaty.

An empirical case: the Commissioner for Energy took the main EU lead throughout the entire 2011 Fukushima nuclear catastrophe with all its multi-sector consequences, not only for Japan but also for other parts of the world.

However, there is a generic problem of impact also inside the external domain itself, now the EEAS, which has existed since before the entry into force of the Lisbon Treaty.

In the normal situation, geographic departments can be expected to be in the lead and the delegation reporting system is coordinated through them and fed into a distribution centre at headquarters level. Of course, many crises are reported through this system and a strong shock to the system is necessary in order for it to move into an overall crisis mode.

Such a crisis mode essentially means calling for assistance from dedicated crisis response bodies and networks. This is a threshold that officials are not likely to cross without authorization from the top political hierarchy. The inbuilt resistance against giving away what you see as your competence, prerogative, and coordination responsibilities is very strong.

This is of course a dangerous instinct since the services on different levels dealing with issues in the normal situation may lack several assets necessary for effective crisis response. First, they may not be trained properly in how to organize and apply standard operating procedures in crisis of the type mentioned above in the description of the situation during the 9/11 crisis.

In such situations, there will in fact be a need for people who are willing to find ways to derogate normal procedures and to take considered risks, including those for ensuring sound financial management.

As noted above, faced with demanding situations in Haiti and later Libya, the HR decided to bypass the normal crisis management structures and set up a new line of command directly responsible to her dealing with crisis coordination.[53]

Second, the services may require additional staff.

The crisis may be man-made but could also result from natural

---

53   see EEAS, *EEAS Review*, 2013,

catastrophes. In dealing with different crises, the methods may in many respects be the same. The role of a pathologist is not very different after a tsunami in Aceh or a terrorist attack in Bali, Indonesia. The pathologist is in both cases not likely to be able to work with victims according to nationality and will need to be able to work in coordination with staff from many countries.

Therefore, the question who can do what in any crisis needs to be dealt with through contingency planning.

The answer to this question has often pointed to the Commission. Not seldom, the issue at hand has been one of mobilizing resources and finding ways to disburse those resources rapidly, be it to the Middle East or Ukraine.

The CSDP setup suffers from being crippled by intergovernmental rules and security restrictions, which makes it difficult for it to be a part of real-time crisis response in the European institutions.

*Functioning in constant crisis*

The more general problem concerning EU capabilities to transition from the procedures of the normal situation to the state of almost permanent crisis management must also be mentioned. Crisis response requires crisis communication.

Suffice it to say here that the EU has on the level of heads of state and government learned how to do just that when handling the financial crisis.

Although this work has required an enormous amount of sensitivity as regards information, institutions have never allowed themselves to be crippled by procedures, as has been the case both in the context of CSDP and in the implementation of other Commission programmes and projects.[54]

54    Lundin, L-E 'From A European Security Strategy to a European Global
       Strategy: Ten Content-Related Issues', *UI Occasional Papers* 11, 2012; Lundin,
       L-E 'From a European Security Strategy to a European Global Strategy: Take
       II: Policy options', *UI Occasional Papers* 13, 2013,

## *Multitasking*[55]

The European Union, as many other decision-making structures, has run into great difficulties dealing with more than one crisis at a time.

To a certain extent this is related to the above-mentioned CNN effect, which tends to concentrate political attention on just a few issues at any given time and where the same issue seldom figures as priority news for very long.

But there is a second problem, related to the fact that the EU has difficulties in handling several crises at the same time for structural reasons, the issue of multitasking (see further 5.3).

## *Crisis as a catalyst for new forms of EU cooperation*

Crises may break new ground in terms of perceived needs for cooperation on the EU level.

Some of these forms of cooperation are very sensitive, touching on the domestic political debate about subsidiarity. A case in point is consular cooperation.

The consequences of globalization are likely to stretch the limits of what is perceived to be acceptable in this regard, notably in areas such as health security related to pandemics, etc.

55   Views expressed by several respondents during interviews in EEAS 2012–2013

# 4. Policy Contexts

This chapter addresses generic problems of impact, starting (4.1) with the dichotomy of intergovernmental and Community policies, with reference to the more general context in which they are produced. For instance, it is noteworthy that CFSP, with its integral part the CSDP, are both intergovernmental policies. They are (4.2) also fundamentally external to the Union. They are to a large extent (4.3) explicit security policies, although the scope of CFSP goes beyond security in a strict sense, including human rights, etc.

## 4.1 Intergovernmental/Community Nexus[1]

*From the EEAS Review 2013:*
There is no shortage of building blocks for comprehensive and effective EU external policies, and in many cases these instruments have helped to deliver a high level of consensus between Member States and the EU institutions, and on this basis, a strong and well-coordinated response to foreign policy challenges.

It is not always easy to achieve this since it requires the establishment of linkages between: related geographic or thematic topics; the work in different institutions, and even the different levels of discussion in the Council bodies (European

---

1   For an overview of CFSP see further the bibliography in particular Cameron, F, *An Introduction to European Foreign Policy*, Routledge, 2007/2012.

Council, Ministerial Council formations, PSC, thematic working groups). At the same time, the Lisbon Treaty left CFSP intergovernmental and therefore subject to unanimity: in the absence of collective political will and agreement between Member States, this is a limiting factor on decision-making.

Moving a step higher on the ladder of overview, this section discusses the policy contexts of decisions relevant to security in the European Union, focusing on the intergovernmental versus Community approaches.

### Developing security-related EU external action in intergovernmental and Community contexts

Thematic policies are, with few exceptions, closely related to Community policies. In addition many of them are mentioned in the framework of the CFSP, notably in article 21 of the Lisbon Treaty.

The overall framework must therefore be coherent:

*From the EU member states' Council Conclusions on the Comprehensive Approach 2014:*
The Council notes that the operationalization of the principles and proposals of the Joint Communication and these Council Conclusions is a joint undertaking, and a shared responsibility for EU institutions and services as well as for Member States, in capitals and on the ground. In this context, the Council also recalls the provisions in the EU Treaty on consistency in external action and with other policies, and the responsibility of the Council and the European Commission to cooperate to that effect. In this context, the Council stresses the role of the High Representative, who is also one of the Vice Presidents of the European Commission.

Below, generic problems of impact are discussed in the intergovernmental context, and then in a second part in the Community, concluding with some further observations concerning problems in the interface between the two, but first a brief illustrative recapitulation.

*Recapitulating areas affected by the*
*intergovernmental/Community divide*

Chapter 1 notes a number of weakly supported Community policies for promoting defence industry productivity. The European Defence Agency had also to work under very difficult conditions in the intergovernmental context.

The intergovernmental domain in general encountered serious problems due to the lack of resources not least due to resistance from the European Parliament.

The sequencing of efforts in the intergovernmental versus Community spheres was a problem for conflict prevention.

Moving on to chapter 2, flows, the intergovernmental/Community divide in the areas of organized crime, nuclear security, small arms, and counterterrorism were briefly discussed.

Chapter 3 referred to problems of coherence of EU and member state postures in bilateral relations with key interlocutors, case in point being China.

As regards effective multilateralism, the fragmentation of intergovernmental and Community efforts were deemed to undercut EU leverage in international organizations.

In some areas, Commission services were unwilling to integrate their bilateral cooperation with other international organizations into their coordination with EU member states accredited to those organizations. A case in point was, at times, Euratom.

Finally, it was noteworthy that the contradiction between intergovernmental and Community approaches undercut crisis coordination between the Commission and the EEAS.

*The evolution of intergovernmental cooperation*

When analysing intergovernmental versus Community approaches to security, the intuitive assessment by many is quick and decisive: security is a fundamental responsibility of governments and thus has to be dealt with and controlled by the intergovernmental framework of the European Union, with its requirement for unanimity in all decisions.

The basis for policies in the intergovernmental context was created with the Maastricht Treaty, ratified in 1992, and the first real test was in the Western Balkans, with reference to the declaration of Jacques Poos, representing the six-monthly rotating presidency of the Council.[2] However, he had proceeded to set the goals before he had access to the appropriate resources. There may have been a legal basis for action but no real agreement existed between the main players in the EU on what could and should be done. Nor was there a structural basis. The budgetary appropriations were missing.

This could perhaps have been dealt with, had the EU member states been united on what had to be done. They would still have been able to put the resources together and create a capacity without being dependent on the EU's resources. However, the member states were strategically not playing the same tune. Some of them were argued to be implicit actors in the conflict by promoting the statehood of Slovenia and Croatia at an early date.

The early 1990s was therefore too soon to introduce serious EU action in the area of CFSP in the Western Balkans. Still, there was progress among the member states on benchmarks for future members of the Union in the context of CFSP, benchmarks that later became important for the enlargement process. In 1993 the member states agreed on the so-called Copenhagen criteria for accession. They introduced what in the OSCE came to be called a comprehensive concept of security including democracy, human rights, fundamental freedoms, and the rule of law.

However, there was an important flaw in the setup. No real continuity was built into the EU efforts. The rotating presidency had a six-monthly lifespan. The Council Secretariat supporting the presidency had more or less a purely secretarial function.

The European Commission was busy developing the internal market programme of Jacques Delors, who as Commission President saw the possibilities to develop the CFSP with caution. Still he deployed several members of his cabinet to build on the Commission side a Secretariat for European Political Cooperation (EPC).

Moving to the end of the 1990s, after the entry into force of the Amsterdam Treaty, the new High Representative Solana was, as could be expected, strongly focused on the Western Balkans. He had

---

2    Guicherd, C, 'The Hour of Europe: Lessons from the Yugoslav Conflict', *Fletcher Forum of World Affairs*, 1993.

left NATO right after having led the NATO operation in Kosovo, and he brought fresh experience from this unprecedented operation.

Solana soon started a shuttle diplomacy, working with his successor as NATO Secretary-General and with the new Commissioner for External Relations Chris Patten.

In parallel, the new institutional structures for CSDP were developed as an integrated part of CFSP. This took place based on what had already largely been agreed in the Western European Union on the scope of military crisis management operations.

Again, in parallel another initially intergovernmental policy, known as the third pillar, started to develop in the European Union towards the end of the 1990s in the context of the Justice and Home Affairs area.

CFSP remained closely related to normal practices of diplomatic interaction through political dialogue mainly pursued by the rotating presidency and assisted by the incoming presidency and the Commission. This dialogue took place whenever possible in the presence of the new structures of the Council Secretariat.

However, these structures were not supported by a field organization. The only existing Council Secretariat permanent presences abroad were at the headquarters in New York and Geneva.[3] These offices lacked diplomatic recognition and had to be accredited under the auspices of the Commission delegation.

Until the entry into force of the Lisbon Treaty, the European Union lacked a legal personality.[4]

The political dialogue thus continued to function in the six-monthly rhythm led by the rotating presidency. The rotating presidency was also in charge of the main EU summits, where the second person in the lead was not the High Representative but the President of the European Commission. Each new presidency had its priorities and wanted to make an impact for instance in the context of relations with strategic partners, notably Russia.

CFSP had little say on 'carrots' or enticements. Its influence was stronger on restrictive policies, including sanctions.

The intergovernmental system could still have been effective had there existed a unified view on the way ahead. By the time

3    Spence, D, 'Effective Multilateralism: the EU Delegation at the UN in Geneva' in J Bátora, & S David (eds.), *European Diplomacy post-Westphalia*, Palgrave, 2015.

4    Piris, J-C, *The Lisbon Treaty: A legal and political analysis*, Cambridge University Press, 2010.

of the Iraq war in 2003, however, it was obvious that such a unified view did not exist on central security-related issues. The first administration of George W. Bush, with its choice to focus on Iraq, split the EU countries and made France and Germany align more with Russia than with the United States.

However, it is important not to underestimate the added value of CFSP to the EU member states and to the Union as such.

European countries not members of the European Union do not participate in constant dialogue on foreign policy issues similar to the one in the EU. They have less opportunity to test their ideas in a wider framework. It is interesting to note that during the 90s such a political dialogue did start to develop in the framework of the OSCE with frequent meetings on the level of political directors in Prague, later replaced by a permanent Council meeting every week in Vienna. However, these meetings over the years tended to develop into a presentation of prepared statements and not really an improvised dialogue, as still was a case in the Council working groups and in the PSC. It was also important, particularly in retrospect, after the entry into force of the Lisbon Treaty that every member state had to prepare itself for a future rotating presidency including a leading role in CFSP. This of course made member states more perceptive and active than they otherwise would have been. Small countries with limited foreign policy interests and presence abroad had to widen their scope of analysis to cover the entire EU framework. The CFSP also included a strategic protected communication network, the COREU system that allowed for continuous foreign policy dialogue between European capitals with increasingly active participation of the Commission and the Council Secretariat.[5]

In summary, one can argue that the CFSP as a paradigm showed considerable promise even before ratification of the Lisbon Treaty, stimulating a strategic dialogue in the context of a broadening concept of security.

5   Bicci, F, & C Caterina, 'The COREU/CORTESY Network and the Circulation of Information within EU Foreign Policy', RECON Inline Working paper 1, 2010.

Furthermore, it created a framework for the European Security and Defence Policy. It was in this framework that the main crisis management operations were deployed.

A new focus on conflict prevention was developed in the intergovernmental pillar.

The security of strategic flows started to be discussed from a political perspective.

Geographic policies were given more political content.

Thematic policies, notably human rights, came to be more integrated into EU external action.

On the multilateral level, Union positions were developed very actively in joint statements in the United Nations and in the OSCE.

However, the impact of the CFSP paradigm was effectively reduced by a number of constraining factors, ranging from treaty and budgetary to structural limitations.

One of the most visible shortfalls in this regard was the lack of support and readiness to mediate on the highest level before and during crisis.[6]

The main interlocutors in the political dialogue, in particular the Americans, frequently pointed out the weaknesses of the intergovernmental approach. Why, they would ask, could not the full scope of issues be discussed with the Europeans in the political dialogue with the United States? As Henry Kissinger asked, what was the telephone number to Europe?

For the Americans it was not least important to develop a capacity in an area where they were weaker, namely in the context of civilian assistance. The US Congress was very restrictive in providing such assets to the US executive, and overall US civilian assistance was smaller than that implemented by the EU.

However, that asset was largely in the hands of the Commission, outside the intergovernmental framework.[7]

6    On mediation: Gourlay, C, 'The European Union as Peacemaker – Enhancing EU Mediation Capacity Background Paper', 2013, ; A Sherriff, & V Hauck, 'Study on EU lessons learnt in mediation and dialogue. Glass half full', FWC COM 2011 – Lot 1 Request n°EEAS.K2.002 2012, ; R Middleton, P Melly, & A Vines, 'Implementing the EU concept on Mediation: Learnings from the Cases of Sudan and the Great Lakes', EXPO/B/AFET/FWC/2009-01/lot5/16, 2011.

7    For an overview of EU external budgets see http://europa.eu/rapid/press-release_MEMO-13-1134_en.htm., Kitt, F, EU *Aid Architecture: Recent Trends and Policy Directions*, World Bank Group, 2010.

*Evolution of the Community framework of relevance to security*

This fact was of course well known to the Commission and led to instructions not to introduce Community assets into the CFSP dialogue for fear that the comitology developed for Community action would be compromised.

The suggestion was not to pollute the pillars, but rather to help the political dialogue partners to understand that there was much to discuss with the Community side – but in another framework.

For many member states, this was an unsatisfactory state of affairs, reducing impact. The European Union was undercutting its leverage in the context of the CFSP by not introducing its main 'carrots' into the equation.

The result was an extensive strategic discussion that prepared first the failed constitutional treaty and then later what became the Lisbon Treaty.

The main idea referring to CFSP was to develop a double-hatted EU capability through the High Representative for CFSP who would also be the Vice-President of the Commission. For some time the view was that this would be a personality who would be the 'foreign minister' of the European Union. However, those who did not want to give the impression that the EU had become a federal structure killed this notion.

Likewise, the initial perception was that the Vice-President of the European Commission would effectively lead the work of a number of junior commissioners in the area of external action. However, the incoming Commission President José Manuel Barroso, in contrast to his successor Juncker, disregarded this idea in 2005. He found it difficult to put commissioners in junior positions.[8]

However, what the Lisbon Treaty achieved was that the Union took over the legal personality of the European Community. The Commission delegations became EU delegations. The High Representative and her new structure, the EEAS, oversaw the work of the EU delegations.

After an acrimonious process of ratification of the Lisbon Treaty, the EEAS was supposed to start working almost immediately (see also section 5.3).

8    Notes from interview in the Commission 2014.

When discussing crisis management and crisis response, the Commission kept a considerable distance from the EEAS. Part of this could be explained by the need for humanitarian assistance not to be securitized:

> *From the EU member states' Council Conclusions on the*
> *Comprehensive Approach 2014:*
> The Council also reaffirms that humanitarian aid must be provided in accordance with the humanitarian principles and international humanitarian law, solely on the basis of needs of affected populations, in line with the European Consensus on Humanitarian Aid.

However, hesitation to coordinate was in other spheres less easy to defend except from the internally perceived need to safeguard Commission independence from the Council.

The fact that after 9/11 member states decided to allow for the development of Justice and Home Affairs policy in the Community context was important and led to the elaboration of the Internal Security Strategy for the EU in 2010. During this period, what had been a small task force in the Commission in the late 1990s had developed into two major DGs for home affairs and justice.

The European Commission also had the main role in developing a number of thematic strategies of great importance for security, including the new transatlantic agenda with the United States.

The most important policies under development in the Union relating to flows, both good and bad, thus became Community policies. Almost all the carrots were Community carrots. This was extremely important not only for enlargement and neighbourhood policies but also for development policies in general.

Relatively few of the intergovernmental constraints are built into the Commission's system. Through the financial crisis, it has learned to act more quickly.

## Renationalization

Finally, there is of course a third alternative to intergovernmental and Community policies: to renationalize EU competencies. This became an important theme in the domestic political debates after the Lisbon Treaty entered into force. This also meant that more emphasis was put on the intergovernmental side of the EU and there was an effort to try to control the work of the European Commission, for instance in the context of the Comprehensive Approach discussed later in this study. Nowhere else is this seen more clearly than in the debate about the relationship of the United Kingdom to the European Union, where the discourse has shifted from efficiency and effectiveness in the spending of taxpayers' money to a legal debate about competencies and strings attached.[9]

## 4.2 Internal–External Nexus

*From the 2013 European Council Conclusions on Defence:*
New security challenges continue to emerge. Europe's internal and external security dimensions are increasingly interlinked. To enable the EU and its Member States to respond, in coherence with NATO efforts, the European Council calls for:

- an EU Cyber Defence Policy Framework in 2014, on the basis of a proposal by the High Representative, in cooperation with the Commission and the European Defence Agency;
- an EU Maritime Security Strategy by June 2014, on the basis of a joint Communication from the Commission and the High Representative, taking into account the opinions of the Member States, and the subsequent elaboration of action plans to respond to maritime challenges;
- increased synergies between CSDP and Freedom/Security/Justice actors to tackle horizontal issues such as illegal migration, organised crime and terrorism;
- progress in developing CSDP support for third states and regions, in order to help them to improve border management;

9    Government, HM, 'Review of the Balance of Competences between the United Kingdom and the European Union Foreign Policy', 2013. Government, HM, 'Review of the Balance of Competences between the United Kingdom and the European Union Development Cooperation and Humanitarian Aid', 2013.

- further strengthening cooperation to tackle energy security challenges.

## The role of internal policies for external action and security

Internal policies can and should constitute the fundamental basis for external relations and external action.

The Europa website of the EU currently (2014) presents an overview of 32 different Union policy areas, ranging from agriculture to transport.

A simple search of the EEAS website, which also includes the websites of EU delegations, brings up thousands of hits on almost every one of these 32 topics. This means that there is hardly any single internal EU policy that does not also have an external dimension.

A comprehensive approach to EU external action therefore necessarily must build on what is traditionally called EU internal policies. This is recognized in article 21 of the Treaty on the European Union (TEU), with its very broad definition of EU external action, which also makes explicit reference to the link to internal policies.

It does not allocate responsibility for the implementation of external action to the High Representative alone; rather, he or she shall assist the Commission and the Council in this regard.

Internal areas receive the bulk of the Community resources. In some areas, the build-up has been quite quick, such as in Justice and Home Affairs. Often this has not left much room for external action.

The legislative and standard-setting capacity of the Union is predominantly deployed in order to harmonize the broad security-related policies of member states in areas such as the environment, consumer policies, energy, etc.

Security policy objectives may not be the most urgent declared objectives of such policies but they often figure in some way.

The overall awareness of all these processes, which together affect European and international security, is limited by the fact that the European Commission and Community policies are largely thematic and implicit as regards security.

The overarching strategies are focused more on growth and freedom in the Union.

The security theme is naturally contradicted by the concern that citizens would perceive the European Union as a federal state.

It is noteworthy in this context that methods defined for intra-European cooperation have important effects on the outside world.

For instance, it has been noted in Norway[10] that close to half and in the future perhaps even more than half the number of laws adopted by the Norwegian Parliament are directly copied from European legislation – for the simple reason that Norway otherwise would not be able to operate in the European market.

The regulation of standards applied by multinational corporations, including companies such as Gazprom, is noteworthy.

The European Union almost from the start also developed several important instruments for supranational control over processes of existential importance for international security, including Euratom.

Indeed, much of what is being discussed in international negotiations and in dialogue between the Union interlocutors and external partners relates to internal processes and standards in the EU. In political science, there is a term for this: comparative politics as opposed to international relations as a field of study.

✤❧✦

9/11 and other catalysts led to the development of an EU Internal Security Strategy from 2010.[11] It contains five major areas: counterterrorism, organized crime, cybercrime, border management, and natural and man-made catastrophes. The motivation for the strategy refers squarely to topics dealt with in the section on bad flows in chapter 2 of this study:

> The European Council is convinced that the enhancement of actions at European level, combined with better coordination with actions at regional and national level, are essential to protection from trans-national threats. Terrorism and organised crime, drug trafficking, corruption, trafficking in human beings, smuggling of persons and trafficking in arms, inter alia, continue to challenge the internal security of the Union. Cross-border wide-spread crime has become an urgent challenge which requires a clear and comprehensive response.

10  Personal notes by the author during a seminar in Norway in 2005 quoting the former Norwegian EU ambassador.

11  Council of the European Union, 'Internal Security Strategy of the EU', 2010.

Action of the Union will enhance the work carried out by Member States' competent authorities and will improve the outcome of their work.

The strategy does not focus on the good flows, nor does it discuss the conflict cycle as such or link up with defence capabilities.

Already in this sense, the strategy rather understates than overstates the importance of internal security issues for external security.

### Recapitulating internal – external links discussed above

First, in the area of crisis management, discussed in chapter 1, the political ownership of capacity building for civilian crisis management missions was deemed weak by justice and interior ministers.

One of the most sensitive topics for discussion in the context of defence is the solidarity clause introduced in the Lisbon Treaty. Whereas some would like to see this clause applied to defence, in the internal security strategy it is conceptually linked to man-made and natural catastrophes.

The references to the need for conflict prevention are not very well developed in the internal domain of the EU. Occasionally, instruments such as regional policy have been used to underpin conflict resolution efforts, such as in the case of Ireland.

Moving on to chapter 2, the lack of internal cohesion among member states on important flow-related standards of the European Union such as those on climate change, undercut EU leverage in external negotiations.

Criticism of the EU structures for lack of democratic legitimacy also arguably reduced this leverage.

The link to the domestic political landscape in EU member states, including the problem of reactionary tendencies related to such flows as migration, is a further problem that makes it difficult for the EU to get its act together.

The management of virtual and other flows such as cyber and energy flows also illustrates the need for increased internal/external coordination.

International cooperation seeking to track flows in order to spot criminal or terrorist activities is highly sensitive in domestic and

European settings, including in the European Parliament, as seen in the debates on data protection and chemical substances.

The governance of research and development efforts supported by the EU through the European Commission is highly focused on the internal context in support of industrial and other interests. The fight against organized crime requires a strong investment in high technology and research on the global level.

A certain confusion about how to coordinate external and internal efforts at the border of the European Union and the Schengen system has been noted. The capacities of EU border management systems are sometimes difficult to deploy outside the Union, due to the intergovernmental/Community divide.[12]

The coordination of internal and external intelligence related to terrorist threats is difficult to achieve on the EU level due to the sensitivities involved. A case in point relates to the many Europeans fighting on the side of the rebels in Syria, some of whom may return to Europe with terrorist experience and ambitions.

In other thematic areas, there is the problem of what is internal and what is external to the Union. For instance in the context of the rule of law and justice, in the past decade a lot of effort has been devoted to developing this portfolio inside the Union, with unclear links to the external side.

The same is true for freedom, which is an objective pursued thematically inside the Union, to a large extent pushed by the European Parliament and supported by the DG Justice. On the external side, implementation is fragmented, partly due to the very different situations as regards democracy, human rights, and fundamental freedoms around the globe.

The weak coordination of thematic and geographic organizational cultures discussed in chapter 3 arguably increases the disconnect between internal and external policy coordination.

The leverage of the EU in international negotiations largely relates to its power to regulate access to the EU internal market. How this can be done effectively in different geographic, thematic, and not least multilateral settings is a major issue.

The power of attraction of the EU also has to do with how suc-

---

12  This has been discussed as regards the role of the Community border management agency FRONTEX in the Mediterranean.

cessful EU internal integration is perceived to be externally; it is clear that the financial crisis in this sense may not have been beneficial for the EU's soft power.

Divisions among EU member states for domestic political reasons regarding EU relationships to key external partners such as Turkey and Russia and the United States have also undercut EU joint effectiveness in external relations.

Commissioners responsible for primarily internal thematic policies hesitate to apply them to the external domain through their own resources.

The EU earns a significant part of its role as an international security actor through the management of its internal security. This has clearly been observed in the G8's work on organized crime and counterterrorism after 9/11. This is an example of the importance of internal policies for EU external action and multilateral effectiveness: the more the EU gets its act together the more it can claim an important place in international negotiations.

Finally, on crisis response, the predominantly internal focus of crisis coordination and the disconnect to the external services, particularly to intergovernmental CSDP structures, needs to be highlighted.

✦⟡✦

By and large the methods developed in the European Union to create more interdependence and thereby prevent war between its members is often seen and defined as the European peace project. This logic has been applied to the enlargement of the Union as a natural way to pursue this project in a wider context.

However, in order to be perceived as a peace project it needs to be inclusive and not define new conflictual borders to the outside world.

## 4.3 Explicit and Implicit Security Policies

*From the European Security Strategy 2003:*
This is a world of new dangers but also of new opportunities. The European Union has the potential to make a major contribution, both in dealing with the threats and in helping realise the opportunities.

## The added value of EU strategies: Pro and con

There are many arguments against conceptualization that clearly link objectives and priorities with desired impact. It is difficult to plan for the future.

> Case in point: de-mining: Obviously it would be desirable to spell out exactly in what order different de-mining projects should be planned and implemented. However, new crises occur that might force a change to the list. It also may not be possible to implement projects in one area due to the situation on the ground, for instance due to a lack of agreement with the implementing partner. There may also be difficulties in the project planning. Therefore, for these reasons it may be more prudent to make general commitments and set general priorities with less negative priorities spelled out.

Conceptualization in the form of strategies[13] is, however, a way to promote visibility and to communicate with partners worldwide. Indeed, it can also influence expectations. It may help to legitimize, contextualize, institutionalize, and bring more resources to specific objectives. So ideally there should be a positive relationship on almost all levels and in all relationships to impact. Lawrence Freedman:

> Having a strategy suggests an ability to look up from the short term and the trivial to view from the long terms and the essential, to address causes rather than symptoms, to see woods rather than the trees.

Nowhere else do governments and international organizations focus as much on the problems and possible impact as in strategies. Strategizing is also a way to define the role of different actors within a system, helping them to decide where they should be on the ladder from a tactical perspective to strategic overview.

Strategies are thus potentially very important since they are in a sense the highest level of impact assessment *ex ante*. They define the vision for the way ahead and indicate major steps towards imple-

---

13 Freedman, L, *Strategy: A History*, Oxford University Press, 2013.

mentation of the vision with a firm view of the end state.

Nevertheless, in the EU they are at the same time politically dangerous since they open an opportunity for political opponents to criticize the European institutions for not living up to their declared goals. It is therefore to be expected that strategies are at times developed in a self-congratulatory way, focusing on what has already been done and codifying what already has been agreed.

Furthermore, strategies are not always welcomed by member states, perhaps in particular the larger member states. EU strategies are by nature explicit but many of the motives for strategies cannot be explicitly declared. The desired impact may be more difficult to achieve if goals are too explicit.

Sometimes member states therefore prefer to develop their priorities internally and then apply their internally developed strategies in the form of both decisions and non-decisions by the EU, adapting to the evolution of the situation.

There are certainly examples of strategic decisions that may tie the hands of the EU unnecessarily.

> Case in point: Russia. Not least before the entry into force of the Lisbon Treaty, it was tempting for every rotating presidency of the European Council to seek to demonstrate some progress in the relationship to Russia. After Georgia and after Ukraine it has turned out that the policies of the Union towards Russia may require more subtlety. Non-decisions, and decisions not to go forward with certain cooperative endeavours may be more important for the EU-Russia relationship than it is commonly understood. In this sense explicit restrictive measures may constitute the tip of an iceberg of a posture that in the long run may create serious difficulties for Russia to continue what in recent years has been perceived as an increasingly aggressive policy towards its neighbours.

Strategies are also not always welcome in the sense that they may themselves promote a Community-type capability of the European institutions, which may be controversial, particularly as regards security.

This, indeed, has led the debate both among scholars and in the political discourse to possibly understate the amount of actual strategy implicit in EU policies. There are many relevant examples indicating the viability of this hypothesis. The European Union of course does not wish to reveal its hand in negotiations with external partners. Well aware of the difficulties in keeping things secret on the EU level, member states may wish to decide on policies without putting them in an explicit strategic framework. In some situations, member states' governments may also wish to do more in the area of security than the treaty explicitly authorizes them to do. So in some situations it may actually be more effective not to have a strategy.

Not having a strategy may, however, mean accepting significant costs in the implementation phase. If staff on all levels are not aware of the long-term goals, other measures of success may become too important.

What the many member states most likely would not like to see in the area of security is a strategic planning capability like that developed by European Commission President Delors and possibly envisaged by President Juncker.

## Development of EU concepts conducive to optimal security impact

Security as an explicit goal of the European Union has its historical roots in the European Political Cooperation (EPC) from the 1970s. This was an informal consultation process between member states on foreign policy with the aim of creating a common approach to foreign policy issues and promoting both the EU's interests and those of the Community as a whole.

This goal was initially formalized in the 1993 Maastricht Treaty, which established the European Union. One part of the CFSP objectives was to strengthen the security of the Union in all ways and at the same time to preserve peace and strengthen international security, in accordance with the principles of the United Nations Charter. Reference was also made to the basic documents of the CSCE/OSCE. A key reference was human rights.[14]

The Lisbon Treaty does not contain a coherent vision for security. The approach is fragmented into different types of policy in different contexts. However, in article 21 it, sets out a general vision of

14   Cameron, F, *An Introduction to European Foreign Policy*, Routledge, 2007/2012. Cameron, F, *Foreign and Security Policy of the European Union: Past, Present and Future*, Continuum, 1999.

external action in the frame of CFSP. FSJ is set out in the Treaty on the Functioning of the European Union (TFEU).

The Treaty of Lisbon thus contains roughly 100 references to the concept of security. Broadly speaking they are situated in four different contexts: the common foreign and security policy, the area of freedom justice and security, national security, and social security. There is also a reference to personal security in the Charter of Fundamental Rights. In the discussion about internal and external aspects of security the main issue is the link between common foreign and security policy and the provisions relating to the area of freedom, justice, and security.[15]

✦❧✦

In summary, one can argue that there are two main tracks of explicit security strategies in the EU, one based on the 2003 European Security Strategy (ESS) in the external domain and one resulting in the 2010 Internal Security Strategy (ISS).

As discussed in chapter 1, the ESS was preceded by benchmarks defined in the context of military and civilian ESDP. Some of the civilian benchmarks are clearly related to the process towards the internal security strategy in FSJ.

In addition, there are a number of thematic security strategies referring to for example cyber system and energy flows (chapter 2). The Strategy against the Proliferation of Weapons of Mass Destruction was adopted at the same time as the ESS, in late 2003, and the 2001 Counter-Terrorism Action Plan was complemented by a Counter-Terrorism Strategy in 2005.

There are also a number of geographic strategies on both the national and regional levels with significant security elements. Member states have pushed for several important geographic strategies that include the Eastern partnership, a European policy on the Arctic, etc. Member states have also intervened with strategic proposals for cooperative frameworks with the southern neighbourhood, in particular the Union for the Mediterranean, which promoted cooperation with some of the leaders who are no longer in power in the Middle East and North Africa.

---

15   European Commission, 'Consolidated Version of the Treaty on European Union', *Official Journal of the European Communities* C 325, 2010.

A number of strategic documents refer to different thematic goals of security relevance such as development, enlargement, trade, etc.

> Notably, several major documents in the area of development were put forward by the Commission, including on Policy coherence on development. The Commission had also put forward a more general policy document called the Agenda for change, which put increased emphasis on these issues. The main director-general responsible for development Cooperation on this basis set up horizontals capabilities in order to address fragility more effectively.[16]

There are also documents that emphasize multilateral cooperation; they have been approved by the European Union and to a certain extent by international organizations. A case in point is the Platform for Co-operative Security adopted by the OSCE[17] in 1999.

Then, finally, there are strategic documents referring to crisis response.

Many of these documents can be described as security-relevant without having security as the priority objective. The latter types of document exist particularly in the Community sphere in the areas of development assistance, human rights, etc.

### The need for comprehensive strategies

> From the EU member states' *Council Conclusions on the Comprehensive Approach* 2014:
> The Council underlines that the comprehensive approach applies to all phases of the conflict cycle, including prevention, early warning, crisis management, stabilisation and longer-term peace-building and development cooperation. Its results are often only reached and sustained in the long term. The Council recalls the 2007 Council Conclusions on Security and

---

16  European Commission, 'Increasing the impact of EU Development Policy: an Agenda for Change', 2011, European Commission, 'EU 2011 Report on Policy Coherence for Development', SEC (2011) 1627, 2011.

17  Lundin, L-E, 'The Charter for European Security from a European Union (EU) perspective', *Helsinki Monitor* 11, no. 1, 2000, pp. 11–21.

Development and the importance of peace and security for development, and vice versa. It also notes that fragility and conflict hamper sustainable development and poverty reduction, create or aggravate humanitarian crises, and can provide a fertile breeding ground for instability and may trigger migratory flows.

The Council notes that the objectives of EU development cooperation remain those set out in the Lisbon Treaty, the European Consensus on Development and the Agenda for Change. It welcomes the progress made in the context of the EU's programming process for the period 2014–20 to further reinforce synergies between development programming and the EU's overall policies and notes that in fragile or conflict-affected states, programming and joint programming must be conducted in accordance with, inter alia, the principles of the New Deal for Engagement in Fragile States, also building on relevant fragility assessments. It notes the need to further enhance the effectiveness and results of EU development policies and programmes, also in line with the principles of the Global Partnership for Effective Development Cooperation. The Council also notes the ongoing discussions in the OECD/DAC and in the context of the post-2015 framework on development financing, including on ODA.

Ideally, strategies should of course be both comprehensive and operational, as illustrated by the Comprehensive Approach, described above.

It should be possible to develop clear priorities for action from these strategies. In this regard, the current set of security-related strategies in the European Union are of very different quality.

The most comprehensive security document is perhaps the 2003 European Security Strategy.[18] The Iraq war and the need to promote an image of greater European unity gave the new High Representative an unprecedented latitude to present a draft European Security Strategy directly to the European Council, bypassing the intermediate decision-making structures for CFSP and

---

18   Solana, J, 'A secure Europe in a better world. The European Security Strategy 2003', *Nato's nations and partners for peace* 2003, pp. 28–30.

allowing only for three think tank seminars from the summer until December of 2003.

Nonetheless, it has been criticized for not being comprehensive enough and because it does not refer sufficiently to Community action, because it focuses on a few types of threat that while they are important are not the only ones, and because it does not sufficiently focus on opportunities for positive action. It leaves several issues undefined. On the one hand, there is an emphasis on effective multilateralism but on the other it is very difficult to derive what this effectively would mean for the European Union.

In contrast, the 2010 Internal Security Strategy is much less comprehensive; it focuses on five enumerated problems but is more clear on follow-up.

There was an effort to update the ESS in 2008 but the uncertainty regarding whether the Lisbon Treaty would enter into force made it difficult to produce a new document. The ambition was therefore limited to a review of the implementation of the 2003 document, which was referred to as still fully relevant. The 2008 document then proceeded to add quite a number of other references, which made the combined body of text very difficult to read, and for this reason the 2008 text was much less well known and referred to.

A few years later the foreign ministers of Sweden, Poland, Italy, and Spain tried to promote a European global strategy approach that would go beyond security and address opportunities.[19] However, this document, which was released publicly in May 2013, came too close to the end of the term of High Representative Catherine Ashton to be seriously pursued. In addition, because of its broad scope it would have required strong support from the European Commission.

Instead, a more limited strategy gradually evolved, focusing on a comprehensive approach for external conflicts and crises. This discourse emerged from the lack of effective military interventions, not least on the Horn of Africa, and the issue of transnational threats, particularly as regards trafficking and terrorism affecting stability in the Sahel region of Africa, as well as maritime security. Regional strategies were developed that were hoped to bring together EU intergovernmental and Community policies to address a wide range of issues relevant for anti-piracy interventions

19   EGS, *Towards a European Union Global Strategy*, UI, 2013.

*From the EU member states' Council Conclusions on the
Comprehensive Approach 2014:*

The EU's policies and priorities should follow from common
strategic objectives and a clear common vision of what the EU
collectively wants to achieve in its external relations or in a
particular conflict or crisis situation. The Council notes that
the regional strategies developed for the Horn of Africa, the
Sahel and most recently the Gulf of Guinea have been valuable
in framing the EU's engagements across many policy areas. In
a similar vein, thematic work on cyber and maritime security
is also being taken forward. The Council would welcome the
continued proactive preparation of such regional and thematic
strategies to frame the EU's comprehensive response to new
political developments and challenges, notably concerning the
EU's neighbourhood. Similarly, the work on Joint Framework
Documents (JFDs), outlining the broad range of EU interests
and priorities in specific countries or regions, should be taken
forward as soon as possible, including in fragile and conflict-
affected states.

## Recapitulating

It is useful to recapitulate some of the generic problems of impact
related to the issue of strategic objectives identified so far in each
section.

Chapter 1 on the conflict cycle refers in section 1.1 to the fundamental debate about whether defence should be an objective for
European integration. Domestic political support for this was low
at least until late 2013 and objectives were implemented with little
strategic reference to this objective.

Moving on to crisis management in 1.2 there was a shift in 2001
from a focus on European security and defence policy to problems
arising after 9/11 and more specifically during the Iraq war. This dis-
sipated focus on the ESDP/CSDP policy development process. When
crisis management situations later started to proliferate and become
more complex during the Arab Spring, in Georgia and Ukraine the EU
stood without a relevant overarching strategy for crisis management.

The comprehensive approach for external conflicts and crises
was essentially developed in another setting, more adapted for

generic crisis management settings in Africa and less explicitly adapted to the EU neighbourhood.

*From the EU member states' Council Conclusions on the Comprehensive Approach 2014:*
The Council notes that the impact of CSDP missions and operations is enhanced when part of a broader EU strategy. Information about and analysis of the conflict and crisis context, including on the ongoing overall EU engagement, should feed into the planning, preparation, implementation and review phases of CSDP missions and operations. The Council also stresses the need for earlier and more coordinated planning for a smooth transition from one form of EU engagement to another, in particular regarding transition from short- or medium- term activity to longer-term development cooperation, and from CSDP missions and operations to other forms of EU engagement, to ensure that the achievements of EU action can be sustained. The ongoing work on transition strategies should therefore be taken forward as a matter of priority. In this context, the Council also stresses the key principle of local ownership and the need for sustainable results. Finally, the Council also underlines the importance to make use of lessons learned from previous operations, missions and programmes.

Section 1.3 on conflict prevention, showed that attention to this objective was reduced from a very significant political focus just before 9/11 to an abolition of the conflict prevention network among European academic institutions just a few years later.

A revitalization of conflict analysis started to take place in the EEAS a few years after the entry into force of the Lisbon Treaty. However, it was applied in an incremental way and again not in the most difficult areas in terms of the complexity of EU roles and objectives in the EU neighbourhood. Above all, an overall cost/benefit analysis of conflict prevention has never been implemented in the EU as a whole.

Moving on to chapter 2 and flow security, this area started to become a major issue in the EU with the 9/11 attacks. Strategic attention was first focused on bad flows related to terrorism and

WMD proliferation. It was only later, from 2006, that serious attention was given to problems relating to flows of energy in the security policy context, in relation to the gas crisis in Ukraine. Further attention to bad flows was systematically developed in the context of Justice and Home Affairs and was finally promulgated in the Internal Security Strategy in 2010. Attention to thematic problems then proliferated to the security of cyber systems through the Cyber Security Strategy in 2013. This problem of course was not new; it had in the context of critical infrastructure protection been a significant topic for discussion during the Clinton Administration in the 1990s.

A generic problem of impact in all these flow-related contexts was the limited inclusion of Community areas in the strategic concepts as well as the need both to focus on threats and opportunities as discussed in the debate on a potential European global strategy

In the third chapter, on organizational cultures, problems were pointed out in 3.1, the geographic context.

> Case in point: The Ukraine crisis illustrated the problem of defining EU strategic partners. This concept started to slowly develop from the European Security Strategy onwards and became a key feature in the discourse of the new High Representative after the entry into force of the Lisbon Treaty. She was soon accused of applying arbitrary definitions in the selection of countries that should be described as strategic partners. But the real problem started during the Ukraine crisis, when top European leaders for the first time after the Cold War hesitated to define Russia even as a potential strategic partner.[20]

The need for geographic strategies as such, however, has not been questioned even though it has not always been possible to develop them.

In the years immediately after the entry into force of the Lisbon Treaty, discussion started, so far without result, about the need for an overall EU strategy on Asia. EU strategies had been developed for regions such as Central Asia and in the context of a comprehensive approach for regions in Africa, such as the Horn of Africa and

---

20  President van Rompuy hesitated to answer a question about this during the Brussels Forum 2014.

Sahel. Several strategic documents were developed over the years for the Western Balkans, for the Mediterranean, for the Eastern partnership and of course for the EU neighbourhood as a whole.

However, many of these documents have been criticized for not being holistic.

In some geographic relationships, the process of accession to the European Union was prioritized to such an extent that conflict analysis arguably became underdeveloped. Whenever there was a conflict analysis the issue whether conflict was related to ethnic and other divisions was not fully analysed in relation to another conflict risk: the contradiction between corrupt elites and impoverished and unemployed populations.[21] Nor was there an explicit political analysis of what the process of enlargement meant in complex cases, such as Turkey. This in turn once again allowed each member state to develop its strategic messaging.

Moving on to thematic policies in section 3.2 it remains to be seen at the time of writing whether the revised MDGs will include a clear reference to security in the context of fragility. In the OSCE area democracy, human rights, and the rule of law were formally accepted as part of the comprehensive concept of security and cooperation developed by the 57 participating states of that organization. These politically binding commitments are furthermore referred to in legally binding documents both in the Council of Europe and in bilateral and multilateral legal documents signed by the EU and a number of its partner countries.

Globally, the status of human rights, democracy, and other value-based priorities, however, is under constant pressure of attention from other EU objectives related to trade, etc.

In the OSCE area, the score is not settled on how to apply these concepts in relation to the need to cooperate and prevent conflict among countries that do not fully accept these principles in practice.

Section 3.3 on international law and the role of the United Nations, pointed out that the EU made a strong statement on the need for effective multilateralism in its 2003 security strategy. However, this statement was declaratory in the sense that it did not fully set out what it meant. It was more a signal to the US administration directed against unilateralism and the need to systematically

---

21   Case in point Bosnia.

support international rule of law. Multilateralism in later EU documents never attributed the same emphasis to this need.

As regards crisis response, 3.4, 9/11 gave a strong impulse towards
a more holistic approach, which resulted in a broad-based counterterrorism action plan.

## EU strategies in the context of major international discourses: generic problems of impact related to continuity, consistency, and logical and institutional coherence

EU strategic discourses also need to be situated in the context of
conceptual debates on the international level.

Notably, the discourse on human security[22] started to influence
the academic and political debate in the early 2000s, also in the EU.

Several other organizing concepts for security-related work in the
EU have been formulated, only to lose visibility some years later. The
fate of the comprehensive approach in this regard is unclear. There
is already the example of conflict prevention, which as a concept
received much attention in the early 2000s – only to be overshadowed by 9/11.

This example illustrates the influence on the discourse in international organizations of policies pursued notably by the US government in recent decades.

At one point during the Clinton Administration peacekeeping
was high on the agenda. It then became an important topic in the
United Nations, NATO, the OSCE, and the WEU.

After 9/11, the war on terrorism was a dominant theme in many
international organizations.

Later it became important for various organizations to have
something to contribute to the problems relating to Afghanistan.
Even organizations such as the OSCE, where Afghanistan is
not a full member, started to discuss their role in Afghanistan.
Organizations such as UNODC started to develop overarching
border management programmes for Afghanistan without really
having the requisite resources.

Then later, of course, the Arab Spring required many international organizations and states to develop an agenda for action.

22  Kaldor, M, & M Glasius, *A human security doctrine for Europe*, Routledge, 2004.

At the time of writing, the possibility to make a difference in the case of Ukraine is being discussed.

These are all political realities but they are associated with a generic problem of impact: lack of follow-up over longer periods.

The EU is also faced with a generic problem of impact related to the lack of consistency between EU and member states' policies. How can one expect an EU strategy to be effective or useful if it is being undercut by member states in their external policies? If the Union decides to pursue a value-based strategy towards China, how can it be effective if some of the largest member states contradict the strategy in their own bilateral relations with China? Similarly, how can a strong and principled posture towards Russia as an EU strategic partner work if individual member states have their own policy towards Moscow, based on national trade and industrial interests or, for that matter, interests related to history, culture, and religion?

Another key generic problem of impact relates to the issue of logical consistency as perceived from outside the Union. The concept of the EU as a peace project – that it exports stability and participates in globalization through increasing integration with the outside world – may of course not be perceived in the same way from the outside.

Finally, there is the issue of institutional coherence. The Commission has so far been careful not to become too engaged in the elaboration of strategic documents in the CFSP context and lately together with the High Representative for fear of the requirement to coordinate with member states before these documents are released to the public, thus compromising on the principle of Community initiative. In the few cases where such documents were successfully produced, they were criticized by member states for not having been properly consulted beforehand and sometimes also for a lack of clarity about the financial implications.[23]

---

23  From the authors notes after interviews in the EEAS and the Commission in
    2012–2013.

# 5. Institutionalization

In the fifth paradigm, discussed in this chapter the focus is on the interplay between the (5.1) legal, (5.2) budgetary/staff, and (5.3) structural problems of impact in EU security-related policies. The legal basis for everything that is being done in the European Union is defined with a point of departure in the treaties. Problems are linked to financial and staff resources at the disposal of the institutions for their administrative and, as regards the Commission, operational budgets. The financing of military CSDP takes place through direct financial contributions by member states. The way static and dynamic structures are set up bring additional problems.

## 5.1 Legal Basis

*Developing the legal basis for EU external action relevant to security*
Formally, all action in the European Union requires a legal basis. For this reason the process of revising EU treaties is fundamental.

When Jacques Delors acceded to the post of President of the European Commission in 1985 he managed to secure the support of Paris and Bonn for essential steps ahead in the European integration process, towards a single market, a single currency, and the free movement of goods, services, and people within the Union.

However, the mandate did not include a security perspective.

Some seven years later the Maastricht Treaty created the basis for the Common Foreign and Security Policy (CFSP), an intergovernmental form of cooperation that came to dominate European integration in the security field over almost two decades. Nevertheless, there was initially little to substantiate the claim that the EU could do something serious. There was no agreement on a legal basis for explicit security action.

In 1998 and 2000 further steps were taken through the Amsterdam and Nice treaties to consolidate this intergovernmental approach and make it more action-oriented, not least in the area of defence. Some of the legacy of efforts by the Western European Union was transferred to the legal framework of the European Union.[1]

At this point, the next step was already actively discussed and was contemplated in the European Commission in a way that would have allowed for a coherent treaty framework, making the intergovernmental and Community approaches fully compatible. Experts close to the President of the European Commission informally proposed a full revision of the treaty.[2]

However, this step went too far for member states and a compromise solution presented in the so-called Constitutional Treaty in 2004 was defeated in referenda in the Netherlands and France.

However, the debate continued in the Convention that was preparing a new treaty.

A new, albeit imperfect solution was negotiated that finally, after a traumatic set of referenda, was ratified and entered into force as the Lisbon Treaty on 1 December 2009.[3]

---

1   Article 4 of the WEU Brussels Treaty stipulated that "if any of the High Contracting Parties should be the object of an armed attack in Europe, the other High Contracting Parties will, in accordance with the provisions of article 51 of the Charter of the United Nations, afford the party so attacked all the military and other aid and assistance in their power." This clause has its succession in the Treaty of Lisbon. A further step was taken through the creation of the European Defence Agency in the second intergovernmental pillar in 2003, a step that was not originally considered possible under the treaty as it existed then.

2   The so-called Penelope project led by the late Director General Francois Lamoureux.

3   European Commission, 'Consolidated Version of the Treaty on European Union', *Official Journal of the European Communities* C 325, 2010.

*Recapitulating*

Legal aspects of relevance to security were referred to in several contexts above:

First, as regards explicit references to security.

Second, the degree to which the legal personality of the EU allowed for efficient coordination.

Third, the issue of representation outside the Union.

On the first point, the entry into force of the Lisbon Treaty was a breakthrough. The treaty contains some 100 references to security in several different areas, in contrast to the fact that the European Commission hardly referred to security in its work before 2001.

Second, the Lisbon Treaty improved the conditions for coordination across the previous pillars. The coherence requirement between the pillars had existed before, but the establishment of the function of HR/VP created a new pragmatic basis for coordination. The Lisbon Treaty also transferred the legal personality of the European Community to the European Union, with the notable exception of the European Atomic Energy Community (Euratom). This exception was an imperfection. Nuclear safeguards are surely a key security activity that the EU performs.

Third, the treaty created an expectation in the international Community that at least at some point the European Union was going to have an enhanced representational role worldwide. The HR/VP function gave a new legitimacy to an overall political dialogue with third parties. The function of President of the European Council provided new continuity on the highest level, complementing the role of the President of the European Commission. The Commission delegations were rebranded EU delegations.

Still, it was up to members of external bodies to admit the EU to international organizations and in other multilateral contexts. Other regional groupings, such as the League of Arab States, were keen to exploit the legal change of the EU to see if they could also improve their own recognition. This complicated the otherwise favourable attitude of the United States towards treaty evolution in the EU.

✦✧✦

The Lisbon Treaty can still be regarded as an intermediary treaty towards an even more thorough revision of the legal basis for the EU.

On the one hand, some believe that the treaty went too far in transferring competencies to the level of the EU, which has provoked a domestic political turmoil, not least in the UK.

Others, who in the spirit of Jacques Delors may wish to call themselves friends of the European Union, believe that the creation of the EEAS has confused some central principles for European integration. It has not taken the Community method as the point of departure and not fully integrated external action into the European Commission. Its close link to the intergovernmental decision-making bodies in the Council tends to compromise the Community method by installing an early requirement of close and continuous coordination with member states in the Council. This arguably undermines the Commission's right of initiative and leads to micromanagement by member states in the implementation of agreed policies. This view has support also from within the Commission and may have contributed to the perception of a less cooperative Commission posture in the fulfilment of the role expected for the HR/VP and the EEAS.

The treaty is vague as regards the interface between the intergovernmental and Community frameworks. The external intergovernmental framework defined as the Common Foreign and Security Policy includes references to a large number of Community areas.

From the standpoint of the Commission, the process of policy development should be a sequence starting with a mandate, as general as possible, given by member states to the Commission. On this basis, the Commission should develop initiatives, which then should be open to debate and subject to approval by the legislative authorities of the Union, the Council, and as appropriate the European Parliament.

The intergovernmental method on the other hand builds on the notion that the Council bodies are continuously involved in the development of the initiatives in order to ensure that there is a seamless integration between member states' national policies and Union-level policies. This is argued to be necessary because of both the sensitivity of security matters and the consequent need for real-time coordination and the need to involve member states' resources in synergetic actions.

## Muddling through

A discussion is currently being pursued on a case-by-case basis of how to develop initiatives in a number of key policy areas. There are already examples of initiatives such as the Communication on the Comprehensive Approach, where some of the normal steps in the policy process have been skipped, such as the *ex ante* impact assessment, partly because of the lack of legal clarity regarding the initiatives.

A legal grey area is thus open that continues to engage the legal services of institutions and the EEAS. This remains a significant problem area,[4] risking delaying action on important issues and clouding the objectives and resolve of EU action in key areas.

The process of negotiation and ratification of the Maastricht, Amsterdam, Nice and Lisbon treaties has already itself caused delay and uncertainty.

At the time of writing, further uncertainty about the way ahead is created by the demand of some member states, notably the UK, to renegotiate the Lisbon Treaty.

At the same time, the absence of an explicit legal basis has not stopped the member states from authorizing the EU to undertake action in important areas, not least in crises. The limited authority of the European Court of Justice over the intergovernmental domain contributes to this. However, there is of course a limit to the flexibility of the treaty in this regard.

The legal analysis of the implementation of the Lisbon Treaty is often biased in the sense that the point of departure of the analysis may predetermine the conclusions, given the considerable lack of clarity in the treaty setup.

Notably, those who emphasize the establishment of the EEAS sometimes tend to lament the lack of authority of the service in coordinating the overall external action of the EU. In the review process of the EEAS in 2013–2014, this led to a number of proposals to enhance this authority.

Those who on the other hand see the EEAS not as an independent institution but rather as a service at the disposal of the Council and the Commission may arrive at different conclusions.

They may also underline the fact that security, not least in

4   Notes from the author's interviews in the EEAS and the Commission, 2013.

terms of crisis response, is not only an issue external to the Union
– it almost as a rule requires overall coordination centred in the
Commission.

In reality the truth may lie somewhere in between: continuous
crisis coordination on the highest level needs to be taken in hand
by the European Council, as has been the case during the financial
crisis since 2008.


## 5.2 Budgetary and Staffing Resources


### Budgets: *The ideal situation*

European institutions, as any others, require financial resources
in order to implement policy decisions taken by the legislative
authorities of the Union.

In order to do this there is a need for impact assessment *ex ante*
that estimates the financial implications of different policy proposals. On this basis, all initiatives should ideally from the start be clear
about financing.

Furthermore, member states' ideal principle was that whenever
a country agreed to a decision in an international organization this
automatically meant providing the resources necessary in order to
implement the decision, according to an agreed scale of contributions.

For this reason many countries devoted a great deal of effort to
negotiate as favourable scales of contributions as possible, knowing
that this would pay off in the long term.


### Budgets: *The real, much more complicated picture*

Very soon, however, the finance ministers of EU Member States
started to refuse the automaticity of budgetary increases. In their
view the international arena should also be a part of the budgetary
discipline managed by them.

Increasingly more contributions also started to be tied to certain
specific objectives close to the heart of the donor. 'Governing by
the purse' became a way of life in international organizations. Not

least in the United Nations, this led to a situation where regular budgets were insufficient for the organization to do its work.

As for the European Union, the real picture is even more complicated, partly because of the different financing systems in place depending on the types of activity in question.

In addition to the role played by finance ministers, enhanced by the financial crisis, the fact that the European Parliament is a part of the budgetary authority of the Union is of special significance. The Parliament often uses the budget as a basis for enhancing its influence vis-à-vis the other institutions and tries to steer appropriations to areas where the Parliament has maximum control, notably towards the Community rather than to the intergovernmental framework.

Despite the increasingly strong Eurosceptic representation in the European Parliament it can therefore be argued that together with the finance ministers the Parliament has over the recent decades more or less systematically tended to favour the Community approach in terms of budgetary appropriations.

When after the entry into force of the Amsterdam and Nice treaties the Council Secretariat sought to build up the framework for the new CFSP, this was met with great scepticism in the Parliament and few resources, overall, were allocated for this purpose.[5]

In addition, the setup with the European Commission as in principle the only institution with an operational budget – all the others had only administrative budgets – made it necessary to find direct financing for a major part of military CSDP.

The budget for the CFSP needed to be implemented by the Commission. After the Lisbon Treaty entered into force this was achieved through a specific body, the Service for Foreign Policy Instruments (FPI), set up by the Commission under the political authority of the High Representative.

It can be argued that in deciding on the overall financial framework the EU puts the cart before the horse. Financial frameworks in the EU are endowed with large budgetary envelopes covering seven-year periods, proposed by the European Commission and negotiated in the Council, mainly by finance ministers and the

---

5   Personal notes of the author participating as a representative of the
    Commission in the EP hearings on the issue.

European Parliament. Normally, one would expect such decisions to be preceded by major strategic debates about the vision and objectives for the budgets in question. However, the process builds on continuity with previous budgets and assumes the need for budgetary discipline affecting percentage changes upward or downward in the main envelopes.

- The total amount agreed for the external relations package is €51,419 million (current prices) over the period 2014–2020.
- Instrument for Pre-accession Assistance (IPA): €11,699 million
- European Neighbourhood Instrument (ENI): €15,433 million
- Development Cooperation Instrument (DCI): €19,662 million
- Partnership Instrument (PI): €955 million
- Instrument contributing to Stability and Peace (IfSP): €2,339 million
- European Instrument for Democracy & Human Rights (EIDHR): €1,333 million
- The Instrument for Nuclear Safety Cooperation will provide €225 million and the Instrument for Greenland €184 million, from the EU-budget.
- A further €30,506 million will be made available for cooperation with African, Caribbean and Pacific (ACP) countries as well as Overseas Countries and Territories (OCT) through the 11th European Development Fund, which will remain outside of the EU budget and also is not subject to the ordinary legislative procedure.
- Overall funding for all above mentioned instruments adds up to €96.8 billion in current prices.
- In addition, there is the CFSP budget, which is likely to encompass more than 2 billion euros for the period, in addition to the direct contributions from Member States to CSDP.[6]

6   http://europa.eu/rapid/press-release_MEMO-13-1134_en.htm

## Money as a problem for EU security action

Is money a real problem for security policies in EU external action? The quick answer should be no: the EU budget is large and should, just as is the case for member states' combined defence budgets, allow for effective security action.

Again, the real situation presents a more complicated picture, as illustrated by the process of setting up the EEAS. This decision was not treated as a reform requiring a careful *ex ante* assessment of the financial implications.

The budgetary authority allocated essentially no change management budget. The concept[7] was to transfer, with minimal financial implications, some of the existing external action services in the Commission and the Council Secretariat. The result was damaging, as discussed in sections below. Once this transfer was made, both the Council Secretariat and the Commission clearly demarcated the EEAS. For tactical reasons it was essential for these two bodies to clarify that no spare budgetary resources existed that could help the EEAS to muddle through in the first period.

The new High Representative was taking on several additional functions and needed to show quick results. Consequently, everything had to be based on the existing structures and the analysis of staffing needs was made on the basis of existing resources. Instead of creating a new administration department bringing together the best possible specialists in order to launch the new ship, the previous Commission department responsible for external administration was taken over as it was, with only a few additional staff.

Costs relating to civilian crisis management and conflict prevention in the intergovernmental pillar had to be financed through the very limited CFSP budget. The competition for funds in that context was fierce when the Council started to promote flow-related programmes in the area of counterterrorism and WMD non-proliferation.

With some goodwill from member states it was possible to agree on financing certain costly types of security-related assistance over the Community budget, such as mine action.[8] However, in other areas it was not possible to reach agreement.

The predominance of geographically defined budget lines in

---

7    EEAS, *EEAS Review*, 2013,
8    Personal notes of the author as head of the responsible unit in the Commission.

addition to an increasingly limited list of thematic objectives for development assistance also made it difficult for security objectives such as conflict prevention to prevail in the process of mainstreaming – despite a 2001 Commission decision in principle to do so,[9] in language very similar to that employed in later years in discussion of the Comprehensive Approach for External Conflicts and Crises.

The focus on speedy implementation of large budgets and sound financial management arguably led to less attention to the substantial impact of programmes. It became an attractive option to transfer large amounts of resources to other implementing agencies or as budgetary support to recipient governments. Both methods were of course difficult to manage in terms of keeping the substantial objectives of the assistance in clear view.

In summary, this study has noted several significant problems for the EU and its institutions. Security remains an underprivileged objective. The financial implications notably of conflict prevention are not properly calculated.

The system for implementation favours large projects with an emphasis on sound financial management. This reduces the ability of the system to accept calculated risks, which often is a necessary condition for working in fragile situations.

There may be enough money in the EU system, but it is not appropriately available for effective action in EU external security endeavours.

Crises are likely to improve the situation at least temporarily, but the fundamental problems remain.

## Staffing problems

Moving to the issue of staff,[10] the situation is even more problematic. Essentially, staff reductions have come to be regarded as a value per

---

9  European Commission , 'Communication from the Commission on Conflict Prevention', COM no. 211, 2001.

10  The EEAS currently (2014) has 3417 staff divided between headquarters (1457) and EU delegations (1960). In addition there are about 3500 Commission staff working in EU delegations. Within the EEAS staff, there are just over 900 AD posts (538 in HQ and 365 in delegations). Other staff include 652 AST posts, 363 seconded national experts, 322 contractual agents, and 1137 local agents in delegations. See EEAS, *EEAS Review*, 2013.

se. Reducing red tape by reducing staff has become a sign of increased efficiency.

This view is closely linked to the discourse on corruption. It started to be a real issue at the time of the resignation crisis of the Santer Commission in the late 1990s.[11] This development, closely related to the quest for more power on the part of the European Parliament, elevated the issue of corruption in European structures to an unprecedented level of attention.

A few corruption cases involving in particular offices of commissioners were translated into a political requirement to limit staffing appropriations across the board in the EU institutions.

It also led to a dramatic limitation of the EU's capabilities to implement its own programmes.

All this is natural and quite understandable when following the domestic political debates in EU member states. Across-the-board budgetary discipline has become necessary.

However, percentage term application of growth should not be deemed appropriate in areas where new services are being set up or new objectives are being pursued.

The current setup again privileges large projects since they require on average fewer staff to implement.

This has made it difficult to implement small and complex projects in key security-related areas, notably in human rights situations.

Effective implementation has not been made easier by the constant reorganization of the main DG responsible for implementation of aid: from the Common Service for External Relations (SCR) to Development and Cooperation (Europe aid) to Devco during a period of little more than a decade.

Savings incurred by reducing staff became a politically irresistible mantra also for the European Commission itself. Particularly during the financial crisis from 2008, across-the-board cuts in staff were decided that were similar to those taking place on the level of member states. It was quickly forgotten that staff costs constitute about 5 percent of the total budget of the EU. In view of the financial framework for the period 2014–2020, the European

11   Ringe, L F, 'The Santer Commission resignation crisis: Government-
      Opposition Dynamics in Executive-Legislative Relations of the EU', University
      of Pittsburgh, 2003,

Commission made the additional overall commitment to cut staff by 5 percent in the EU institutions.

The past decade has witnessed a significant outsourcing of implementation capacity of large programmes to other international organizations, member states, and NGOs. It has become normal practice for the EU to decide on a strategy for implementation only to transfer the right to decide on implementation to another actor.

The most significant example is of course the assistance money transferred to the United Nations system, which in the past decade sometimes exceeded €1 billion per year. This would have been good had it been coupled with an explicit joint strategy promoting multilateral effectiveness. Instead, financing decisions by the EU were often taken as a last resort, as a way to spend the money without going through drawn-out tendering procedures.

Steps were also accepted for political reasons that compromised the integrity and quality of staff, thereby actually decreasing the inbuilt protection against corruption. Initially, it was believed necessary to have a European civil service to ensure the integrity of the European institutions, offering safe employment conditions that were also competitive with other major employers internationally.

Particularly after the entry into force of the Lisbon Treaty, more short-term appointments of staff who keep their allegiance to their national governments have deliberately undercut this loyalty to the institutions.

The risk is that the natural concern for achieving geographic balance in the staffing tables of the institutions (thereby creating space for the newer member states) will in the end undermine quality and integrity. The informal fast track career path of members of cabinets, 'parachutage', had already created fairness problems for selection boards.

The issue of gender balance is in this regard a different matter. The institutions no doubt for a long time needed to be more aware of issues in this domain.

*Recapitulating*

Staffing problems are referred to in several contexts in this book.

Chapter 1, the conflict cycle, explained that one of the most visible shortfalls was the lack of support and readiness to mediate on the highest level before and during a crisis. A sufficient conflict prevention capability in terms of staff has still not become an overall priority.

When discussing crisis management in the framework of CSDP it was notable that the requirement for a proper staffing table for the EU military staff before it was deemed operational was not implemented with the same resolve in the civilian domain.

Chapter 2, which focuses on flows, showed that the availability of staff to provide the liaison between geographic departments and delegations and the thematically organized Commission was a very visible problem. For example, only a few staff supported the counterterrorism coordinator.[12] In addition, the joint communication on cyber security with the Commission had to be taken in hand by only one national expert in the EEAS.

Moving to chapter 3, the first priority for the EU after the entry into force of the Lisbon Treaty in 2009 was to promote representation of the EU worldwide by strengthening smaller delegations, now sometimes equipped with only one official[13] from Brussels. Focus on sound financial management and the personal responsibility of heads of delegations to assure this objective has left little room for political analysis. Heads of delegation essentially need to set negative priorities themselves.

The priority in terms of staffing of the EU Commission thematic Directorate Generals is still the development of internal capacities in the Union. Little thematic expertise has been deployed to the delegations. Whenever serious negotiations on important topics has had to be carried out, staff have to be deployed from headquarters to the international organization in question on short-term missions.

---

12  The entry into force of the Lisbon Treaty left counterterrorism in the external dimension in some respects in a limbo. The first counterterrorism coordinator who had his own political profile from a national parliament had been replaced by a senior official in the Council Secretariat, still with very limited institutional support in the Council structures. Given the fact that he was also coordinating with Council formations dealing with internal EU counterterrorism matters, formerly in the third pillar, his post was not transferred to the EEAS.

13  EU delegations are often configured with just one or two officials from Brussels, largely focused on financial and contractual issues, often not with the right training, and supported by local staff lacking security clearance.

The way the permanent representations of member states to the European Union are set up with permanent thematic expertise present at all times was not implemented on the international level in the EU delegations. Instead, the delegations were dependent on the deployment of member states' national experts on the topics, which again meant less continuity, coherence, and ownership as regards what the multilateral delegations were doing in relation to the European Commission.

Multilateral staffing requirements received low priority, leading to staffing levels even after the entry into force of the Lisbon Treaty that were much lower than those of the Russian and US delegations.

## 5.4 Structures and Activities

### Creating and managing structures for EU external action relevant for security

The previous sections of this chapter noted how legal and budgetary provisions have shaped some of the conditions for EU security-related policies.

This section focuses on structures and activities. Beyond limitations created by budgets and staff, and beyond what has been discussed about legal basis, what can be said about generic problems of impact of structures and activities related to security?

The next chapter focuses on the process from problem definition to impact assessment, using the SMARTER acronym (characteristics that are specific, measurable, achievable, relevant, time-relevant, allowing for evaluation, and reevaluation). Some aspects related to this discourse also appear in this section.

At this point, it is appropriate to focus on issues that more specifically relate to the types of structure and activity set up by the EU. Again[14], there is a need to focus on structural and dynamic charac-

14  For an interesting analysis of the inclusion of CSDP structures in EEAS see Méran, F, & A Weston, 'The EEAS and Crisis Management: The Organisational Challenges of a Comprehensive Approach' in J Bátora, & S David (eds.), *European Diplomacy post-Westphalia*, Palgrave, 2015, This important contribution made available to the current author at the end of the drafting process for this book contains quite a number of empirical references to

teristics that have a shelf life that is longer than only a few years. As noted in the introduction, some of the problems discussed before entry into force of the Lisbon Treaty are no longer very relevant.

Several types of problem stand out when recapitulating the discussions in the previous chapters and considering the medium term organizational recommendations in the *EEAS Review*.

*Medium term organisational recommendations in the EEAS Review:*
1. Overhaul management and procedures for CSDP operations (streamline planning functions for civilian and military missions; reduce intermediate steps in consultation of Council working groups; simplified procurement and financial procedures). The December European Council debate on security and defence could also cover structural issues (*e.g.* integration of CSDP structures within the EEAS, reporting lines, mission support);
2. Create a shared services centre to provide logistical, procurement and administrative support for all CSDP missions and EUSRS.
3. Clarify system of political deput(ies) for the High Representative (either within EEAS structures or through clearer responsibility for HRVP over other Commissioners). Conclude formal arrangements for existing practice where Foreign Ministers, members of the Commission and senior EEAS officials can deputise for the HRVP (including having formal representation rights in EP, Council and Commission meetings);
4. In future allocation of Commission portfolios, strengthen HRVP position in Commission decision-making on external assistance programmes, to ensure optimal coherence with EU foreign policy priorities and clarify the HR/VP's lead responsibility for relations with Western Balkans and ENP countries.
5. Streamline EEAS top management structure in particular the composition of the Corporate Board and the division of labour between Managing Directors and Directors. Merge

---

problems in the new CSDP setup in EEAS, supporting observations throughout this study.

posts of Executive Secretary General and Chief Operating Officer into a single post of Secretary General. Reduce number of Managing Directors.

## Line of command, coordination, and a sense of ownership

Starting from the top, the *line of command* issue is of course central not only for security but also and perhaps in particular for crises relating to security problems. There is also a continuous need for *coordination* and a sense of *ownership* as regards a number of security concerns.

The need for a clear line of command, not least in crises, was highlighted in the 9/11 attacks in 2001 and the ensuing crisis.[15]

After the Lisbon Treaty entered into force, this was a question of the role and authority of not only the HR/VP but also, and notably, the president of the European Commission and the president of the European Council.

In turn this is closely related to the question whether the security issue is seen as external or both internal and external to the Union. The language of the treaty is confusing in this regard, not least to outsiders, with the formula 'common foreign and security policy'.

A problem on the next lower level is the unclear relationship between the HR/VP and other commissioners dealing with security-relevant issues. Ideally, organization of the Commission in clusters would facilitate coordination and constitute a clear line of command as envisaged in the new Commission from 2015.

A number of DGs in the Commission have chosen to develop their own links with the outside world for the purpose of coordination of internal policies with those of other countries.[16] Several DGs have also built up capacities to instruct EU delegations that include significant Commission staff elements.

On some of these issues, the *EEAS Review* is quite frank:

---

15 Lunch with the 9/11 Commission
16 Their websites currently (2014) only to a limited extent take into account the existence of the EEAS.

*From the EEAS Review 2013:*
Close co-operation between the EEAS and the Commission is
also vital on the various global issues where the external aspects
of internal EU policies have a growing foreign policy dimension.
This includes areas such as energy security, environmental protection and climate change, migration issues, counter-terrorism,
financial regulation and global economic governance. The EEAS
is increasingly expected to provide the Foreign Affairs Council
with ideas and policy proposals in these areas. Yet, following
the allocation of responsibilities and resources at the creation of
the EEAS, virtually all the expertise and capacity to manage the
external aspects of these policies remained in the Commission
services. The EEAS[17] is not calling into question the lead
responsibilities of Commission services in these areas. However,
as their political significance and potential impact on the wider
foreign policy agenda continues to grow, the EEAS will need
to continue to reinforce its capacity to deal with them in the
future.[18]

The Lisbon Treaty brought a welcome rebranding of the Commission delegations as EU delegations, still performing the task of
the Commission delegations but also politically empowered to lead
the work of member states in most settings, both multilateral and
bilateral. Nonetheless, there are still problems on this level, notably
as regards the status of the head of delegation in relation to other
EU principals, be they EU Special representatives, heads of crisis
management operations, etc. EU Special representatives, in addition, are torn between the loyalty to the member States in the PSC
and the EEAS and often appointed for very short periods of time
allowing little time for strategic planning.

   In summary, there is the problem of the roles of several
actors, which relates to the system for intergovernmental versus
Community coordination. It is in this context possible to see even
more clearly the complications brought by the Lisbon Treaty, as
discussed in section 5.1. Essentially, article 21 of the treaty provides

17   Just before the entry into force of the treaty the Commission excluded impor-
     tant thematic entities from the structures to be transferred to the EEAS, for
     instance in the area of energy.
18   *EEAS Review* 2013

a CFSP perspective to more or less the entire external action domain, including trade, etc. This article creates the expectation that the High Representative, assisted by EEAS and EU delegations, is able to ensure overall coherence of EU action externally.[19] Seen in this way, the EEAS is not a service but rather an institution on the same level as the European Commission.

This paradigm can be said to be at the heart of the so-called comprehensive approach developed during the first five years after the entry into force of the Lisbon Treaty. This is of course difficult for the European Commission to accept. It contradicts the notion of the treaty that the EEAS should assist the Commission and the Council in the coordination of external action. It also seems to elevate the HR/VP from the role of a vice-president of the Commission to a position on the same level as the presidents of the Commission and the Council. It risks in the longer term undermining the Community method with the right of initiative developed over many decades. Today, the European Commission requires that inter-service consultation takes place in the Commission before the Council is consulted. For the EEAS it is natural to base most initiatives on prior discussion in the PSC.

The president of the European Commission has given a special status for the High Representative as vice-president of the Commission in relation to other commissioners dealing with external action and security. The *EEAS Review* contains a clear recommendation to this effect.

*From the EEAS Review 2013:*
In addition to the HR/VP and within the overarching strategic objectives defined by her, the EEAS works closely with the Commissioner for Enlargement and the European Neighbourhood Policy and the Commissioner for Development. The division of labour has generally worked well. Designating a Commissioner for the neighbourhood when the geographical responsibilities for these countries were transferred to the HR/VP and EEAS risked confusion. The EEAS has full responsibility for relations with all countries across

---

19   Issue discussed in interviews in EEAS. Also under discussion during the drafting process of the Comprehensive Approach Council Conclusions.

the globe including the ENP countries where it provides support to both the High Representative and the Enlargement
Commissioner and the ACP countries where it provides support to the HRVP and to the Development Commissioner. DG
Enlargement has policy lead for relations with pre-accession
countries in relation to the enlargement process, while more
political aspects of relations with the Western Balkans and
Turkey are handled by small geographical teams in the EEAS.
DG DEVCO has the policy lead for cross-cutting development programmes. The current arrangements in terms of lead
responsibility work mainly because of the good and close working relationships between the HR/VP and her Commissioner
colleagues. But the division of responsibilities is potentially
unclear and should be clarified. The allocation of portfolio
responsibilities in the next Commission presents an opportunity for the President of the Commission to review the situation.

For such an effort to be effective there will also need to be more
agreement with member states and the Parliament on who can truly represent the Union in crises and in high-level shuttle diplomacy.

The absence of a clear line of command in the EEAS itself is a
further issue raised in the *EEAS Review*, as seen above.

There is also the issue of the line of command through the
organizing cultures as discussed in chapter 3, with a primary role
for geographic services. Ideally, this geographic setup should be
fully supported by the other resources of the EU. This concept was
promulgated in the beginning of the millennium in the context of
the DG for External Relations of the Commission. The informal
doctrine was that the departments directing geographically defined
delegations would be at the forefront, supported by other types of
entity in the rear. In addition, after the Lisbon Treaty entered into
force it was decided to set up single geographic desks in the EEAS,
as discussed in section 3.1.

This was coupled with efforts to develop *comprehensive approaches*
ranging from border management, to geographic and thematic
strategies and of course to the specific comprehensive approach
on external conflicts and crises elaborated mainly in Africa. There
are also transregional strategies based on programmes such as the
Instrument for Stability.

The situation in these regards remains unclear in a number of the areas discussed in previous chapters. For instance, in the DGs for Development, Enlargement and Trade, a whole range of geographic units and directorates have been set up directly instructing EU delegations. The Commission is elaborating thematic strategic documents, and its services totally dominate the contributions to joint security-related thematic documents, such as those in the area of cyber security. The Commission represents the EU in several key international negotiations on international legal instruments relating to Community competencies. It also leads negotiations with the United States on the Transatlantic Trade and Investment Partnership (TTIP). The Commission has its own crisis centre for humanitarian assistance and civil protection as well as its own overall crisis coordination system, ARGUS, which does not include the EEAS.

## Multitasking

On the issue of *multitasking* capabilities on the part of the leadership on different levels, there is a risk that the Lisbon Treaty in some respects represents a step back in relation to earlier capabilities. The multitasking capability required in order to prevent and manage conflicts worldwide is difficult to create under the current treaty. Second-best solutions are being tried, such as deploying commissioners, ministers from member states, or senior officials.

In periods of a strong rotating presidency it could put many capabilities into the presidency role for a short time, for instance by deploying special envoys and other high-level representatives.

This became much more difficult after the Lisbon Treaty entered into force. The HR/VP has taken on the functions of a number of different personalities – the previous High Representative in the Council Secretariat, the previous Commissioner for External Relations in the Commission, the role of the rotating presidency in chairing the Foreign Affairs Council as well as the leadership role in the Commission for External Relations, previously assumed by the president of the European Commission. At the same time the level of ambition has increased. The EU is supposed to do more in the area of security.

As mentioned in section 1.3, the first High Representative to be appointed after entry into force of the treaty tried to experiment with several different solutions to the problem, including asking foreign ministers to represent her in serious crisis situations, such as Ukraine. However, this did not bring continuity and the mandate was seldom clear. Commissioners were seldom if ever empowered to represent member states. Senior officials in the external action service were occasionally deployed in different troubleshooting missions, but again with a limited level of recognition and an even more limited possibility to act on the highest levels. The EU special representatives were also not given highest-level recognition: on the contrary, there was an effort to integrate them and their staff into the EEAS.

Expectations that the new High Representative would be highly visible in the media had sometimes absurd consequences for the allocation of her time. Despite the fact that the Union had a dedicated Commissioner for Humanitarian Assistance she was still expected to devote considerable attention to the humanitarian catastrophe in Haiti, for example.[20]

The new High Representative developed an incremental approach, focusing on high visibility deliverables in a few areas such as Iran and Belgrade-Pristina and she worked effectively with only a few troubleshooters in this effort.

The level of intervention was also from time to time elevated to the president of the European Council and the president of the Commission, but there was no consistent or continuous overall leadership on the part of any one EU representative. The problem in the case of Ukraine was that the crisis played out during a transition year when all three major figures in addition to the president of the European Parliament were in transition.

On the level of EU delegations the new system created after the entry into force of the Lisbon Treaty continued to place unreasonable expectations particularly on the heads of delegations and staff who were to do political reporting. Heads of delegation were still

---

20  This was actually in some respects a result of the domestic political problem in the United States: that the new President Obama wanted at all costs to avoid the criticism levelled at President Bush for a lack of attention to the Katrina catastrophe a few years earlier. This not only led to an enormous pressure on the US Defense Department to send immediate assets to the scene, but also forced the US Secretary of State to spend a lot of time on the Haiti issue, which in turn forced the European High Representative to do the same.

burdened with extensive administrative duties and in some countries worked almost on their own.

## Strategic overview

A third issue is the need for *strategic overview*, a necessary condition for leadership. This is not an asset that at least the larger member states necessarily want the EU institutions to possess. They do not share intelligence with the European institutions on the level necessary for these institutions to have such a capability. The implicit assumption is clear: strategic thinking is for governments of member states, the real strategic motives cannot be openly discussed among 28 states.

Commission President Delors, who built up a cabinet with powerful and strategic analytical capability, did not accept this notion, an ambition that was not fully pursued by his successors. The president of the European Council has no real strategic planning capability in the EU system and is mainly dependent on briefings from the EEAS.

The High Representative chose to dismantle the powerful policy unit that was at the disposal of Javier Solana.[21] In addition, the thematic security entities had less staffing. Staff support for the EU special representatives was also cut.

At the time of writing new efforts are being undertaken in order to improve conflict analysis,[22] pursuing a comprehensive approach. The process of conducting a cost/benefit analysis of conflict prevention requires strategic overview and coordination. Before the Lisbon Treaty entered into force, there were few opportunities for geographic desks and EU delegations to fully engage in forward-looking scenario analysis. Training budgets that would allow more capabilities to do this have rather decreased than increased.

## Contingency planning capabilities

The area of *contingency planning* is another example of a possible deterioration after the entry into force of the Lisbon Treaty. One

---

21  With one representative from each of the member states and the Commission often bringing important intelligence into the system.
22  In cooperation between security policy officials and geographic departments.

particularly visible aspect relates to the need to prepare for high-level
mediation.

The limitations of EU mediating capacity were particularly visible before and during the 2008 Georgia war, when the main role
was played by the President of France as rotating presidency but
only after the war had already started. Mediation work before the
war was limited to the level of the EU special representative and
other service-level officials.

Whenever a conflict prevention effort reached a more serious stage requiring high-level shuttle diplomacy combined with
coordination of all relevant EU long- and short-term efforts, the
European Union has only very gradually improved its capabilities
but its potential is seriously diminished by its lack of multitasking
potential.

Ideally, EU delegations and other EU presences should promote
contingency planning for such mediation efforts but the European
Union has so far been slow in promoting such a capacity. EU
officials below the political level can normally not be effective as
mediators at the top level in crisis and even less in a conflict prevention situation.

Even finding mission money to go to the various crisis locations has turned out to be a difficulty. Logistic support for mediation efforts is weak. Logistic requirements for shuttle diplomacy
between states and regions in conflict are typically very demanding.

*Flexibility*

As noted above, the CSDP area is burdened by problems relating
to micromanagement, information security, etc. In addition, the
need to act quickly makes the general procurement procedures
that are in place in the EU very unsuitable. This compares unfavourably with the flexibility of organizations such as the OSCE.
Notably, it also compares unfavourably with the much less strict
crisis response procedures developed in the Commission in support of the European Council, dealing with the financial crisis.
The question might be raised, as noted above, whether the link
to NATO in this regard has introduced some unnecessary practices
into the EU.

## Mainstreaming

A number of security concerns need to be *mainstreamed* into different geographic and other programmes. This is a requirement in quite a number of policy areas, such as conflict prevention, non-proliferation, human rights, mine action, etc., but the literature is often critical about the effectiveness of these policies.

It has turned out to be difficult to protect the level of thematic funding for niche projects such as mine action when they were integrated into larger programmes, often geographically defined and with few central benchmarks that were related to security.

As regards more long-term conflict prevention measures, they were supposed to be mainstreamed across all Community external programmes from 2001. However, this required an overall strategic capability to do such mainstreaming, including in the *ex ante* assessment process, which often was missing.

There are examples of cases where commissioners have resisted the inclusion of clauses not to make trade and other negotiations too difficult.

Commissioners with thematic responsibilities in the Commission relating to key security areas such as FSJ have generally not assumed the responsibility to contribute staff to external delegations or to ensure that mainstreaming is successful.

There is a constant conflict of interests in the EU institutions, not least between various DGs in the Commission, on how to keep mainstreaming decisions alive and relevant over the years.

Studies have been made on the mainstreaming of conflict prevention, for instance on clauses concerning non-proliferation and human rights. Strategic compromises have sometimes been made, notably when it comes to India and nuclear energy cooperation, which has made it difficult to continue to push for effective and principled mainstreaming. Some may be focusing specifically on aspects of security relevance in strategic documents while others may shy away from such considerations, trying not to introduce too many complications in the definition of measurements of success.

Chapter 4 shows how in policy contexts the Community option may help the EU to be working more consistently over longer periods in areas such as conflict prevention, enlargement, and development assistance. In addition, the intergovernmental approach may bring more coherence with member states' policies at any given time and mobilize political attention on acute problems, particularly in crises. Here again the contexts in which policies of mainstreaming are being implemented are important.

## Reporting and analysis

The staff dealing with *reporting* and analysis need to be trained.

The extent to which officials were trained to feed headquarters and hierarchy with relevant information is a problem that has received additional attention in recent years, in particular with the entry into force of the Lisbon Treaty. Commission staff did not necessarily have this background and were often not expected to carry out political reporting.

> *From the EU member states' Council Conclusions on the Comprehensive Approach 2014:*
> The Council notes that the starting point for the EU's comprehensive approach must be early, coordinated and shared analysis of each country and/or regional specific context, the conflict dynamics and the root causes of a crisis situation. This early joined-up analysis should in particular build on existing mechanisms and processes and systematically bring together all relevant domains of EU external action, including diplomacy, security, development and, as appropriate, humanitarian assistance, justice and migration, at headquarters and on the ground. EU Delegations, Member States' representations and EU Special Representatives all have a central role in contributing to this joint analysis and making recommendations for EU action, including in the field of conflict prevention. EU Delegations, in particular, have a key role to play, drawing on their expertise on a range of issues, including on security and defence issues where appropriate, and also engaging Member States' representations.

Guidelines for political reporting have been promulgated by the executive secretary general of the EEAS but much training is necessary in order to realize the objectives set out in these guidelines. In particular the tendency to apply only one or just a few of the perspectives discussed in this study needs to be counteracted systematically.

The amount of time available to the hierarchy on almost all levels to take a wider view is very limited. The highest-level officials and political leaders literally deal with hundreds of issues every day. Great care needs to be taken to synthesize the basic important information.

This need for training is particularly obvious when one considers the complexity of the substance. In national EU representations typically three ambassadors cover the entire spectrum of EU policies, in the EU permanent representatives committees, COREPER II and I, as well as in the PSC. Even a small EU Council presidency has several hundred staff in Brussels covering about 300 different working parties in the Council. The complexity is no less visible in the Commission and the EEAS, where some 1 000 heads of division and other units cover the entire ground, assisted by over 140 EU delegations abroad. Even on this level it is not unusual for a single middle-level official to cover an entire policy area.

A constant differentiation of topics at some point needs to lead to more integration.

The security discourse in the EU is already enormously more complex than it was at the beginning of the ESDP in the late 1990s. Even on the highest level this may lead to confusion and non-decision. There is therefore an obvious need to promote awareness and overview and find ways to simplify the problems.

It has been difficult for the EU structures to create the capacity to properly analyse all these problems. This is partly seen as a problem of political reporting and strategic analysis, further hurt by the lack of staff in general not only in the EEAS but also to a certain extent in the European Commission. It is also affected by a lack of open exchange of reports and analyses between member states and the difficulties in promoting and effectively using academic research, partly due to the longstanding perceived lack of legal basis in the European Commission to promote security-relevant research beyond support to technological capacities.

The problem of budget and staff starts in the EU delegations, often configured with only one or two officials from Brussels, largely focused on financial and contractual issues, often not with the right training, and supported by local staff who lack security clearance. At the same time a holistic overview needs to be developed on this level. Lack of mission money to visit delegations from headquarters, staff

rotations, and overburdening of the system with briefing requirements, etc. all make it difficult for desks at headquarters to carry out
the necessary political reporting.[23]

The same problems characterize the level of the geographic desk
in the EEAS and the Commission, where posts are included in
mobility schemes, with insufficient training between posts, a lack
of mission budget, etc. This is further compounded by the lack of
resources in the thematic, crisis response, and multilateral desks
both in the EEAS and in the Commission

## Safety of staff and business continuity

Finally, staff security and the assurance of business continuity as
illustrated by the 9/11 crisis are likely to become a more important
problem in the future.

Organized crime presents important security problems for staff
in civilian missions and programmes deployed by the EU or implemented by other international organizations such as the OSCE,
UNDP, etc. Increasingly, civilian workers are the target of crime
including hostage taking. Given the high level of corruption in
most countries with which the EU has development and other
programmes, confidentiality of reporting becomes an important
problem, in particular the protection of sources. There are many
examples of international operations and missions where the most
rampant forms of organized crime involving corrupt elites in the
country in question are not faced openly by mission personnel in the
country for personal security reasons. This was for a long time the
case not least in Central Asia.

Business continuity is also related to the readiness of the organization to function effectively.

Unfortunately, it also means being wary of radical reorganization proposals. The different actors' suspicion of attempts to create
new conceptual hierarchies is very strong.

---

23   There are exceptions to this situation of course in the EU system for external
     action. The most well-known and appreciated systems are perhaps related to
     the progress reports on EU enlargement where significant efforts are made
     to systematically evaluate developments according to certain precise criteria.
     There are reports written for the European Parliament, etc. There are line
     speeches being written which should be making strategic analysis.

By default, many see such conceptual constructs in organizational contexts as ways to change power structures and reallocate competences. Once some of these proposals actually result in a reorganization, it may take a long time for the benefits to be reaped.

From the point of view of the media, while drastic reorganizations often look good they drain organizations of their energy and reduce effectiveness for a long period of time. In the case of the setting up of the EEAS the period of time may be not one or two but maybe five or ten years.

# 6. From Problem Identification to Impact Assessment

This chapter addresses the issue of impact assessment as a way to identify generic problems of impact in EU security-related policies.

The European Commission has established a methodology for impact assessments and adopted some more general practices in place in other international organizations, such as the World Bank.

Typically, there are two main stages in this process: impact assessment *ex ante*, discussed in section 6.2, and impact assessment *ex post*, discussed in section 6.3.

## 6.1 Focusing on the Problem

It is essential to have a constant focus on the overall objective in order to achieve effective implementation. However, officials on all levels and in all stages of implementation are tempted to be detracted from the strategic purposes of the defined actions and to seek intermediate measurements of success.

In EU impact assessment methodology, even one further step back is promulgated: identifying the problem. Before programmes are discussed, the proponents should describe the problem at hand.

*Focus on problems rather than instruments:*
*The SMARTER approach*

A few decades ago, when foreign ministries were first subjected to the type of programming requirements that were implemented in public service, it was not uncommon for senior diplomats to claim that foreign policy cannot really be planned.

At the level of the EU, this reasoning has also often been voiced in response to calls for more strategic planning and overall strategic documents in the Union. The typical argument is: how do we know how things will develop? If we had fixed a strategy at a point in the past we could very well have been caught in a paradigm that would not have been appropriate for the current situation. Even to decide who is and who is not an EU strategic partner has proven difficult: a prominent case in point is Russia. It may be necessary to keep the definition vague since one never knows when the character of a relationship between the EU and world powers may change or when the role of those players may develop in one or another direction.

When strategies and programmatic documents are developed and formulated, there is a natural tendency not to pinpoint the desired end state too precisely since this may tie the hands of those implementing the policy in question.

*Case in point*: Heads of EU delegations to multilateral and bilateral bodies receive mandates for their work. When these mandates are developed there is a tendency to include as much as possible in these documents, brainstorming any possible contribution such a delegation can bring to all the different interests at headquarters level. A prioritization of these objectives is much more difficult to do. However, planning and prioritization are a necessary condition for the implementation of something more than ad hoc political dialogues and reporting.

Even the early issue of focusing on the desired impact is a significant problem for EU security-related policies.

To illustrate the issue one can image a normal meeting of EU officials discussing a possible initiative on any given topic. In such an inter-service meeting, it is common for participants to bring issues related to their area of competences to the table. They speak about instruments they are responsible for, and seek to protect and develop their role in the organization. They often tend to just address one part of the substance under discussion. They also may use a conceptual framework for their presentation that fits and underlines their competences.

It will then be up to the chair of the meeting to bring the issues together and try to find a common point of departure. However, he or she may in the end still find it only possible to produce a paper that enumerates the number of different areas discussed during the meeting. The result may very well be an enumeration of possible actions according to available instruments rather than a conceptually coherent document.

This difficulty is not specific to the EU, but most likely a problem facing almost all large organizations. The literature on the issue is abundant, not least in the context of project management.[1]

As a guideline, the SMARTER acronym will now be used, as developed in project management literature, applied to the context of EU external action.[2]

The 'SMART' concept refers in project management to criteria related to impact: Specific, Measurable, Attainable, Relevant and Time-bound. A later version goes two steps further by introducing the criteria of Evaluation and Re-evaluation with the acronym SMARTER.

In interviews with EU institutions carried out by the author in 2012–2013, respondents referred to many relevant aspects in this paradigm: they saw a need for Specific expertise, clearer Measurements of success, Attainable goals in terms of EU leverage, Relevance of EU interests and values and, that it was Time-bound as regards the need for longer-term goals, Evaluations denoting the need for a more systematic approach to lessons learned, and Re-evaluation in situations when earlier policies have failed.

---

1   Gudda, P, *A Guide to Project Monitoring & Evaluation*, Authorhouse, 2011.
2   A shorter version of this analysis specifically applied to CSDP appears in Lundin, L-E, 'CSDP Senior Mission Leaders and the Comprehensive Approach. A need-to-know guide', *folkebernadotteacademy.se*, 2013.

*Examples of measures of success*

Some measures of success defined on the levels below the political, influenced by administrative and other organizational cultures, may also significantly impact on the vision of the desired end state. This requires:

- An official responsible for the implementation of aid programmes: ensure that the statistics for implementation of the budget are satisfactory to the Parliament and Court of Auditors
- A programmer: propose something that can be implemented — make sure to introduce enough flexibility to allow for adjustments
- A project implementation official: follow the so-called internal control standards — implement the project correctly — choose large projects with well-known partners in as favourable conditions as possible
- A military official responsible for a strategic concept: propose limited risks with appropriate resources

Impact as a result of planned action should normally be rated by clear measures of success. However, it is often difficult to keep to this practice. Success is often defined by reference to intermediate measures of success. When it comes to the ultimate measures of success it is much more difficult to pinpoint impact:

- How can efforts be argued to have led to the strengthening of the non-proliferation regime?
- How can efforts be shown to have led to a reduction of the drug trafficking out of Afghanistan?
- How can results of counterterrorism efforts be determined?

*S – specific expertise*

*Specific expertise* needs to be available in a number of security-relevant areas.

*From a report the current author has produced after a series of interviews in the EU institutions in 2012:*

The need for *specific expertise* is also a major problem. The study already referred to the need to develop geographic expertise able to cover country and regional situations through political reporting which is developed in continuity over a longer period of time, which can form the basis for risk management analysis. Then there is the issue of thematic expertise. This is clearly a major problem. Given the fact that geography must be given predominant priority in the staffing of EU delegations and in the organization of the EEAS at headquarters level, limited resources remain in order to promote thematic expertise. One centrally placed respondent, however, noted that sooner or later more emphasis needs to be put on developing the global issues department, which engage with thematic issues in the Commission line DGs. This includes quite a number of thematic areas ranging from development, human rights including elections etc., non-proliferation and disarmament issues, mine action and small arms, cyber, energy, environment, etc. The importance even of the work of individual experts was referred to in different examples in areas such as the nexus between security and development, the development of transnational threats policy (drugs, organized crime and terrorism). Clearly it is of great importance for the institutions to be able to recruit over a longer periods of time eminent expertise from the member states to help develop policies in these areas. The institutions can probably not develop such expertise fully in-house from the early part of their career but more adequate systems than the current short-term secondments need to be found. In this context, it was noted that the Joint Research Centre is too much focused on technical issues. Several respondents referred to the possibility to develop more thematic expertise in DEVCO. Several of the drivers of energy policy in the Commission were moved to DEVCO just before the setting up of the EEAS. As can be expected there is a resistance in DEVCO to do this given the pressure on the project management side in the house. The third possibility is of course to develop and use more systematically expertise in the line directorate generals. The limits of this potential were discussed with a representative of DG HOME. He testified to the impossibility to put systematic focus on external work. Already cooperation with the United States had threatened to put his agenda off-track and efforts to develop more and more sectoral dialogues with key partners such as China clearly is a threatening perspective for a DG mainly focusing on legislative endeavours inside the Union. The risk is that an overall perspective to the need for thematic expertise is not applied. It would seem useful to propose a dedicated study on this in the EU.

Staffing was a central issue when the new structures were set up after the Lisbon Treaty had entered into force, including staff contributions from member states with due regard to gender and geographic balance. These criteria were relevant when it came to broadening EU expertise in an ever more complex security situation. In addition, in this context there was a need to improve pooling and sharing of expertise. The EU enlargement process showed the way through deployment of EU experts (twinning) to different governmental institutions of host countries, helping them to harmonize with EU standards. This methodology was later applied in the EU neighbourhood and as far away as Central Asia, in border management and other programmes.

Nevertheless, there are still significant deficits. Geographically, there is a concern that political reporting, from both the field and desks at headquarters level, has not been developed with the requisite continuity and in-country knowledge. Thematically, there is a dramatic shortfall of expertise in many areas, ranging from non-proliferation and counterterrorism in multilateral delegations to experts on corruption, organized crime, and drugs in key geographic contexts.

The Commission services focus mainly on work in the Union. External departments such as DEVCO are tied up in the management of huge financial programmes. The priority in the EEAS is to secure a minimum of two diplomats in each of the 140 delegations. The member states still hesitate to share reporting and intelligence with the EU institutions, partly because of problems with security of information, but they do second national experts, which in many policy areas makes a vital difference to promoting policy development. These are issues to a certain extent brought up in the *EEAS Review*.

Senior staff need to take this into account and as much as possible seek to mobilize staff with significant expertise and encourage staff to grow in the job. Staff mobility programmes need to cater for continuity of expertise.

### M – *measure of success*

The issue of performance against targets constitutes one of the issues addressed in the 2013 *EEAS Review*. Again, the key is to focus on the problem and look at the end state, not allowing for intermediate measures of success to develop that would cloud vision of the ultimate goals. There is a natural hesitation to be clear about this and instead make *ex post* evaluations of success. It is worth noting in particular the following factors which have constituted problems in EU delivery.

First, there is too intense a focus on competencies. The issue of who does what has sometimes been deemed more important than what is being done.

The EU also has a history of ambivalence when it comes to implementation. In a first phase, it is typically seen as important for the EU to deliver and act quickly. Sometimes just announcing the commitment of funds has been considered a sufficient measure of success. Later, in a lesson learned and evaluation phase, criticism is often launched against hasty action or insufficient attention to factors hampering the effectiveness of the programme or operation, be it corruption or other problems. The legacy of any operation is plainly related to the sustainability of its result, and this must at all times be at the top of the attention of the leadership.

### A – *attainable leverage*

Current efforts in the concrete elaboration of the comprehensive approach also need to look at EU comparative advantages in relation to other actors. Sometimes it can be more effective to support others, from international organizations to NGOs, that may have more leverage than the EU in terms of power of attraction or other elements of soft power. The notion mentioned for instance in the context of the EU Global Strategy report of the EU's need to take comprehensive security responsibility in its strategic neighbourhood is otherwise not understandable: the EU must make smart coalitions with others. All the EU actors, including those in the CSDP, may also benefit from situating their work in the overall EU and international context, not least when conducting external political dialogue.

## R – relevant values and interests

The EU is on the level of the Lisbon Treaty a strongly value-based organization. These values can in turn be linked to a series of strategic interests. Contradictions may appear in concrete situations and in relationship to actors with less value-based approaches. EU approaches may sometimes be seen by partners as either unrealistic (for instance as regards democracy) or dualistic (that EU trade interests are pursued in contradiction to development goals). All of this is complex and needs to be carefully calibrated, benefitting from a comprehensive approach.

In the context of a CSDP mission, for example, it is therefore important to link up closely with geographic and thematic services through the EU delegations and on the level of headquarters in order to correctly situate the work of the mission.

## T – with continuity over time

The transformation timeline in the conflict cycle ranges from short-term interventions to long-term peace and stability where development assistance, security sector reform, dialogue, mediation, and crisis intervention/return assistance/shuttle diplomacy constitute intermediate stages. A persistent deficit in CSDP is deemed to be the result of not having attributed sufficient attention to issues of not only sequencing (see above) but also continuity.

The link to when the Commission can deploy its instruments is particularly important. There are examples where the decision has been taken to intervene through ESDP, for instance through rule of law missions, with arguments that this could be better done in CSDP than through normal Community efforts. However, when the mission has come to an end, the Commission has been expected to seamlessly take over. This is an automaticity that is resisted in the Commission or for which it may not be prepared early enough.

This is thus a problem that is highly relevant to CSDP and Community action, which should be considered at an early stage in every relevant mission and project. In the political dialogue this includes the issues of continuity of coordinating formats, of reporting and of outreach.

## E and R: evaluation and re-evaluation

Lessons learned must be an inbuilt process in each endeavour, be it a project or a CSDP mission. It needs to take the overall measures of success into account and should be combined with evaluations over the longer term of Community programmes and ad hoc Council decisions.

There is no joined up approach to this in the EU that can provide decision makers with relevant evaluations before important decisions are made. On the Community side, evaluations are often so voluminous and cover such a long period (a decade of assistance or more) that they are difficult to digest for those who need to read them. At the other end, political evaluations of a string of Council decisions in the CFSP area are not often made or are partly confidential.

Still, those responsible for these policies need to face the fact that outside evaluations are often more critical.

Re-evaluation is a different process altogether. In science, as documented by Thomas Kuhn, it is a process often leading to new discovery through agonizing reappraisals.[3] In the EU, it is an effort typically required in crisis and difficult to animate in the normal situation. However, as discussed in the context of the Arab Spring, re-evaluation is key, as a part of the continuous political dialogue within and outside the EU.

## Recapitulating

This chapter recapitulates the difficulties in defining the overall and longterm desired impact clearly beforehand.

3    Kuhn, T S, *The Structure of Scientific Revolutions*, 2 ed., University of Chicago Press, 1970. See also for a discussion of Kuhn's critique of the positivist school: Buzan, B, & L Hansen, *The Evolution of International Security Studies*, Cambridge University Press, 2009.

As regards defence and crisis management it is important to note that the need for a crisis management operation may be perceived more in terms of capacity building than in terms of the conflict itself. This was arguably the perspective of many engaged in the Western Balkans in the first years of the CSDP. The possibility of adding another crisis management operation to the list of success-ful CSDP missions may also for some decision makers and planners have overshadowed the question of where the need for an opera-tion was most clear. Specifically, the need to be able to describe the operation as a success in the sense that it was possible to undertake and end it may have weakened the interest in other measures of success.

This is also related to conflict prevention: the extent to which the issue is defined as an end state pointing at conflict resolution rather than just military disengagement, without necessarily paving the way for further conflict resolution efforts.

Moving to chapter 2, flow security, the definition of the issue may be different depending on the predominant paradigm of the beholder. If the view is that interdependence is good, the focus may be exclusively on price when discussing agreements on energy and other flows. If there is a concern that a flow may not be sustainable and secure, a more composite definition of the issue may follow, including not only questions of diversification of dependence but also potential problems relating to crime, including corruption and terrorism. Developing efficient networks has in recent decades been seen as something inherently good in terms of creating greater interdependence and cooperation, which is seen as something that should prevent conflict. Then this paradigm has been contrasted with the one of trying to avoid too much dependence, which could lead to flows being used to influence another country.

The way military operations may unintentionally promote organized crime, corruption and terrorism is an area that has received considerable attention in recent years. Cases in point have been military operations in order to eradicate drugs trafficking, the use of drones, etc.

Another example is the acceptance and even use of certain types of corruptive influence in order to keep warring factions at peace. In the context of the former Soviet Union and the Western Balkans, the post-cold war experience has shown that solving one problem through creating a balance between different ethnic groups can create another problem, leading to uprising against corrupt elites.

From the geographic paradigm alone, there may be a focus on relations between organizations and states as they develop over time. In the thematic paradigm, the focus may be more centred on specific benchmarks determined by conditionality or by economic and other calculations. In the multilateral domain, the focus may sometimes be on the definition of negotiating positions, the achievement of more or less prominent roles in a negotiation, etc. In the crisis response paradigm the issue is strongly related to contingency planning, how to get the EU to get its act together if things go wrong. All this relates to the difficulties involved in balancing different security-related and not security-related objectives.

Examples in the literature include the links between:
• Development and security,
• Development and counterterrorism,
• Human rights and counterterrorism
• Trade and non-proliferation
• Transnational threats and crisis

Moving into the area of policy contexts, examined in chapter 4, the scope of concern on the part of decision makers and planners may be very different. Overall, decision makers may see a value in developing the intergovernmental domain versus the Community domain *per se*. The EU has come a long way towards broadening and adapting its problem definition in the context of the discourse on the comprehensive approach. However, it still suffers from a certain disconnect between these spheres.

As regards the internal/external nexus, it was observed how the focus on internal problems sometimes has diminished attention to the outside world. Some may look mainly to the internal situation, the Union, and to the harmonization of member states' policies or the development of the acquis. Notably, when the Commission has focused on the rule of law in its internal policies, it has done so mainly with reference to legislation of the member states, not to the overall problem as such.

In terms of explicit and implicit security policies one of the main issues is of course that of mainstreaming security aspects, as discussed in chapter 5.

Sub-cultures focusing on legal issues, on sound financial management or on staffing policies will have their own issues at the top of their agenda. In any discussion of structures and activities it is also unavoidable that personal considerations of career and institutional power will appear.

For political leaders in the EU institutions, media impact is of course important. To show focus and the willingness to prioritize what is deemed important for the moment is key. But media attention shifts almost daily from one topic to another. It is therefore not unusual to hear about initiatives being developed that indicate only the start of a process.

"You are dammed if you do and you are damned if you don't" is an expression often applicable to EU external action programmes and operations. The political pressure to implement them may be high, many may lament the slow procedures, recipients may clamour for the money, and the media may ridicule EU bureaucratic hurdles.

Considerable political courage is required to keep the focus on the forest and not just the trees.

All these examples illustrate the need for an open and differentiated debate about how to best focus on different security-related problems in different contexts. The EU's ability to pursue such discussions in different policy contexts and using different paradigms is both a strength and a weakness.

What it does require is openness to allow for vibrant academic and political debate and sufficient resources for strategic planning in different places in the various EU institutions. Above all, strong engagement on the part of member states is extremely important. The institutions cannot replace the creativity provided by active participation in the debate by 28 member states, their national parliaments and their civil societies.

## 6.2 Impact Assessment Ex Ante

*Evolution of the Key Objective: Screen Proposed*
*Initiatives Before the Decision*

*Ex ante* impact assessment has been a standard requirement in Community programme projects for a number of years – projects must be carefully examined *before* they are put into motion.

This has led to the development of a methodology that puts the burden of proof on the Commissioner or DG proposing a certain initiative. In recent years, in particular the Secretary-General of the Commission has been instructed by the Commission President to be quite tough in the scrutiny of all initiatives in order to counter proposals for unnecessary or inefficient regulation.

For higher-level actors the impact assessment procedure is an important tool to ensure that the level of risk-taking is appropriate, that the best initiatives go ahead, etc.

The process of impact assessment also, of course, promotes more careful thinking and consideration of options that otherwise might fall under the table. The support for such an approach will increase if the impact assessment procedure truly poses the right questions and provides more than a bureaucratic methodology to answer them.

After the entry into force of the Lisbon Treaty, the impact assessment procedure was, however, not systematically applied to joint communications elaborated by the High Representative and the Commission.

This led to less attention for instance to financial implications and staffing requirements for implementation. The discrepancy between goals and resources was not sufficiently addressed.

A case in point was the Joint Communication to the European Parliament and the Council: The EU's Comprehensive Approach To External Conflict And Crises. The recommendations were not fully operationalized and did not include calculations of the financial impact of implementation.[4]

---

4    There are, as extensively discussed in the case of the intergovernmental CSDP rule of law operation in Kosovo EULEX, clear consequences of a hasty deployment decision. The Court of auditors of the EU noted that some of the most important problems related to corruption in Kosovo had not been properly factored in when setting up the programme, which in the end cost over 650 million euros. See http://www.eca.europa.eu/Lists/ECADocuments/SR12_18/ SR12 _ 18 _ EN.PDF.

Security objectives almost by definition include a higher risk-taking level where a real cost benefit analysis needs to be carried out, going beyond criteria for sound financial management. Sometimes the risk of later criticism of bad implementation or unsuccessful implementation must be accepted.

## 6.3 Impact Assessment Ex Post

*Evolution of the Key Objective: Evaluate the Impact*
*of EU External Action after Implementation*[5]

The European Commission has developed a structure for evaluation, which as regards development assistance is situated in DEVCO, the Directorate General for Development Cooperation.[6]

On the intergovernmental side, evaluation is often undertaken through lessons learned exercises, which are often not open to the public and not outsourced to external evaluators. Instead, intergovernmental policies are typically analysed by think tanks based on public material.

The literature on evaluation of impact is huge. Sophisticated models have been built, sponsored by international organizations such as the World Bank.

There is also a significant scientific literature that deals with validation of the impact assessments, for instance the effectiveness of various types of development assistance in different theatres. Not seldom, sophisticated statistical methods are used.

Such research is important since there are many different conclusions about causal links between different policy areas which are based on circumstantial evidence.

As an example it seemed clear from the dialogue with different actors in Indonesian society after the terrorist bombing attacks on Bali in 2002 that a diminished respect for the rule of law may have inspired terrorists and increased support in the population for terrorism. However, research in for instance Afghanistan on the links between different types of assistance and counterterrorism is still underway and inconclusive.

---

5    On impact evaluation see further the bibliography.
6    Examples included in the bibliography.

The list and full texts of impact assessments produced by the European Commission are available on the Internet. They often have more or less the same structure and often cover a long period of project implementation, which in the Community area can extend over a decade or more.

They are carried out according to an established and prioritized programme whereby large tenders are put out for competition between different consortia of think tanks specializing on these types of evaluation and using standardized methodology.

Security relevance is not a prominent feature in the current list of evaluations, with the exception of topics such as conflict prevention and security sector reform. Relatively few security experts seem to have been involved in the evaluations. The periodicity of the evaluations is such that they lead to voluminous products, which are not easily accessible for those responsible for future policy development.

The results are sometimes summarized in general terms, describing the Commission approach as more or less effective in relation to set policy objectives and in meeting the needs of partner countries.

*Case in point*: A major neighbourhood policy evaluation undertaken in 2009 included many of the countries later involved in the Arab Spring. A main problem turned out to be that the evaluation focused on the needs on the country level, with their governments at the time. The objectives pursued were deemed not always to correspond to the main priorities of each of the neighbourhood policy countries. This resulted in a lack of commitment by the partner countries, leading to a negative impact on the ownership and sustainability of the efforts.

The example above illustrates the need also to evaluate evaluations. There clearly is a need for a more developed security analysis in EU evaluations, where the overall conclusions in retrospect may appear too schematic:

This is noteworthy when looking at individual country evaluations. *Case in point*: Egypt, where the evaluation of assistance to that country covered a large envelope, €1 billion for bilat-

eral interventions to Egypt over the period 1998 to 2008. The
evaluation concluded that the EU Commission's cooperation
strategy with Egypt was highly relevant to the realization of the
EU-Egypt agreements objectives.

This was a general conclusion, which in the fine print later
is coupled with important reservations such as the finding that
the results of the various interventions had been difficult to
capture due to

(i) Interventions being focused mostly on the measuring and
monitoring of activities rather than of results and impacts and

(ii) Attribution problems, the financial support of the
Commission generally representing only a small contribution
relative to the financing of the Government of Egypt (GoE)
and other donors in a specific area.

Similarly, in the area of human rights, democracy and the
rule of law, the Commission and the GoE had made great
strides forward in opening up the political dialogue about
these sensitive issues; the Commission's support had become
increasingly overt but its effectiveness (strengthened capacities
of government and non-government bodies in the management and implementation of activities and CSO (civil society
organization) participation in political dialogue) could not
be evidenced. In addition, in the end it is noted that human
rights projects constituted only around 5% of the total project
money allocation over the period.[7]

Finally, evaluations seem to validate the existence of the problem
discussed in chapter 5 as regards staffing and structural problems.
The Commission's institutional setup, human resource capacity,
and programming tools and guidance were not commensurate with
its policy commitment and its level of funding for JSSR (justice
and security sector reform). The Commission's programming cycle
and procedures[8] were not deemed sufficiently efficient, flexible, and
long-term in orientation to respond adequately to the dynamic and
political nature of justice and security sector reform.

7  Which again links up to the notion that the Commission prioritizes large programmes.
8  ADE, *Thematic Evaluation of European Commission Support to Justice and Security
   System Reform*, 2011.

# 7. Power and Influence

Living next to you [the United States] is in some ways like
sleeping with an elephant; no matter how friendly and even-
tempered is the beast, if I may call it that, one is affected by
every twitch and grunt. Even a friendly nuzzling can sometimes
lead to frightening consequences.[1]

This quote from Canadian Prime Minister Pierre Trudeau vividly
illustrates the need to think slowly and carefully[2] about power and
influence when discussing the European Union as a security actor.

There are many schools of thought in this debate. The scope of
this study does not permit a full analysis of all the various aspects
examined in the literature on this huge topic. What is done here
is to provide some references to prominent issues of particular
relevance to the EU.

Again, starting as in section 1.1 with the most obvious and traditional way to look at power, there are those – a comparatively small
group – who believe that the EU should be an actor in defence,
projecting power directly through very conscious strategies. The
main constraint in this perspective of course is capacity, and then
mainly military capacity in addition to the problem of convincing
the sceptics.

A second school is against equipping the EU with such capabilities but is still convinced that it is (or should be) a powerful actor,
but not primarily on the basis of military capabilities.

---

1    Pierre Trudeau speech, Washington, May 25, 1969. Retrieved from https://
     www.nelsonbrain.com/content/9780176644628.pdf
2    Kahneman, D, *Thinking, fast and slow*, Macmillan, 2011.

The protagonists of this view include Euro-sceptics who want to repatriate EU powers to the member states, notably in the justice and home affairs area. For them the EU is too powerful.

Then there are the Friends of Europe, who focus on the leverage of the EU internal market as a huge asset of power.

And finally, there are those who are convinced of a potential significant EU role in civilian conflict prevention and crisis management.

Outside the Union and perhaps particularly in the EU neighbourhood, many perceive a strong European influence in positive or negative terms.

In this second school of power and influence there are many, not least scholars, who are intrigued about the complex way in which the EU influences other actors directly or indirectly, in intended or unintended ways, including with implications for democratic legitimacy.

Then there is evidently a large third group of people who do not see a major role for the EU as an international security actor. This group is extremely important since, together with those in the second school who want to diminish the EU's influence, they may have a decisive influence on EU impact by default. The way in which expectations on the part of European constituencies and of strategic partners such as the United States, etc. influence the EU's impact on security is itself a major field of study.

As noted, the influence of specific EU policies or actions may also be perceived in widely different ways. For some, EU enlargement and neighbourhood policies are a way to project stability and security, while for others they are methods for the EU to enlarge its zone of influence. This again may constitute an important drawback in the effectiveness of these policies.

When seeking to explain the EU's impact on security in terms of power and influence, quite a number of research traditions have played a part for some time. Some scholars derive EU influence from the implementation of strategies and policies based on values and interests.

Others see the influence much more as a result of the way the EU institutions function, sometimes quietly developing capabilities, supported by epistemic communities.[3]

---

3   See Cross, MKD, *Security Integration in Europe: How Knowledge-based Networks Are Transforming the European Union*, The University of Michigan Press, 2011 for an analysis of the role of epistemic communities in security integration.

Some see influence as a complex and dynamic process of interaction where some of the generic problems of impact met by the EU relate to a lack of flexibility.

As shown in previous chapters and sections of this book, the relevant toolbox of the EU is rich in opportunities but equally abundant in constraints.

This chapter considers the toolbox and its associated generic problems of impact from different perspectives, again referring to the overlapping ovals in Figure 1.

First, from the notion that an actor seeks to influence another to do what he does not want to do, this is central to the discourse of power, discussed from an EU perspective in section 7.1.

Second, looking at enabling influence as a central feature of EU external action, this is partly an issue of capacity building, as discussed in the area of defence in section 1.1. But it is also a paradigm of fundamental importance for military and civilian assistance: to enable someone to do what he otherwise *could* not do, which includes the possibility to delimit that enabling influence to what the donor wants to enable and little else. This perspective is discussed in section 7.2.

Third, there is the issue of the EU as a normative power, a major school of study in the EU. This is discussed in section 7.3.

Section 7.4 considers perceptions of the EU as they may impact on the behaviour of others in intended or unintended ways.

The analysis is similar to Joseph Nye's[4] focus on soft power and his definition of smart power as a combination of both hard and soft. Of specific importance for the discussion to follow is the understanding that hard power can also be based on economic resources, that power is strongly related to how actors and actions are perceived and that ways to exert influence include international organizations, states and non-state actors in a complex and dynamic interrelationship. Furthermore, Nye sees two faces of power additional to the traditional (Robert Dahl) notion of changing the behaviour of others through threats or awards, namely, influence on beliefs and perceptions as well as influence on agenda setting. An important element of this analysis, finally, is also the many different possible actions, ranging from aid to physical violence. Nye

4    Nye, J S J, *The Future of Power*, Reprint ed., *PublicAffairs*, 2011.

thus does not exclude development or even humanitarian assistance from the arsenal of possible tools. If for instance humanitarian assistance increases the power of attraction of the donor, then this is smart power.

Against this background it is perhaps not surprising that Nye appreciates the potential role and influence of the European Union, referring partly to its economic resources and partly to its power of attraction, particularly in the enlargement context. He also notes the combined resources of the EU member states in all relevant dimensions, including the military, which taken together with a higher degree of unity of purpose would only be matched by the United States.

Again, following Nye, it is important to go beyond the two typical approaches, still very common in the security policy debate in Europe:

- First, referring to power and influence in terms of resources and equating the ambition of building up influence with capability commitments; and
- Second, making an *ex post* analysis of the importance of different actions, sometimes in a self-congratulatory way, defining them as outcomes of comprehensive approaches.

From the standpoint of EU citizens, the main question is not necessarily the extent to which the Union, through its policies, can be more of an actor or exert more power and influence in the world. The constituency of the European Union may have other or additional questions: it would like to learn what the effects of Union policies are, whether they are intended or not, how the Union is perceived, what this means for European and international security and whether EU actions are based on democratic legitimacy.

There are many follow-up questions here which are debated in specific contexts. Just to mention one: if the European Union is seen as exerting power and influence, can it at the same time be perceived as a bona fide development or humanitarian assistance actor? Can the Union be perceived as a force for good if it is perceived as acting mainly in its own interest?

In addition, as noted above with reference to governments, there is the question of the extent to which there will be global powers in the future, whether power and influence need to be seen in each specific local and regional context in order to be meaningful concepts.[5] Governments may still wish to promote the image of being powerful in what they may define as their sphere of influence. This is true for Russia as regards most of the area of the former Soviet Union. It may also be true for one or several of the former colonial powers in Africa or the Middle East. It is manifestly true for the United States, not only in the Western Hemisphere but also in some other areas. However, is it meaningful when discussing the European Union?

The lack of influence, in fact the lack of success, in foreign and security policy in several spectacular cases also illustrates the limits to power, cases in point being the crises involving the United States in Vietnam and the Soviet Union in Afghanistan. It can be argued that the Vietnam War was not only lost on the battlefield – it was also lost in the hearts and minds of millions around the world.

As noted in earlier sections, the issue of the influence of China will be hotly debated in the coming decades. The question will continue to be put whether a country can be more successful in pursuing a policy of no values in external relations than declared value-driven actors such as the European Union. The answer is not obvious. It may play a role in determining the extent that a country such as the United States, China or Russia is being perceived as a positive actor in the international system, particularly in a world where individuals and NGOs play an increasingly important role.

Whether the European Union should have been awarded the Nobel Peace Prize in 2012 is up to each reader to judge. Literally speaking, according to the will of Alfred Nobel, the Peace Prize should be awarded to 'the person who shall have done the most or the best work for fraternity between nations, for the abolition or reduction of standing armies and for the holding and promotion of peace congresses'. The European Union is of course not a person but it became a legal personality with the entry into force of the Lisbon Treaty. Once the decision was taken to award the prize also to international organizations, such as the Red Cross, which has received it three times, the next question arises: Is it how these organizations act in support of peace that merits the prize or is it what they

5    Kupchan, C A, *No One's World*, Oxford University Press, 2012, Naím, M, *The end of power*, Basic Books, 2013.

constitute as a factor for peace in the world? For the current author it is easier to justify awarding the prize to the EU with the second interpretation as long as the process of European integration and enlargement is seen from the eyes of the beholder.

The logic of this becomes more obvious when looking at another region: would it not be desirable for ASEAN (the Association of Southeast Asian Nations) to develop in the direction of the EU in order to enable the countries of this region to work more effectively together with China and the United States and to solve, or at least prevent, escalation of the disputes in and around the South China Sea? Would it not be useful for the African Union to develop further in order to support its member states in managing conflict in Africa?

It is important to state at the outset that there is a considerable risk of overestimating rather than underestimating the impact of EU policies. Particularly in crisis situations, the power of one actor in relation to another is dependent on the price people are willing to pay. Even a superpower has limited possibilities to prevent small groups of people to act in their own interest if they are willing to accept much higher casualties than the superpower. The power to stop things from happening is often easier to exert than the power to make things happen, with all the requirements in terms of necessary and sufficient conditions in today's complex world.

## 7.1 Actor Capability and the Objects of Power

*Actor Capability*

*From the European Security Strategy 2003:*
As a union of 25 states with over 450 million people producing a quarter of the world's gross national product (GNP), and with a wide range of instruments at its disposal, the European Union is inevitably a global player.

This section comments on several central issues in the discourse on the EU and power. First, there is a need to discuss the issue of actor capability itself, an academic and political discourse already at least 40 years in the making.

Does the EU really need such an actor capability? This is evidently a particularly sensitive and controversial issue when it comes
to security. It could be argued that member states with access to
significant military resources can coordinate these resources in the
context of the wider CFSP and thus exert power in informal coalitions of the willing, without subordinating their capabilities to the
European Union. This is also what they have generally done so far.

The paradigm of leverage through military resources is not a
prominent power asset of the European Union. The actual use of
military resources is not described in doctrinal terms in relation to
defence but rather to military crisis management.

Leverage in international organizations or in other multilateral
and bilateral contexts is an entirely different matter. Here, the EU
member states have had the choice either to align as junior partners
with the United States or to try to build a European leverage. With
globalization, the US pivot to Asia, and the fact that European vital
interests are not necessarily the same as the USA's vital interests has
increased the perceived need to develop an EU leverage.

### Leverage

On what assets and using which methods can the EU build its leverage? This is a much wider question than one of coercive influence.

EU actor capability also cannot be defined simply as the capacity
to deploy programmes, projects, operations, or missions based on a
mandate from member states. It cannot just be seen as an issue of the
HR/VP implementing what member states are asking him or her to
do in the area of security.

Oddly, it can also be defined as non-decisions: the power not to
grant others access to the EU internal market, the most important
basis for EU leverage to the outside world according to the president
of the European Council, Herman Van Rompuy.[6] This essentially
means that the existence of the internal market itself can be seen as
a fundamental power asset for the European Union, far exceeding
the importance of ever so harsh sanctions or other types of restrictive measures. Again, this also illustrates the wide power base of the

6    President of the European Council, *The future of Europe – great challenges of the
     European Union.*

European Union through the interplay of different policy contexts, discussed in chapter 4.

It is also a smart power base in the sense that it can be used precisely through non-decisions. In the context of a conflict with Russia, it is sufficient for the EU not to continue certain policies or not engage in new endeavours in order to have a significant impact in the medium to long term.

The EU member states themselves can therefore have a strategic policy vis-à-vis Russia without making that policy publicly explicit. In fact, many would argue that more impact is achieved by not making it explicit since Russian counteractions that may cancel out the impact of EU policies will be more difficult to motivate on the part of the Russian leadership. If Russia can project the image of an enemy in the West, it may be able to create more unity and stability inside the country. If it is more difficult to point to such an enemy image, this may be more cumbersome.

All this is closely related to the issue of zero-sum vs mixed-motive games. International relations are seldom just bilateral; what is being done in one bilateral relation will be perceived as good or bad by others depending on their cognitive frames.

It must be a major objective of the EU to promote mixed-motive game perceptions and a comprehensive approach, as illustrated by the Ukraine crisis. Judging from the debate around the crisis this is, however, far from accepted. Notions such as 'isolating Russia', focusing on hard security are favoured by many. And the possibilities to win Russian hearts and minds in support of EU policy objectives are often appreciated as very limited. At the same time it is noteworthy that Russia itself puts considerable emphasis on the importance of trade, etc. in its appreciation of European influence on Russia. And the Russian discourse seems to be moving more and more towards a comprehensive approach, seeking to identify and exploit weaknesses of Western positions in a broad spectrum of situations.[7]

On the level of international organizations, two of them, for example the EU and NATO, do not even need to have a formal relationship in order to be important for each other. Similarly, the EU does not have to have formal relations with any particular country

7   For a recent discussion of Russian policies in these regards see Starr, SF, & Cornell, SE, Putin's grand strategy: the Eurasian Union and its discontents, Central Asia – Caucasus Institute Silk Road Studies program, 2014.

in its neighbourhood in order to be important for that country. The EU does not have to have a formal regulatory authority over any person, NGO, or corporation outside the EU in order to be important for that entity as long as it has a regulatory authority inside the Union itself. The examples of Microsoft, Google, and recently Gazprom illustrate the global implications of a European regulatory authority.

The impact of the European Union on the crisis in Ukraine does not actually need to be built on material projects and programmes implemented in that country. It may be an issue of hopes and expectations for the future, well-founded or not. What the European Union actually does in Turkey through its delegation and through its enlargement negotiations may actually play a limited role in comparison with its impact on the perceptions and expectations of the Turkish authorities and population.

There are many examples of the impact of the European Union and its policies on its neighbours and the world at large.

However, the EU of course also needs to have capabilities to implement its programmes and operations effectively. This book identifies a large number of generic problems of impact. In the literature, the need for epistemic communities to develop in order to support efforts for the EU to become more effective is an interesting recent finding.

Actions and communication strategies need to take into account the effects of globalization. Each actor, including the EEAS, needs to multiply its channels of communication. Perhaps the notion of the EU enabling the work of other bodies, including those within the Union, to be more effective is a more realistic way to achieve leverage than the perception of a centralized actor capability in the EU institutions.

Similarly, the impact should to a large extent be geared towards creating and meeting expectations, creating hopes and reducing fears, influencing perceptions, and creating empathy – all issues closely related to the concept of soft power. EU officials need to speak more in terms of *We* than *I*.

There are many ways to exert influence, starting with the way EU performs internally, setting an example for others. This is an important perhaps even vital aspect of the link between internal and external aspects of security policy in the EU.

The constant effort to go to the root of the problem, to take up defence in depth in terms of time, space, and concepts, seems vital.

The literature on the various types of sanctions is sobering. Sometimes sanctions may galvanize resistance against the international community and mobilize support inside a country/grouping for the leader(s) who are under international criticism. Negative side effects in the EU may also undercut support for continued sanctions.

The European Union is undoubtedly a major source of influence as long as it can coordinate its policies, particularly in the CFSP domain, in a way that also includes member states' bilateral relations with the countries in question.

There is a clear need for more intelligent and flexible concepts, requiring strategic analysis and good political reporting, as discussed in previous sections. Here the EU has a shortfall, as witnessed by several leading representatives in recent years.[8]

Sometimes, the EU has to adapt its posture very quickly from one of a cooperative relationship towards one of more distance and conditionality. The way this is done in the short term needs to be improved. The notion of local ownership in development assistance or the notions of *more for more* and *less for less* in neighbourhood policy may not always be applicable.

Another example, which also has been widely discussed and studied, is the impact of an EU military presence. Ideally, in the context of a comprehensive approach, such military presence should complement other actions and bring together a net positive impact. Often, however, serious complications arise, short-term and long-term.

It may be a problem of how to keep the work of humanitarian actors and development assistance efforts separate from the military action whenever the EU may be perceived as an actor in the conflict.

Then there is the link between security actions and human rights. If security actions, for instance in the counterterrorism field, counteract human rights, this may also produce risks for conflicts and may undermine the efforts that the EU is trying to support.

Inversely, if EU actions in support of human rights and democracy are perceived by a population to be destabilizing and threatening, this may also undermine the desired impact of the policy in question.

8    Including by the EEAS executive secretary Pierre Vimont.

## A wider spectrum of actors

This book seeks to promote more recognition for the possibly diminishing relative importance of governments in a globalized world. It may be that international power exerted by major actors such as the United States is diminishing as one of several mega-trends in the coming decades.

Instead, there is a need to appreciate more fully the importance of the individual, civil society, business, and non-governmental organizations, not only on the state level, etc. The EU may also need to look to international organizations – from the United Nations to smaller, regional bodies – to help create some sort of order in a world increasingly influenced by multinational and transnational activities and actors. Some of these actors have legitimate objectives, but where some regulation may still be necessary, for instance in the interest of consumers. However, there is also a large sector of criminal activity, including terrorism and corruption, with no easily defined headquarters location.

The notion of the security of the citizen became popular in the EU some 10 years ago, in particular after the 9/11 terrorist attacks. But the individual is not just an object but also an actor who influences the security of others in a positive or negative sense. In a gender perspective, this is particularly important in a wide spectrum of situations ranging from violence inside households to the actions of individuals in war.

## Coercion or just influence?

Arguably, even in its assistance policies the EU may be perceived to attempt to coerce other actors. However, from the EU's perspective the notion is of course another: there are agreed commitments made either jointly or on the level of international organizations and treaty regimes. Therefore, if the partner in question no longer honours these commitments it is not 'coercion' on the part of the EU if the EU decides not to go forward with its assistance.

## Object of power and problems of impact

In many situations, there are enormous difficulties involved in achieving the desired impact. From the pessimistic point of view, one might argue that the necessary and sufficient conditions will never be present.

As seen in the example of *layered defence* applied to the vital area of nuclear security, there is great sense in trying to reduce the probability that terrorists can ever lay their hands on nuclear capabilities. However, this focus on a single priority is very difficult to implement in all areas, for instance in border management.

Consider as an example of difficulties in achieving necessary and sufficient conditions the following: in the context of drugs trafficking from Afghanistan, there is a phenomenon called the balloon effect. If drugs trafficking through Iran and Pakistan are interdicted, drugs may be transported through the northern route, through Central Asia and Russia. It has proven difficult to stop the cultivation of opium poppy inside the country through alternative development schemes. Finding comparable sources of income for farmers through other crops is almost impossible. Corruption inside and outside Afghanistan reduces the willingness to do something drastic about the situation. Some would then argue that an effective line of defence needs to be set up in order to interdict drugs trafficking, as has been tried by Iran. Border management models have been developed for this purpose and implemented in different regions by the EU, including in Central Asia. But if one visits the border between Afghanistan and Tajikistan[9] one can see the problem. There are controlled border crossings on the road between Kabul and Dushanbe. However, drugs do not require lorries to be transported; it is sufficient for mules to cross a deserted long border at night in areas when electricity often is shut off. Once the border is crossed there are so many different routes that transport can take. Literally millions of migrant workers try to support their families in Central Asia by working abroad, primarily in Russia. Some of them are no doubt trafficking heroin. In addition, young people are being forced to traffic drugs also through Iran in order to find refuge abroad, be it in Sweden or elsewhere. Informal payment systems are being used to finance the trafficking, including the so-called hawallah system. So it

9    As the current author did in 2011.

looks almost hopeless in terms of affecting in a serious way
the trafficking itself through any one method. Once the Soviet
air force had destroyed much of the Afghan agriculture from
the air in the 1980s not many positive alternatives remained.
Similarly when looking at demand in the countries where drugs
are consumed, starting in Afghanistan itself, the rapid development of alternative synthetic and other drugs makes control
very difficult. Therefore, the picture is gloomy, indeed, where
no single solution can be seen. Even as promoted by Russia the
most radical method such as eradication of drugs from the air
or through military operations on the ground can have its drawbacks, including through radicalization of the population and
the recruitment of new terrorists

Then, which are the *objects of power*? This discourse has changed
dramatically in recent decades, perhaps in particular after 9/11, when
the focus on security of the citizen and human security became very
important also inside the EU.

Frightening perspectives for major powers include the prospect
of international actors that one cannot control with seemingly
rational power approaches, an international anarchic system where
mutual constraints do not work the way they were expected to,
where the willingness to accept casualties, as noted in section 1.1
may be without (rational) limits and where values may relate to the
next world rather than this one.

The Arab Spring reminded EU decision-makers once more, as
in the case for instance of Belarus, that the EU needs to develop a
relationship to civil society.


## 7.2 Enabling Assistance

*Increasing the effectiveness of EU external assistance*

The bodies of the European Union and its member states provide
more than half of all development assistance. It would be natural
to assume that this fact alone would make the EU a powerful international actor. This section points to a number of generic problems
of impact nuancing and conditioning this assumption.

For a start, money does not always buy influence and as regards development assistance should not be steered by this motive.

Development assistance presupposes close cooperation with the recipient of assistance and sound financial procedures in the implementation of assistance programmes, which reduces the risk of corruption.

The notion that development and security can be directed from a distance through large assistance programmes or peace support operations is most likely a fallacy. It leads policymakers to define end states which are too short-term or shallow in their measures of success.

Influence on how others behave and develop is instead in most cases catalytic.

Donors may enable others to reach their goals, but they have to do the bulk of the work themselves. Donors must also understand that by enabling others to do things they may in fact enable them to do things they do not want them to do. Sometimes one can see this over time – assistance provided to a friendly actor at one point may some years later help this actor to turn against the donor or the donor's interests. Weapons delivered to a friendly actor may come into the hands of an unfriendly actor, coalitions may change, and money may help a country to increase its military budget disproportionately.

A general problem is the discourse on budgetary support, which of course by improving the recipient's general state finances allows resources to be freed up for other less desired causes by the European Union, including perhaps military expenditures. To a certain extent, this can be remedied through close consultation with the country in question but often the European Union will find itself in a less powerful position to influence such decisions.

Furthermore, any international assistance policy needs an analysis of the necessary and sufficient conditions for progress from the point of view of the donor. More often than not, the donor will find that a key condition for effectiveness is missing. Does assistance reach the intended recipient in the periphery? How does the recipient see the donor? These questions have been researched in many different development contexts over the past 40 to 50 years.

In recent years, additional difficult questions have been added to the list. Will armed protection for development workers be needed in the future in places other than Afghanistan, Iraq, the Horn of Africa and Sahel? How can the specificity of humanitarian assistance be protected in a world where hostage taking for monetary ransom is becoming increasingly frequent? How can the EU work with highly corrupt governments? Can European expeditionary forces be active in warlike environments, which require a high degree of willingness to accept casualties?

It is also noteworthy that there may be a considerable time lag between the decisions on assistance policies and actual delivery. In the EU policy cycle, the span from inception to implementation of policies can be up to a decade. Problems that the donor wanted to address at the time of the decision may have completely changed in character once implementation is underway.


## 7.3 Values

### Promoting agreed values in EU external action

The discourse on normative power is often critical of the EU. The EU is often deemed to be unclear about its values, and the translation of values into interests and concrete action is often criticized. The normative school discourse, however, does not necessarily question whether the EU is a normative power; it often sees value-based EU policies as a soft power asset.

A question that is frequently asked is whether the EU is an ethical power.

The European Union has not decided to take a passive approach to its relationship with the outside world. It does not seek autonomy. It seeks interdependence based on fundamental principles that are enshrined in the UN Charter and in documents such as those agreed in the CSCE/OSCE and the Council of Europe setting out a comprehensive concept of security, including freedom and the rule of law.

Value commitments in the EU are to a large extent treaty-based.

But this is probably not enough: they also need to be perceived as genuine interests, which is easier said than done in such areas as trade and agriculture.

In order for these to be effective objectives, they need to be supported not only in letter but also in spirit.

Can an EU driven by values function effectively in a world where other major actors take a more geopolitical approach?

Should trade be more or less decoupled from value-based considerations?

Can sanctions be effective in a world where some major actors argue that non-interference in the internal affairs of states should be a primary principle?

Even beyond this, values most likely need to be perceived to be not only in the interest of the EU as a whole but also in the interest of various stakeholders that are important for the implementation of EU policies.

Commercial interests will sometimes dominate the discourse. In other cases, these interests need to stand back for policies dominated by other values and interests.

Even in the enlargement context, there has been a need to make an overall assessment of the balance between different EU values and interests when reacting to changes in the policies of important candidates, such as Turkey. Turkey plays a significant role in many security and economic contexts, and it is often seen as a powerful potential ally of European interests, not least in the wider Middle East.

Linking values with interests has proven to be a complicated process in many areas, such as human rights and non-proliferation.

The practice of seeking to include clauses in mixed agreements between the EU and its partners has been diluted through trade and other interests.

The foundation for value-based cooperation between the EU and its main partners has even within the OSCE area been undermined by spectacular breaches of political and legally binding commitments.

Recent examples include the way in which former President of Ukraine Viktor Yanukovic met the opposition on Euromaidan right after the 2013 Eastern Partnership Summit, held in Vilnius. Another example is the way President of Belarus Alexandr Lukashenko hit on his opposition in a matter of weeks after the 2010 Astana OSCE Summit. Then came Russia's annexation of Crimea in 2014.

Do these events signal the end of value-based international cooperation? Proponents of the realist school of politics probably would argue that they do. However, the counterargument would point to the situation during the cold war when precisely value-based arguments such as human rights constituted an important support to civil society in the Warsaw Pact (case in point Solidarnosc in Poland and Charta 77 in Czechoslovakia), eventually contributing to a completely new situation.

## 7.4 Perceptions

*Promoting perceptions of EU external action*
*in line with agreed objectives*

This section deals with impact of perceptions and how they change over time as measured in opinion polls such as the Eurobarometer, within and outside the EU.

Perceptions can also be discerned in the context of a conflict where messaging between conflicting parties may be perceived in several unintended ways.

Soft power typically includes the notion of trying to influence the perceptions of others, through the media, by using opinion builders, etc.

In order to be effective, the policies dealing with perceptions must also include a significant amount of real-time feedback to the EU about how EU actions are interpreted by others.

Significantly, perceptions of EU policies may require them to be more or less explicit in the sense discussed in section 4.3.

More awareness in the future about how the European Union is perceived as an actor outside its borders clearly is necessary. This perception may be very different from what might be expected.

In the context of the debate about zones of influence, the real intentions and effects of EU policies may be perverted in the political information policies of other states, for instance those of Russia.

It was of course never an explicit objective of the EU to develop a 'Fortress Europe', a concept that has been discussed among peace researchers since the 1960s.

*From the European Security Strategy 2003:*
It is not in our interest that enlargement should create new dividing lines in Europe. We need to extend the benefits of economic and political cooperation to our neighbours in the East while tackling political problems there.

However, if this has been the perception of some observers, it is nonetheless relevant.

Similarly, it has never been an explicit intention of the EU to establish spheres of influence outside its borders or through enlargement.

Importantly, however, this is how many have perceived EU policies – and this alone makes this perception important.

The power of attraction of the EU and other international organizations is often questioned. The literature on evaluation promotes the argument that power of attraction is closely linked to hopes and expectations for the future.

Once steps have been taken to clarify both the real basis for these hopes and expectations and the requirements that have to be met by the EU partner or member, however, the enthusiasm may be much less, as can be seen in opinion polls undertaken in the EU.

Then there is the issue of power and influence through EU external action. Increasingly, it is argued that what brings impact is not the material content of actions but rather how actions are perceived. This notion of soft power raises the essential question of quality rather than quantity, a major generic problem of impact in an EU that is short of staff.

It is clear that it is the recipient of assistance who does 99 percent of the work. It is also clear that it is difficult to reach the real intended recipient in a thoroughly corrupted world.

There have been evaluations of EU visibility in its external action programmes. The more the better seems to be the underlying assumption. This is, however, clearly a simplistic notion if one considers the issue of perceptions. Visibility can be important to show the European taxpayers the results of their investments, but it must not be conducted in a self-congratulatory way.

Visibility of EU programmes can also help to promote hopes

and expectations for the future.[10] The way the message is being promoted makes a major difference as to how it is perceived. If assistance is being promoted so as to enable the recipient to reach commonly agreed goals, then this will in most cases be helpful.

It is important to continue to work on the multilateral level to consolidate commitments regarding values. It is a process with its setbacks and successes over time.

The extent to which overall support for the European project is developing in Europe will no doubt fundamentally also influence perceptions outside the EU.

In particular, working on the issue of democratic legitimacy of the EU is a key issue in this regard.[11]

---

10  This is likely to be one of the reasons why e-diplomacy is emerging as a new feature of international relations. The United States adopted this policy some time ago.

11  C Kantner, & A Liberatore, 'Security and democracy in the European Union: An introductory framework', *European Security* vol. 15, no. 4, 2006, pp. 363–383; L-E Lundin, & K Revelas, 'Security and Democracy: From the Perspective of Commission Officials Working at the Interface between ESDP and Community External Action', *European Security* vol. 15, no. 4, 2006, pp. 423–430;

# 8. Timelines

The new millennium brought quite a number of new developments that either could not have been foreseen or where the outcome was uncertain. First, as regards European integration it should be noted that almost the entire first decade of the 2000s was characterized by intensive debate on the legal basis for European integration.

It was only on 1 December 2009 that the Lisbon Treaty could enter into force, after a series of domestic political battles in a number of member states.

Even earlier, several important steps in Union enlargement had taken place so that by the end of the decade the EU stretched across nearly the entire European continent.

The decade started with the traumatic 9/11 attacks in the United States. The US Administration entered two significant periods. In the first, the Bush Administration was unilateralist and at the same time integrating internal and external elements of security through the Homeland Security Program. In US foreign policy, attention was squarely on counterterrorism and weapons of mass destruction (WMD).

For the EU, during the decade the focus in security moved in the southern direction also outside the European area, first to Iraq but also to a certain extent to Africa and Afghanistan. In parallel, and partly in response to developments in the USA, even the EU sceptic United Kingdom moved towards a more communitarian approach to the Justice and Home Affairs area, the so-called third pillar of the Union.

Divisions in the EU on strategic approaches to the Iraqi situation forced it to adopt not one but several new security strategies.

The first one was the European Security Strategy adopted by the EU heads of state and government in December 2003. The second was the Strategy Against the Proliferation of Weapons of Mass Destruction, adopted the same month. During this decade the focus was on the same issues that occupied the US administration with the important addition that the EU was supporting international rule of law and effective multilateralism.

For a short period, the leadership in security policy moved up to the level of heads of state and government. Later, the financial crisis came to dominate the agenda, only to be again replaced by a focus on external security from early 2014.

✦✧✦

Each of the preceding chapters contains a more or less explicit chronological perspective. As noted initially, this is not simply a way to describe the interplay between the perspectives in the chapters. It is also meant to allow for the possibility that time itself may be a factor that influences impact.

In chapter 1 the study takes as a point of departure capacity building in defence with a focus on the Union's member states. Clearly, there has been a development over time towards greater acceptance of a European role in promoting this process.

The resistance against using such capacities in EU crisis management missions was overcome, starting in 1998.

The scope of such operations extended eventually into the civilian area, increasingly complemented by Community actions.

The need to promote early action to prevent conflict and achieve more sustainable impact was a mainstreaming objective across the board from the start of the 2000s.

In parallel, the focus broadened to encompass the security of flows as discussed in chapter 2, both good and bad. Clearly, this emphasis was related to globalization; consequently, the efforts needed to be both global and local, requiring coordination of geographic, thematic, multilateral and crisis response policies, as discussed in chapter 3.

However, security is not only an issue of protection against threats. It also requires promoting good relations and developing non-zero-sum solutions in such relationships.

It is also not only an issue of security of states but also of human beings, of human security. In addition, states are not the only security actors.

Security problems are not only military and generally are not served by military solutions.

In all these and other respects the security discourse has differentiated enormously over recent decades. It has become impossible to delimit security responses to any one compartmentalized area of the EU, intergovernmental or community-based, as discussed in chapter 4.

It has become less and less feasible to pursue a straightforward policy of external action in security.

Policies have increasingly been recognized both internally and externally to have at least implicit security relevance. This includes notably not only development policies but also humanitarian assistance.

The complications increase even further when one considers the notion of soft power, discussed in chapter 7 – the fact that what is important may not be how things are being done but how they are perceived. In addition, the impact on security may not be actions alone but also non-decisions. The posture of an actor may be the decisive element determining a fundamental development.

The EU and security, as the topic for this book is defined, is therefore clearly a fascinating field of study. It is also in its full scope a relatively new field; until recently the security discourse was not recognized as a paradigm for the EU.

The enormous differentiation of the discussion makes the issue of learning from the past extremely important. Progress in terms of capacity building in different contexts can easily be cancelled out by bad decisions, late decisions, and non-decisions.

Capacity building in terms of structures is not a numbers game; it is an issue of increasingly organic synergy, of contingency planning and a willingness to face new situations.

In measuring progress one must also take into account the priorities, actions, perceptions and capabilities of others, not only state actors but increasingly non-state actors, notably those involved in organized crime and business and individuals migrating for good or bad reasons.

Assumptions about future trends are of course essential. Important studies have been carried out, also within EU structures dealing with security, on factors that are relevant for the long-term vision of the EU and security.

However, as was the case towards the end of the cold war it may be just as important to question assumptions about trends as to take them for granted. The euphoria about democratic developments in the world just after the cold war seems not to have been warranted.

Similarly, the widespread notion that (after a period of weakness in the 1990s) Russia and now also China have a linear future towards more and more power may also turn out to be incorrect.

Problems and megatrends relating to demography, the environment, energy, economy and technology may complicate this process in several directions. On the one hand, they may lead to internal instability, weakening capabilities. On the other hand, they may lead to more autocratic and aggressive external policies.

Whatever happens, one can be sure that the EU member states will need to be prepared for a wide range of possible outcomes.

Each member state will, while trying to focus on its own problems, perceive itself as smaller and smaller in the international community, not only in relation to other states but also in relation to non-state actors and in relation to trends and developments that are not local but at least regional and often global or virtual.

To survive in the long term in such a world, coalitions are necessary. In addition, they cannot just be coalitions of the moment but long-term cooperative relationships.

European countries will also need to cope with relationships that cannot be built fully on trust, such as the one with Russia, and which may develop in surprising directions.

Such relationships need to be founded on the fundamental recognition that states are not individuals. States do not think as one person.

Moreover, the conflict resolution can seldom occur through regime change alone or through deterrence alone.

All of this requires slow thinking as well as a preparedness to act quickly and decisively in crises.

The European states are all far too small to be able to develop such capabilities on their own. Such capabilities must most likely also have a certain institutional resilience similar to the one promoted through European integration.

Conflict prevention is a long-term endeavour, which cannot be governed by the CNN effect.

Most likely, cooperation on the global level in the United Nations, supported by regional organizations, is for the foreseeable future very dependent on Europe as well. Again, there is a need for long-term approaches supporting international law and developing international consensus as far as possible on major thematic topics, not least those relating to human security with vital gender and other aspects.

And as regards gender-related issues it is important to note that these relate not only to objects of security concern but also as an important reflection of how security policies are carried out and by whom.[1]

The way the EU works is in important respects cyclical. Periods of time in office, financial perspectives, treaty revision processes, project implementation cycles, and periods of reorganization all contribute to a lack of continuity.

Strategies are therefore a *sine qua non* even if they often will not be totally comprehensive or explicit.

The EU's and member states' leaders need the political courage to say that, in order to respond to all of this, the EU needs not only money but also personnel.

The lessons from the financial crisis may show just that. More analytical capability is clearly necessary in order to see the way forward for the EU in today's globalized world.

Democratic legitimacy will also by necessity be related to the quality of the EU's work.

Richard Betts,[2] in a review of three studies that have influenced the debate over the past 25 years, notes the close link to events such as the end of the cold war (Fukuyama),[3] the 9/11 attacks

---

1   It is noteworthy that in his security studies overview Barry Buzan makes 100 references to gender and has one section dedicated to feminism, stressing the bottom up and broad security definitions of such approaches. Buzan, B, & L Hansen, The Evolution of International Security Studies, Cambridge University Press, 2009 Buzan, B, & L Hansen, *The Evolution of International Security Studies*, Cambridge University Press, 2009.

2   Rose, *The Clash of Civilizations?: The Debate.* Council on Foreign Relations 2013.

3   Fukuyama, F, *The End of the History and the Last Man*, Reprint ed., Penguin, 1992.

(Huntington)[4] and the rise of China (Mearsheimer).[5]

This is a useful final reminder that the cognitive world of security elites is a topic worthy of continuous future study – it changes over time as agonizing reappraisals are made.

4   Huntington, S, *The Clash of Civilizations and the Remaking of World Order,* Simon & Schuster, 2011
5   Mearsheimer, J, *The Tragedy of Great Power Politics.* Revised ed., W W Norton, 2014.

# 9. EU and Security

## 9.1 Towards Wider, Comprehensive Approaches

*Pursuing a comprehensive concept of security including development, justice, freedom, and peace*

A book about security needs to spell out its concept of security. If the book is about the European Union and security, it must address issues that are prevalent in the mainstream discourse.

On the European level, this essentially involves protecting the way ahead that has been agreed among EU member states for the European idea on the levels of the Union itself, its member states and its citizens.

In the external dimension, this refers to important aspects of freedom embodied in the comprehensive concept of security that was formally agreed in the OSCE for the Eurasian space 'from Vancouver to Vladivostok'. The essential ingredients are respect for democratically elected governments, non-recognition of policies that undermine the freedom of citizens to interact with the outside world based on international rule of law, and the right to work politically within countries based on freedom of belief.

This is of course much more than a defensive concept of security focused on negative peace, that is, only the absence of war. It is a concept aimed at securing freedom, through trade and investments abroad, communication, freedom of movement, etc. It is founded on the basic recognition that there are no internal state affairs in the area of human rights and fundamental freedoms.[1]

The concept entails freedom to pursue further integration in and around Europe while respecting other forms of integration. It rejects the notion of a zero-sum game in international integration. It must be possible for countries in the eastern direction around Russia to integrate with Russia and at the same time to integrate with the European Union. Pursuing this concept in a consistent way implies caring about the security of the EU's neighbouring states and citizens.

Notably, it also suggests caring about the neighbours of the neighbours, not least because instability in those countries, in some cases leading to a situation of failing states, may undermine security in the countries neighbouring on the European Union and in the Union itself.

For example, Europe cannot be indifferent to the spread of HIV in Russia due to drugs trafficking from Afghanistan. In a globalized world where piracy in the Malacca Strait may be as serious a threat to European trade interests as piracy in the Mediterranean area, this implies in some respects a global security concern.

It also presupposes a fundamental emphasis on the need for an international legal order and a strong United Nations.

This is a discourse that is controversial, not least with some of the countries on the territory of the former Soviet Union. It is controversial with China and some other countries in Asia, but above all it can be seen as idealistic when it comes to the relationship between Europe, the Middle East, and large parts of Africa.

Nevertheless, not using this concept when discussing the link between the EU and security suggests not accepting the fundamentally agreed basis for relations among states in the OSCE region and some key commitments embodied in the Charter of the United Nations. It also indicates disregard for the legal basis of the treaties in place in the European Union and the carrying ideas underpinning legally agreed cooperation in the Council of Europe.

## 9.2 Conceptualizing Security Policies

On this basis, one can ask what this must mean in terms of security policies.

---

1    The OSCE Moscow Mechanism.

These policies obviously must encompass much more than seeking military solutions to military problems,[2] managing crises or preventing conflicts. They need to include securing flows and meeting threats emanating from flows. Innovative forms of international integration in the context of geographic, thematic, and multilateral policies must be pursued. Both intergovernmental and supranational formats for cooperation in the European Union and with the outside world are required. It implies linking up and exploiting synergies between internal and external policies of the Union. It means taking into account EU security interests also in policies that do not explicitly address security objectives but which are security relevant. It means developing strategies to communicate these policies to the outside world, to create strategic awareness for the implementation of the policies of the European institutions and anchor them democratically in the European Union. It means creating a viable system for crisis management and response, respecting the formats for cooperation within these various spheres. In more general multisector crises, it requires coming together and creating coherent responses in cooperation with the international community.

In analysing what security could mean from these different perspectives one finds that the EU and its member states are organized differently in different contexts. In some cases, one paradigm is dominant, leading to one type of legal, institutional, and financial basis for EU actions. In another case, the format may be completely different.

> The lack of a comprehensive approach over time may lead to the problem often encountered when searching dossiers in diplomatic paper archives in the past. New dossiers covering correspondence and position papers are constantly developed making it very difficult to see the whole. One type of correspondence may be classified over time under different headings in the archive depending on the way issues are being discussed at the time. Thus, one issue may fall under a geographic heading at one point, under a thematic heading at another, under a multilateral heading, in the context of an on-going crisis, an ad hoc conference, in an internal context or an external,

---

2    As stated in the 2003 European Security Strategy.

in an intergovernmental or Community context, in a security related dossier or in a dossier which does not explicitly relate to security.

Even with the arrival of electronic archives, hyperlinks, etc., there is a substantial risk that the security potential of EU actions is underestimated. In addition, institutional memory may suffer.

This historically becomes an even greater risk given the fact that using security as a declared objective for a very long time has been without a perceived legal basis in most European policy areas.

Many know for instance that a generic border management regime can be very important in fighting terrorism. However, to say it explicitly, for instance in the development context has for a long time been deemed to lack a legal basis.

Fundamentally, European institutions need to choose the format in which different problems are to be addressed. If nothing else, this book should assist those who find it difficult to form a view on this and on the format to be created in order for different services to cooperate with each other.

The issue of who is in the lead should not cloud the need to create a cooperative culture.

The fight for competences and the relentless pursuit of more institutional power make many actors in the European system think in vertical rather than horizontal dimensions of cooperation and coordination.

This study examines how different types of security-related policies are organized and conceptualized, moving from the more traditional perspectives in the intergovernmental sphere focusing on defence, crisis management, and conflict prevention towards innovative approaches also in the Community domain.

Fundamentally, security policies not only require implementing operations and missions, or programmes and projects, which aim to have an impact on a situation within or outside the EU borders. They also include influencing perceptions and decisions. This means in turn that the European posture in terms of capacity building, values, and other elements of importance for how the EU is perceived by others is vital.

This necessitates the combination of hard and soft power into what sometimes is called smart power.

Importantly, the European Union should be perceived as a force for good with a strong power of attraction.

That this is increasingly questioned in the general debate on the development of the Union is itself a threat to the positive relationship between the European Union and security.

## 9.3 Focusing on the Problems Rather than the Instruments

This book is about the security of states and peoples and the added value that the European Union can bring, but it is also about all the things that can detract attention from this simple goal. There is a need to focus on the security of information, the security of infrastructure, sound financial management, the respect for procedures, the political security of leaders, etc.

However, it is vital not to lose track of the reason for the investment of European taxpayers in the first place. Taxpayers contribute a great deal to the EU's budget, although in percentage terms this contribution is smaller than many believe – around 1 percent of the national income of member states. Nevertheless, in absolute terms, the EU's budget is enormous, more than €100 billion per year, and tens of thousands of EU officials work in Brussels and in more than 140 delegations around the world.

In the comprehensive approach of the EU to external conflicts in crisis, there is an agreed determination to focus more squarely on the problem rather than on the instruments and to focus on impact.

## 9.4 The Added Value of Thinking Both Fast and Slow

Daniel Kahneman has in his best-selling book on thinking fast and thinking slow[3] elaborated on his findings in the area of decision-making, in particular in relation to economics. He notes the importance of thinking fast, making intuitive decisions. However, he also

3  Kahneman, D, *Thinking, fast and slow*, Macmillan, 2011.

stresses the vital role of a second system in the brain, thinking slow, analysing things more carefully before taking a decision.

Recent memoirs by US decision-makers, such as Robert Gates, former head of both the Defense Department and the Central Intelligence Agency, illustrate the importance of the second system. Gates laments the lack of learning potential in US decision-making and underlines the fact that huge resources do not guarantee success.

He also notes, as did General Eisenhower at the end of his presidency, the enormous difficulties created by special-interest groups, for instance the military-industrial complex. In the midst of two major wars, in Iraq and Afghanistan, the issue for many members of Congress was more the question of how much defence money would go to their own constituency than to the war itself.

It was evident during the cold war that these interest groups can destroy slow thinking, for instance in the context of arms control. The United States benefits from an academic tradition analysing, in-depth, Soviet negotiating behaviour, applying game theory and other techniques to determine the best course of action. In spite of this, interest groups, with their fixed cognitive frameworks, in many cases arguably determine the way forward, case in point being the US posture on the control of small arms. Governments' declared strategy is thus reduced to rationalizing the already decided policy. And this is not unique to the USA.

The arms race does not continue in the same way as it used to. However, there is still a need for slow thinking. The intuitive answers are not necessarily the correct ones. In many decision-making situations, there is merit and reason to think slow and to extensively debate the way forward.

Also in this new post-cold war situation and not least in view of the current crisis in Ukraine, it is important to consider carefully how to construct non-zero-sum situations where the action of one actor does not automatically provoke a negative reaction on the part of another actor which would cancel out the value of the first action.

This implies analysing the perceptions and formats for decision-making and negotiations. The academic community can help and there are interesting examples in the literature of game theory being applied to situations such as how to internationalize responsibility for the future of the Arctic region or to how to create motives for corrupt individuals to reduce their corruption.

The media sometimes ridicule the European Union for its slow decision-making procedures. However, these procedures allow decision-makers to ponder alternative solutions through internal and intergovernmental considerations among 28 member states.

Extensive public consultations also improve democratic legitimacy.

The European Union provides the possibility of applying many different perspectives to the same problem.

In some areas, extensive research underpins the way forward in areas ranging from protection of bathing waters at public baths across Europe (where the recent directive was based on new research findings) to careful monitoring of the production and consumption of drugs inside the Union (the EU has a special observatory in Portugal for this purpose).

In major areas for external action such as non-proliferation, there are academic networks with participation also from outside the European Union.

The US examples cited above stress the importance of careful consideration. In fact, the same is true for Europe. There are many examples where there has been tremendous pressure for early and quick decisions on spending large amounts of money, for instance on aid through donor conferences. Even the commitment to spend this money is often described as a measure of success. However, just as often a short time after such a commitment has been made it has transpired that not enough analysis underpinned the commitment decision. The impact assessment *ex ante*, a standard operating procedure in the European Commission, is often not been made carefully enough because of political pressure. After this happens or during this process of slow thinking, of re-evaluation, it is sometimes possible to correct the situation by simply not spending the money. There are examples, for instance from Central Asia in the 1990s, where large amounts of money were committed but never spent for the simple reason that the conditions for assistance were not met.

It is understandable that the media and politicians working to make an impact in the European Parliament and national parliaments do not portray this in a positive way. The notions of corruption and bureaucracy are often applied in the public discourse, sometimes for domestic political purposes, to ridicule the often deliberately slow procedures – the many signatures necessary for a decision to be implemented.

Indexes of how fast assistance money was being spent were proposed after the crisis and resignation of the Santer Commission in the late 1990s,[4] leading to even more outsourcing of funds to other implementing agencies.

This does not meant to imply that it is wrong to outsource funds or other capacities to other actors. This is regularly done by EU member states themselves, including outsourcing to the European Union and to a number of international organizations. This goes even for organizations with consensus decision-making systems, systems that may be necessary to keep these organizations alive, for instance in contexts where vital national interests are involved. As an example the EU members' staff – and fund – organizations such as the OSCE to a very large proportion.

However, it is wrong to outsource to other actors if it is only because of a lack of implementing capacity due to irrelevant staffing constraints.

## 9.5 Who, When, What, How, Where?

These are all questions that from different perspectives are put forth in the political and academic debate on security and defence. The situation determines the answers. In a real crisis situation it is natural to look for help (who); when you find that you have reacted too late you look for earlier and possibly also more sustainable solutions (when); when finding that solutions have so far been insufficient, you look for a broader or a more targeted problem definition (what), a broader set of instruments (how) and more or less defence in depth (where).

The logic varies and is not least influenced by the available resources. When the financial crisis hits, the focus may even be on that crisis itself, which may lead to less appetite for complicated

---

4   Measured in terms of outstanding commitments through the so-called RALS
    index. See for instance:http://www.europarl.europa.eu/document/activities/con
    t/201403/20140319ATT81312/20140319ATT81312EN.pdf.

(strategic) approaches in all the dimensions mentioned above. In defence, for instance, there may be less support for international operations taking up defence in depth, prioritizing national defence solutions.

In one respect, however, a financial crisis such as the one experienced by Europe and the rest of the world since 2008 does require more strategic approaches. It becomes increasingly difficult to convince political leaders to take serious action in any one area, such as defence, without a strategic overview of the priorities and the consequences of decisions. In the absence of any real analysis of security threats and challenges, this results in primacy for finance ministers and across-the-board solutions such as those that have drawn on both national and EU budgets in recent years. Budgetary discipline is then translated into general cuts in percentage terms for broad categories of expenditure, including notably staff, without a clear analysis of the cost/benefit of such decisions.

If on top of this political leaders are acting in an election year both on the EU level and in their own country, it is even more difficult to pursue complex reasoning. There is less appetite for balanced approaches. On national defence, simple illustrations take even clearer preference over complex ones. The point of departure becomes even more rigidly defined.

## 9.6 The EU as One Option for Security Action

The European Union provides for its member states and their citizens one of several options for pursuing security. There are national solutions, there are sub-regional solutions such as the Nordic framework, there are regional solutions such as the OSCE, and there are solutions within NATO and within the United Nations.

At the time of writing there is a strong preference for the European Union when it comes to civilian security solutions above the level of the state, whereas the support for military solutions carried out by the EU is very weak. The previous strong interest in international military operations deployed by the EU has diminished and been replaced by more emphasis on the national level and as regards international operations on the global level of the United Nations.

The situation on the civilian side is very different. A number of geographic, thematic, crisis-oriented and multilateral challenges are being responded to on the EU level. Again, there is limited support for far-reaching ambitions, notably reducing the EU to more of a regional than a global power. Except for development assistance, environmental solutions and the regulation of virtual transactions (finance, cyber) much is defined in the context of the EU Neighbourhood, and sometimes also the Neighbourhood of the Neighbourhood, areas such as Somalia, Sahel and Central Asia.

## 9.7 Democratic Legitimacy, Education, and Research

The democratic legitimacy of security policy is very much undercut by many of the factors mentioned above. The complexity of the topics, the secrecy of much of the discourse, the lack of consistent media focus beyond the CNN effect of the day, the existence of parallel often very disparate logics on the public and elite levels, and the tendency to focus on local politics all undermine support for security policy among the general public.

In financial crises with serious repercussions in terms of unemployment and social security, more extreme views are supported by reference to dangerous effects in terms of xenophobia, etc. The discourse on migration, an essentially good flow, is increasingly perverted.

The result may be more confrontation over security policy solutions and more simple paradigms. Those who have no experience of any recent war on their territory may put a low priority on military security. Those who have lived in freedom may assign low priority to threats against democracy, human rights, and indeed freedom of speech. Those who have lived in relative affluence and have had little exposure to others living in poverty may assign low priority to development assistance. Those who live in secular societies may have little interest in the situation in countries where there are violent clashes between different religious beliefs. Those who live in environments that are not in crisis in terms of climate change or energy security may put less emphasis on these problems. Those who live relatively autonomously from communications and cyber networks may see these issues as less of a problem. Those who enjoy a relatively healthy life may be more worried about their pensions than threatening pandemics. In addition, those who have not experienced the fundamental importance of migration for European economic and cultural development after the Second World War may only see the threats and not the opportunities.

The further Europe moves away from the existential concerns people had during and after the Second World War, during the cold war, and from the period of widespread poverty and low life expectancy inter alia due to pandemics, the greater is the need for education and research in order to visualize and clarify not only the opportunities but also the challenges and threats to human life.

## 9.8 A Smaller Europe in a More Complex World With a Diffuse Distribution of Power

The world has become smaller and more interdependent but at the same time more complex. Each country has also consequently become smaller, less self-sufficient and more dependent on wider solutions. Decision-making systems on the highest level, on the level of the United Nations and in particular the United Nations Security Council, have so far blocked efficient action in many of the serious security-related areas of global importance.

The configuration of the international system in terms of power is not stable. The current predominance of a single superpower is constantly challenged by failures to address key security issues.

The power to say no is stronger than the power to say yes, the power of the small willing to sacrifice everything including human life in order to reach goals is stronger than the power of even huge military actors if they have no similar latitude of decision in their political systems.

For European countries and citizens this implies the need to look for broader cooperative solutions. So it is legitimate to ask what the added value of the European Union is for security.

The European Union may only be beginning to address many security issues systematically and explicitly. Depending on the support for this in Europe, the EU's current Treaty of Lisbon provides a broad scope for potential action.

Therefore, history does not fully answer the question of the added value of the EU. The issue of the potential for the future also needs to be discussed. The answer to the question how much of this should be done by the EU is a matter of political preference and cannot be given an objective answer.

If one asks what the EU contributes to security, the answer may be that the EU High Representative leads international negotiations on Iran or that the EU High Representative mediates between Serbia and Kosovo. This could be what Daniel Kahneman would call the intuitive answer from the brain using its first system, the fast one, designed for this purpose.

Mobilizing the second system, constructed for more careful reflection, would give more complicated answers. Some would perhaps refer to the EU as a peace project or to EU crisis management operations in various parts of the world. Some of those who are interested in defence might be dismissive, arguing that only NATO plays a role in the provision of security. Others might say that the EU should focus on the financial crisis and do a better job in that context. But few would probably have a fully developed view.

## 9.9 The Risk of Over-Securitization

Over-securitization of EU policies is often discussed in the academic literature.[5] Section 3.2 of this study refers to this briefly when examining the relationship between thematic benchmarks and security. On the one hand security can be an important condition for achieving such benchmarks, notably development and freedom. Development and freedom can also be important conditions for security.

There is, however, strong resistance on the part of many scholars against framing the debate about development and freedom in the context of security. This resistance has not least become visible in the discussion of the concept of human security. It has sometimes been argued that this discourse is intended to usurp development resources for security purposes or to subordinate freedom, notably

5    Buzan, B, & L Hansen, *The Evolution of International Security Studies*,
     Cambridge University Press, 2009.

the integrity of the individual, to counterterrorism and other purposes. This is a valid and an important debate. However, it does not negate the need to analyse the link between different objectives.

# 10. Personal Note

I am a former diplomat who returned to political science/international relations research in 2012 after some 35 years in public service.

I have seen the European Union as a black box from the outside and then from the inside both from the intergovernmental and the Community perspectives. I have lived for some years in four European countries in addition to my own, Sweden, and spent an important year at an early stage in the United States as well as lived for a brief time in Africa.

❊❊❊

My awareness of the world essentially started to develop as an exchange student in Michigan in 1964–65. Some 75 percent of my male schoolmates there were sent to the war in Vietnam and some did not come back or were severely injured.

This did not automatically lead me to choose political science as my field of study when I entered the University of Göteborg in late 1967. However, I missed all other potential courses for trivial reasons. The choice of topic for my first thesis was less of a coincidence. There was a big debate ahead of the 1968 Swedish elections about the (lack of) objectivity in the reporting by the Swedish radio and television on the Vietnam War. My professor, Jörgen Westerståhl, had started to build up a research team to study the Swedish media and was asked to find a way to analyse this issue. He argued that objectivity could not really be measured and decided to examine how radio and television reporting was situated in relation to the Swedish print media. As a very insignificant spin-off effect of this work, I was involved in a small study of the reporting of the Swedish prestige newspaper *Svenska Dagbladet* on the war in Vietnam. As I started my thesis work towards the end of 1968, I managed to get material from the first eight months of the year.

This was one of the most interesting periods in recent international history. The year started with the Têt offensive in Vietnam in January, which captured the headlines of this newspaper for almost a full month. But later in the year other topics demanded headline attention: the murder of Martin Luther King and the gold crisis in March, the Paris student demonstrations in May, the assassination of Robert Kennedy in June, the Vietnam negotiations in Paris, the Soviet invasion of Czechoslovakia in August and, after millions of people had been killed, some media also reported on the war in Biafra. It so happened that a Swedish pilot was active in the war and when he died this finally heightened the attention of the Swedish media. When trying to describe what happened in the war in Vietnam according to reports in *Svenska Dagbladet* I found that, although the level of casualties was argued to be very different in a comparison between US and North Vietnamese sources there was broad agreement about the trends. It turned out that there had been three major offensives during the year: in January–February, May and September. Only the first period had been competitive in terms of headline attention.

Therefore, the Swedish media had most likely given the public a very selective and partially incorrect picture of events in that year on which to build perceptions of how the war was developing. One of the main reasons for this was no doubt competition from other news.

This put me on to the type of security policy questions that came to dominate my work for over 40 years, starting with the importance of information, perceptions and cognitive frameworks. This had to do not only with the bias in media reporting due to the so-called CNN effect, often referred to in this study, but also with the predominant cognitive frameworks in place. In the United States, I was effectively cut off from information from my own country. In the mid-1960s it was nearly unheard of for ordinary people to make a telephone call to Europe. This was something that only the wealthy could afford. Since the mid-1950s the cost of a three-minute transatlantic telephone call has gone down from around $100 to currently less than $1. The books I read in my studies of American history and American government were not only very patriotic but you could also here and there find quotations from J. Edgar Hoover inserted as mementos in captions. In contrast, when I returned to Sweden, social democrat Olof Palme, who was strongly engaged in the issues of the Vietnam War, was on the rise to become Swedish Prime Minister in 1969 and the climate for debate was very different. I started to realize that the information you have is essentially related to how you think and that being ambivalent and willing to take in different points of view is a vital asset. This is an important theme in this study because it links up with another difficulty related to the willingness of observers to acknowledge change. Whereas some diplomats in the past, particularly during the cold war, favoured the expression 'plus ça change, plus c'est la même chose' (the more things change, the more they stay the same), after the cold war other qualities came to be more appreciated.

❧❦

In the scholarly debate, changes in the international system started to be perceived as a real possibility after the cold war and during a period of transformations in Asia, largely unforeseen by Swedish Professor Gunnar Myrdal in his work on 'the Asian drama'.

The possibilities to study these changes developed dramatically. When I wrote my dissertation in the 1970s on Soviet attempts to use military assistance to influence North Vietnam and Egypt, international relations research was so much more difficult, particularly on this sensitive topic. I was relatively isolated in my work, library searches were painfully slow, and there was no Internet. Since I was focusing on very recent international events, I was fighting an uneven struggle to keep up with new publications. In the last year of drafting, I was working for the Swedish Foreign Ministry and was posted to Angola, trying to motivate myself in a tropical climate to once more hammer out my ideas on a manual typewriter. I did manage to finish the dissertation but I felt a strong dissatisfaction with my lack of real life experiences and the difficulties to find material to study recent international history.

I can now claim to be in a much more privileged position after 35 rich years in public service and living in a new period of real-time international communications also on sensitive topics.

I have been very fortunate throughout my career. In the interviews for the entry examination to the Swedish Foreign Service in 1975 I was asked how I saw my future life as a potential diplomat. I said that I would like to focus on security policy. A hearty laughter followed my future ambition. The chair of the board explained: "Young man, you would at some point in your career come close to security policy, but mostly you would deal with other things across the globe." Well, it turned out that I was right and he was wrong.

I was twice called back from bilateral postings to the same security policy unit in the ministry where I started to work in 1976 and was regularly assigned to work over the years on increasingly Europe-focused security policy issues for Sweden and for 15 years for the EU.

Having returned to research after leaving active service as a diplomat, I now find that some of the questions that I posed in my work as a practitioner have been thought through and discussed by scientists in almost every detail. This does not mean that the questions that I have put in this book have already been answered. However, there is clearly a theoretical framework to benefit from. I cannot claim that I am even close to being able to use the available material on the theoretical level, but at least I have tried to follow up a number of ideas and concepts.

❧❧❧

How did I come closer to the European issues beyond the fact that I was assigned certain postings? It maybe useful to describe this process in some detail because it also describes both assets and drawbacks in my background that may affect the analysis in this book.

Perhaps it is true to say that someone who has been on the outside is more perceptive and curious when entering a new environment than someone who has been on the inside all the time. The first 15 years of my career as a diplomat did not bring me close to European issues. I was much more influenced by the transatlantic dimension, by the situation in what was then called the 'Third World', and in my work during the 1970s and 1980s by the cold war confrontation between the United States and the Soviet Union. It was only in the early 1990s, when I was working on wider European issues, that I started to be truly aware of the relevance of the European Union for security policy.

For a number of years my cognitive frame conditioned me to perceive Sweden as a nonaligned, mediating actor operating in a strategic environment dominated by NATO and the Warsaw Pact, where globalization in terms of trade etc. had mainly economic dimensions.

I was aware of and very interested in energy security for instance as a diplomat in Finland in the early 1980s but I cannot say that the EU aspect of that issue was really on the table in security policy terms until much later. In this perception, I was far from alone.

As a young research assistant at the Swedish Institute for International Affairs in 1972–73 I had participated in an interview study of Swedish security elites managed by Thomas G. Hart[1]. With only one exception, the 80 respondents saw security mainly as a military issue in the light of the bipolar confrontation between the two superpowers. It was only after the energy crisis in September 1973 that perceptions started to change; in particular, this happened towards the end of the cold war.

As a Swede, I have thus followed the EU from the outside during the period 1970 to 1995 with increasing interest, as noted particularly from the early 1990s. From 1976 to 1996, I was a Swedish diplomat working mainly on security policy issues in bilateral (with Angola, Finland, Germany) and multilateral (with the UN and the CSCE/OSCE on arms control) settings. During the early 1990s I had the opportunity to participate in building a new international organization, the OSCE, where Sweden had the chair in 1993. I also worked with the accession of Sweden to the Partnership for Peace (PFP) in NATO and the Council of Europe.

During these years, I started to perceive my position more clearly in some respects as that of an outsider in European security policy. What did diplomats in the EU member states deliberate in their

1    Hart, T G, *The Cognitive World of Swedish Security Elites*, Scandinavian University books, 1976.

many coordination meetings? What went on inside the sound, protected walls of NATO caucuses? What could the European Union do for peace, for instance in the conflict between Armenia and Azerbaijan on Nagorno-Karabach, where I was involved as a so-called Minsk Group ambassador in the mid-1990s. Was it true what my British colleagues told me – that the EU could have no role in this context except possibly after a settlement had been reached? Could the EU help with incentives in bringing a settlement closer?

This question was difficult to analyze for an outsider who could not clearly see what was inside the big black boxes in Brussels. I had already in the early 1980s found it very difficult to understand the complexities of the CSCE process, with its different 'baskets' and a myriad of historic relationships between the then 35 members. I had seen the enormous detailed knowledge that was necessary to understand disarmament and non-proliferation work on the level of the United Nations from the mid-1970s. I was even more impressed by the need for detailed and the same time strategically broad knowledge in order to deal with the arms control challenges on the European level. I saw this in the context of the Stockholm Conference on Confidence- and Security-building Measures and Disarmament in Europe, which started in January 1984 and where I served as a member of the Swedish delegation for three years. As part of the mediating team during the Stockholm Conference, I had been briefed by experts on important data relevant to the NATO and Warsaw Pact positions in those negotiations. I started to feel that similar insights into the work of the EU was a necessary condition not only for understanding EU positions but actually, as in the Stockholm Conference, for reaching tangible results in the areas of European security where I was working.

❧❧

On the basis of these different experiences I succeeded, after the accession of my country to the EU in 1995, in the competition to become the first dedicated European Commission head of delegation to the international organizations in Vienna, including the OSCE and the International Atomic Energy Agency (IAEA). The Vienna post was probably not seen as very attractive in terms of the number of staff or responsibility for budgets. As the years went by, however, I found the experience of working with member states in Vienna very rewarding, not least in view of the important 1999 Istanbul summit of the OSCE where the Charter for European Security was agreed.

There was no lack of other interesting experiences. Already towards the end of 1996, for instance, I participated in a mission led by former Spanish Prime Minister Felipe Gonzalez to Belgrade, seeking to explore possibilities for the Serbian leaders to embrace the new democratic movement in the streets of Belgrade. They chose instead to focus on Kosovo as a way to bridge the gap to the opposition led by Draskovic, Djincic, and Pesic. The road towards the end signalled by the NATO humanitarian intervention in 1999 was opened. The example illustrated the need for an understanding of the intricate relationship between domestic and foreign security policy and the need for a broad concept of security. The most important follow-up action for me personally from the Belgrade mission was to promote EU support for the B92 radio and television station in Belgrade. Media freedom was seen as one of the most important possible contributions to mobilize popular support for a peaceful way forward towards a stable and democratic Western Balkans region. It was obvious to everyone during that trip that Gonzalez was enormously frustrated by the lack of willingness of the Serbian leaders to learn from Spain's road from the Franco regime to democracy.

To my surprise and I think even more to the surprise of my colleagues in Brussels, I was in the year 2000 appointed as head of the Security Policy Unit in the Directorate-General for External Relations, serving under Commissioner Chris Patten. This was a position previously held by a French colleague, and he and a few others expressed surprise that the post had not been allocated to someone from a NATO country. After all, my team was supposed to be responsible for the very sensitive relationship of the European Commission to NATO and the Western European Union (WEU). We were also expected to manage the representation of the Commission to a number of hard UN Security Council bodies discussing issues where Sweden was still considered an outsider. Sweden was in the centre of the peacekeeping debate, in the context of both the United Nations and the OSCE. It had also through its foreign minister together with the Finnish foreign minister promoted a later agreed definition of the Petersberg tasks. But it certainly was not

engaged in the kind of considerations dominating French thinking at the time: how to build further on the agreement with the
UK and indirectly with the USA and NATO on promoting military
burden sharing with the United States and at the same time create
an embryo autonomous European military capability. However, the
position and main objectives of my hierarchy in the Commission
had another focus. Lord Patten's predecessor, Commissioner Hans
van den Broek, had an eminent personal expertise from leading the
work of the WEU just a few years earlier. He chose a low profile on
these issues as Commissioner, however, deliberately staying outside
the first informal meeting of EU defence ministers, which took place
in Vienna in 1998. Instead, the Commission had a very hands-on
objective to promote its role in key processes that were underway,
notably in the Western Balkans after the 1999 NATO intervention. It wanted to create a climate for good cooperation with the
intergovernmental side of the Council, while at the same time not
undermining the right of initiative of the Commission. My appoint-
ment was probably seen as a small step towards creating a team of
interlocutors with the Council who would not be seen as totally
indoctrinated Community representatives. My director-general had
been instrumental in building up the Commission's representation
in the European Political Cooperation (EPC) in the previous decade,
and three deputy directors-general in succession were recruited
as Commission political directors from the outside, coming from
ambassadorial positions in member states. The head of the newly
established directorate for CFSP had also been working closely with
these issues and a diplomatic adviser to President of the European
Commission Romano Prodi succeeded him.

Over the period 2000–07 my role in this context as head
of a 15 to 20 persons team dealing with more general issues of
security policy expanded to also be the acting Director in 2005
and Deputy Political Director for the Commission in 2006–07.
In this work I was closely involved with the development of the
security policy dimension of the EU, in both the intergovernmental and Community pillars, until 2007. I helped to represent the
Commission in the EU's Political and Security Commission (PSC),
was the first representative in the Military committee and in a
number of other Council formations dealing with security-related
issues as well as in several external contexts, including a unique

insight into the work of the G8 on non-proliferation, organized crime and counterterrorism.

In 2007 the Commission took the unusual decision to appoint me once again as head of delegation to Vienna in anticipation of the possible adoption of the Lisbon Treaty, which was expected to dramatically change the way the EU was represented in these international organizations. After many months of uncertainty, I then had the privilege to serve as the first EU ambassador to the international organizations in Vienna from late 2009 until the end of September 2011.

✦⟡✦

In 2002 I was elected to become a member of the Swedish Royal Academy of War Sciences. This gave me an opportunity to write a chapter in the annual proceedings of the Academy about the EU's role in security. My views were met with a certain lack of enthusiasm in a context where the emphasis was mainly on military matters. My argument was relatively simple: the civilian aspects of security had been grossly underestimated in the security discourse in the EU and indeed in Europe. I pointed not only to the intergovernmental aspects of security but also to the whole field of Community action. I remember a comment by a senior Swedish ambassador at a peacekeeping seminar in Oslo in the early 1990s. He noted that peacekeeping may be important, but for Europe the enlargement process was no doubt the most important development in terms of security.

As an illustration of this, it is interesting to consider the perception of the EU and the Commission in the high-level meetings with member states and other countries in which I had the opportunity to participate over the years. Throughout the period 1983–2011, I was fortunate to be able to participate in a large number of ministerial and summit meetings in different configurations. In some of these meetings on the ministerial level both within and outside the EU, I was appointed to represent the European Commission in the absence of Commissioners. This included quite a number of meetings of EU defence ministers, an EU–NATO ministerial meeting in Reykjavik where I was seated next to Colin Powell, etc. I thus became privy to high-level discussions also in informal settings, particularly in meetings of EU defence ministers. During this period, I experienced an increasing curiosity on the part of both officials and political leaders as to the potential role of the European Union in the area of security. I saw Jacques Delors, Hans van den Broek (representing Jacques Santer) and Romani Prodi at the table in summits in the 1990s with no formal coordinating role. In contrast, I saw Herman van Rompuy represent the entire EU at the OSCE Astana Summit in 2010. In hindsight, this looks like a dramatic shift from a peripheral to a central role for the EU. However, this perception might be wrong. Perhaps others saw the EU leaders' presence at the summit meetings in the 1990s as equally or perhaps even more important than the presence of the EU at the summit in 2010. After all, in the 1990s the issue of EU enlargement had not yet advanced fundamentally, and the EU's role in its neighbourhood remained unclear. Many around the table in meetings in the 1990s started to develop strong expectations of coming closer to the EU. So maybe the presence of the Commission at the earlier summits was perceived as more important than generally acknowledged at the time.

# 11. Acknowledgements

This book has mainly been written after my leaving active service in the European Union in late 2011. Connie Wall has skilfully edited it. The publisher Torbjörn Santérus has been very helpful. Magnus Ekengren, Kristin de Peyron and Ola Sohlström have made valuable comments on the whole manuscript and helped to position it academically and the definition of the potential readership. Ian Anthony, Lina Grip, Christian Leffler, Lisa Lundin, David Spence, and Andrew Sherriff have commented on individual chapters. I am indebted to Jacob Westberg who contributed constructive criticism on the overall approach in several stages.

The Swedish National Defence College, SNDC, has been the main sponsor of the project and I am particularly indebted to Jan Mörtberg and Magnus Ekengren for this invaluable support. Several other institutes in Stockholm, UI (Mark Rhinard, Johan Eriksson, Anna Jardfeldt), ISDP (Svante Cornell, Niklas Swanström), SIPRI (Ian Anthony, Lina Grip) and the Folke Bernadotte Academy (Sven-Eric Söder, Anneli Eriksson, Lina Frödin) have supported studies, the results of which have fed into the book.

The Swedish Foreign Ministry commissioned work on the follow on to the European Security Strategy and the EU Comprehensive Approach (Peter Ericson, Johan Frisell, Erik Widman, Åsa Pousard), which enabled essential collection of material for the study.

Several debates have taken place in the Swedish Royal Academy of War Sciences based on contributions from my side, the first one already in 2003.

I have recently participated in three parallel and synergetic book projects of direct importance to the study, where my own contributions have been enhanced in particular by Anders Bjurner and David Spence.

I am grateful for a great number of interviews given to me not only in Brussels but also in other major multilateral and bilateral capitals. One such interviews series was undertaken in 2012 on behalf of the Irish Chair of the OSCE (Eoin O'Leary, Alan Owens). A second round was in several stages undertaken in the context of studies on the follow-up to the European Security Strategy. A third one was undertaken to support my analysis of the comprehensive approach in 2013. I have committed not to explicitly quote individual respondents in these interviews, but I am grateful to them all.

CPDS (John Hemery and Serena Hemery) has invited me to participate in training of EU officials, which has given me opportunities to maintain contacts with many earlier colleagues.

Beyond the political leaders under whose auspices I have served, I have learned from many senior officials throughout the years working for the EU notably Claude France Arnould, Lodewijk Briet, Günther Burghardt, Anthony Cary, Robert Cooper, Catherine Day, Pieter Feith, Annalisa Giannella, Christoph Heusgens, Eneko Landaburu, Stefan Lehne, Guy Legras, Karel Kovanda, Vasco Ramos, Dominique Ristori, Stefano Sannino, Helga Schmid, Nick Witney, Fernando Valenzuela, Angel Vinas and Richard Wright.

During earlier years I have received important advice from senior colleagues in the Swedish Foreign Ministry including Anders Bjurner, Staffan Carlsson, Jan Eliasson, Nils Eliasson, Ingmar Karlsson, Folke Löfgren, Lars Norberg, Anders Oljelund and Björn Skala.

I have benefitted from the wisdom of a large number of colleagues throughout the years. Many have directly or indirectly contributed thoughts and ideas to this book including (and the list is far from complete) Francois Alabrune, Krister Andrén, Frank Asbeck, Juha Auvinen, Adebayo Babajide, Pierre Philippe Bacri, Alyson Bailes, Eitvydas Bajarunas, Veronika Bard, Thierry Bechet, Christian Berger, Mats Bergquist, Sven Biscop, Marc Perrin de Brichambaut, Jan Blomqvist, Pierre Borgoltz, Christian Bourgin, Christian Brumter, Dirk Buda, Inger Buxton, Jacek Bylica, Frazer Cameron, Sven-Olov Carlsson, Patrick Child, Ian and Carol Cliff,

Pierre Cleostrate, Markus Cornaro, Balacs Csuday, Vilmos Cserveny, Christian Danielsson, Ron van Dartel, Marc Deffrennes, Daniela Dicorrado Andreoni, Michael Doczy, Gilbert Dubois, Bruno Dupre, Björn Elmér, Björn Fagerberg, Cornel Feruta, Karen Fogg, Florika Fink-Hooijer, Erwan Fouere, Björn Fägersten, Hubert Gambs, Kjell Goldmann, Richardo Gosalbo Bono, Thomas Greminger, Fernando Andresen Guimares, Istvan Gyarmati, Joelle Jenny, Carl Hallergard, Tom Hart, Carl Harzell, Gunilla Herolf, Patricia Holland, Gabor Iklody, Bertil Johansson, Jonas Jonsson, Norbert Jousten, Kirsten van Kaathoven, Ian Kelly, Daniel Keohane, Michalis Ketselidis, Riina Kionka, Toivo Klaar, Stephan Klement, Lotte Knudsen, Veronika Kuchynova Smigolova, Ricard Kühnel, Michael Köhler, Eric Lebedel, Didier Lenoir, Angela Liberatore, Rüdiger Ludeking, Hans Lundborg, Björn Lyrvall, Alexander Maclachlan, Robert Madelin, Mara Marinaki, Ana Martinho, John Mattiussi, Maria McLoughlin, Michael Matthiessen, Adrian van der Meer, Dunja Mijatovic, Hugues Mingarelli, Pierre Mirel, Antonio Missiroli, György Molnar, Pierre Morel, Luigi Narbone, Renatas Norkus, Cesare Onestini, Jean-Marc Pisani, Maciej Popowski, Reinhard Priebe, Gunnar Sjöstedt, Frank Recker, Geneviève Renaux, Kyriakos Revelas, Andrea Ricci, Lorenzo Rilasciati, Adam Daniel Rotfeld, Gerhard Sabathil, Michael Sahlin, Herbert Salber, Keith Sangway, Pierre Seailles, Peter Semneby, Pedro Serrano, Olof Skoog, Simon Smith, Annika Söder, Pirkka Tapiola, Daniel Tarschys, Richard Tibbels, David Tirr, Johan Tunberger, Antti Turunen, Niamh Walsh, Veronika Wand-Danielsson, Lars Wedin, Hans Bernhard Weisserth, Annika Weidemann, Alison Weston, Gunnar Wiegand, Lars-Gunnar Wigemark, Cornelis Wittebrood,Wolfgang Wosolsobe, Gert-Jan Van Hegelsom, Bert Versmessen, Guttorm Vik, Vladimir Voronkov, Andrei Zagorski and many more. They all, in different ways, have contributed to the epistemic communities supporting a comprehensive concept of security.

# References

Abed, G T & S Gupta, *Governance, corruption and economic performance*, International Monetary Fund, 2002.

Acemoglu, D & J Robinson, *Why Nations Fail: The Origins of Power, Prosperity, and Poverty*, Crown Business, 2012.

Adamson, F B, 'Crossing borders: international migration and national security', *International security* 31, no. 1, 2006, pp. 165–199.

ADE, *Thematic Evaluation of European Commission Support to Conflict Prevention and Peace Building*, 2011.

—, *Thematic Evaluation of European Commission Support to Justice and Security System Reform*, 2011.

Adler, E, 'Imagined (security) communities: cognitive regions in international relations', *Millennium-Journal of International Studies* 26, no. 2, 1997, pp. 249–277.

Adler, E & M Barnett, *Security Communities*, Cambridge University Press, 1998.

Akbaba, S, 'Measuring EU actorness through CFSP and ESDP: Civilian power EU', Ankara *Avrupa Çalısmaları Dergisi, ULAK-BM, World Political Science* pp. 1.

Allison, G & P Zelikow, *Essence of Decision: Explaining the Cuban Missile Crisis* (2nd Edition), 2 ed., Pearson, 1999.

Allison, R & Jonson, L, *Central Asian Security: The New International Context*, Brookings Institution Press, 2001.

Anastasakis, O & D Bechev, 'EU Conditionality in South East Europe: Bringing Commitment to the Process', *South East European Studies Programme* 2003, pp. 1–20.

Anderman, K, Frisell, E H & Pallin, C V, *Russia-EU external security relations: Russian policy and perceptions*, FOI-Swedish defence research agency, 2007.

Anderson, S & Williams, J, 'The Securitization of Development Policy or the Developmentalization of Security Policy? Legitimacy, Public Opinion, and the EU External

Action Service (EAS)', European Union Studies Association Conference, Boston, 2011.

Andersson, JJ, Brattberg, E, Häggqvist, M & Ojanen, H, 'The European Security Strategy: Reinvigorate, Revise or Reinvent?', Occasional UI Papers, 2011.

ECFR, *European Foreign Policy Scorecard 2014*, 2014.

Anderssson, JJ, 'The Transatlantic Relationship', UI Brief 19, 2013.

Annan, K, *Interventions: A Life in War and Peace*, Penguin Press, 2012.

Anthony, I, 'Sanctions applied by the European Union and the United Nations', *SIPRI yearbook* 2002, pp. 203–230.

Anthony, I & L Grip, *Strengthening the European Union's future approach to WMD*, SIPRI Policy paper 37, 2013

Apap, J, *Justice and Home Affairs in the EU: Liberty and Security Issues after Enlargement*, Edward Elgar, 2004.

Archick, K, *Cybercrime: The Council of Europe convention*, 2005.

Armitage, R L, *A Comprehensive Approach to North Korea*, DTIC Document,1999.

Arnswald, S, *EU enlargement and the Baltic States: the incremental making of new members*, Ulkopoliittinen instituutti, 2000.

Ashton, C, 'Preparing the December 2013 European Council on Security and Defence Interim Report by the High Representative', 2013.

—, 'Remarks by HRVP Ashton at the presentation of the ENP package 2012.

—, 'Catherine Ashton, EU High Representative for Foreign Affairs and Security Policy and Vice President of the European Commission Address at the United Nations Security Council', United Nations, New York, 8 Feb. 2011.

Association, WN, *The Nuclear Renaissance*, 2011.

Atran, S, 'A failure of imagination (intelligence, WMDs, and "virtual jihad")', *Studies in Conflict & Terrorism* 29, no. 3, 2006, pp. 285–300.

Avery, G & F Cameron, *The enlargement of the European Union*, Burns & Oates, 1998.

Aybet, G & R R Moore, *NATO: in search of a vision*, Georgetown University Press, 2010.

Bailes, A J K, 'The EU and a 'better world': what role for the European Security and Defence Policy?', *International Affairs* 84, no. 1, 2008, pp. 115–130.

—, 'The European Security Strategy, An Evolutionary History'. Stockholm, SIPRI Policy Paper, 2005.

Baldaccini, A, E Guild & H Toner, *Whose freedom, security and justice?: EU immigration and asylum law and policy*, Hart Publishing, 2007.

Balfour, R, 'Principles of democracy and human rights' in S Lucarelli & I Manners (eds.), *Values and principles in European Union Foreign Policy*, Routledge, 2014.

Balfour, R & H Ojanen, 'Does the European External Action Service Represent a Model for the Challenges of Global Diplomacy?', *IAI*, 2011.

Balzacq, T & S Léonard, 'Information-sharing and the EU Counter-terrorism Policy: A "Securitisation Tool" Approach', In: *European Security, Terrorism and Intelligence: Tackling New Security Challenges in Europe* 2013, pp. 127.

Balzacq, T, *Security and the two-level game: The Treaty of Prüm, the EU and the management of threats*, CEPS, 2006.

Balzacq, T, *The external dimension of EU justice and home affairs: Tools, Processes, Outcomes*, CEPS, 2008.

Baran, Z, 'EU energy security: time to end Russian leverage', *Washington Quarterly* 30, no. 4, 2007, pp. 131–144.

Barfield, T, *Afghanistan: A Cultural and Political History* (Princeton Studies in Muslim Politics), Reprint ed., Princeton University Press, 2012.

Barham, J (*et al.*) *Evaluation of DG Echo's action in Uganda*, alnap. org, 2011.

Barnes-Dacey, J & D Levy, 'Syria the Imperative of Deescalation', *Open Democracy*, 2013.

Barnier, M, *For a European civil protection force: Europe aid*, 2006.

Barquin, J, J-M Glachant, F Lévêque, F Hölzl, WJ Nuttall & C von Hirschhausen, *Security of Energy Supply in Europe: Natural Gas, Nuclear and Hydrogen*, Edward Elgar Publishing, 2010.

Barry, L, *European Security in the 21st Century: The EU's Comprehensive Approach*, IIEA 2011.

Bassiouni, MC, 'Comprehensive Strategic Approach on International Cooperation for the Prevention, Control and Suppression of International and Transnational Criminality', *Nova L. Rev.* 15, 1991, pp. 353.

Bastick, M & K Valasek, *Gender & Security Sector Reform: Toolkit*, DCAF, 2008.

Bayne, N, Hanging in There: *The G7 and G8 Summit in Maturity and Renewal*, The G8 and Global Governance Series, Aldershot: Ashgate, 2000.

Beckman, J, *Comparative legal approaches to homeland security and anti-terrorism*, Ashgate Publishing, 2013.

Beeson, M & AJ Bellamy, 'Globalisation, security and international order after 11 September', *Australian Journal of Politics & History* 49, no. 3, 2003, pp. 339–354.

Bertsch, G K, *Crossroads and conflict: security and foreign policy in the Caucasus and Central Asia*, Routledge, 2000.

Bicci, F & C Caterina, 'The COREU/CORTESY Network and the Circulation of Information within EU Foreign Policy', RECON Inline Working paper 1, 2010.

Bickerton, CJ, B Irondelle & A Menon, 'Security Cooperation beyond the Nation State: The EU's Common Security and Defence Policy', *JCMS: Journal of Common Market Studies* 49, no. 1, 2011, pp. 1–21.

Biermann, R, 'Rivalry Among International Organizations, Bringing Power Back In', Paper prepared for the Panel 'The European Union and Transatlantic Relations' of the Pan-European Conference of the Standing Group on International Relations in Europe, Turin 14, 2007.

Bigo, D, 'Frontiers and security in the European Union: The illusion of migration control', *The frontiers of Europe* 1998, pp. 148–164.

Bildt, C, 'Carl Bildt at Center for Strategic and International Studies, Washington DC', 2012.

Bingham, T, *The Rule of Law*, Reprint ed., Penguin Global, 2011.

Birnhack, MD, 'The EU data protection directive: an engine of a global regime', *Computer Law & Security Review* 24, no. 6, 2008, pp. 508–520.

Biscop, S, 'The UK's change of course: a new change for the European Security and Defence Identity.', *European foreign affairs Review* 4, no. 2, 1999, pp. 253–268.

—'Opening up the ESDP to the south: a comprehensive and cooperative approach to Euro-Mediterranean security', *Security Dialogue* 34, no. 2, 2003, pp. 183–197.

—, Euro-Mediterranean Security: A Search for Partnership, Ashgate Publishing, 2003.

—'Able and willing? Assessing the EU's capacity for military action', *European foreign affairs review*, no. 4, 2004, pp. 509–527.

—, *The European security strategy: implementing a distinctive approach to security*, Centre d'études de Défense, 2004.

—, *The European Security Strategy: A global agenda for positive power*, Ashgate Publishing, 2005.

—, 'E pluribus unum? Military integration in the European Union', Royal Institute for International Relations, 2005.

—, 'Permanent Structured Cooperation and the future of the ESDP: transformation and integration', *European Foreign Affairs Review* 13, no. 4, 2008, pp. 431–448.

—, 'The value of power, the power of values: a call for an EU Grand Strategy', *Egmont paper* 33, 2009.

—, 'And What Will Europe Do? The European Council and Military Strategy', *Egmont Policy Brief*, 2013.

Biscop, S & JJ Andersson, *The EU and the European security strategy: forging a global Europe*, Psychology Press, 2008.

Biscop, S & J Coelmont, *Europe deploys towards a Civil-military strategy for CSDP*, Egmont Paper 49, 2011.

—, *A Strategy for CSDP Europe's Ambitions as a Global Security Provider* (Egmont Paper 37), Academia Press, 2010.

Biscop, S, F Francioni & K Graham, *The European Union and the United Nations, Partners in Effective Multilateralism*, Institute for Security Studies, 2005.

Bjurner, A, 'On EU peacemaking – challenging or complementing the UN?' In: P Wallensteen & A Bjurner (eds.), *Regional Organisations and Peacemaking Challengers to the UN*, Routledge, 2014.

Blair, A, 'The CFSP: History, Overview, and Prospects', *Organizing Europe's place in world affairs: the European Union's Common Foreign and Security Policy* 3, 2001, pp. 16.

Blavoukos, S, 'Capturing the EU International Performance: an

Analytical Framework' in: *The EU and the non-proliferation of nuclear weapons: strategies, policies, actions* Blavoukos, S; D Bourantonis & C Portela (eds.), 2013.

Blavoukos, S & D Bourantonis, 'Do UN Sanctions Strenghten the International Presence of the EU?' http://www.wiscnetwork.org/porto2011/papers/WISC_2011-651.doc.

—, 'The EU's Performance in the United Nations Security Council', *Journal of European Integration* 33, no. 6, 2011, pp. 731–742.

Blix, H, *Weapons of Terror: Freeing the World of Nuclear Biological and Chemical Arms*, United Nations, 2006.

—, *Why Nuclear Disarmament Matters*, The MIT Press, 2008.

Blockmans, S & R A Wessel, 'The European Union and crisis management: will the Lisbon Treaty make the EU more effective?', *Journal of conflict and security law*, no. 2, 2009, pp. 265–308.

Blockmans, S, C Hillion, M Cremona, D Curtin, G De Baere, S Duke, C Eckes, B Van Vooren, R A Wessel & J Wouters, EEAS *2.0: A legal commentary on Council Decision 2010/427/EU establishing the organisation and functioning of the European External Action Service*, 2013.

Blockmans, S, *The European Union and crisis management: policy and legal aspects*, TMC Asser, 2008.

Boin, A, M Ekengren & M Rhinard, 'Protecting the union: analysing an emerging policy space', *European Integration* 28, no. 5, 2006, pp. 405–421.

—, *Security in transition: towards a new paradigm for the European Union*, Försvarshögskolan, 2008.

—, *Functional security and crisis management capacity in the European Union*, Citeseer, 2006.

—, *The European Union as Crisis Manager: Patterns and Prospects*, Cambridge University Press, 2013.

Bonaglia, F, A Goldstein & F Petito, 'Values in European Union development cooperation policy' in S Lucarelli & I Manners (eds.), *Values and principles in European Union Foreign Policy*, Routledge, 2014.

Bossong, R, 'The action plan on combating terrorism: a flawed instrument of EU security governance', *JCMS: journal of common market studies* 46, no. 1, 2008, pp. 27–48.

Braun, J, 'EU Energy Policy under the Treaty of Lisbon Rules: Between a new policy and business as usual', *EPIN Working Paper*, 2011.

Bremer III, L P, 'with Malcolm McConnell', *My Year in Iraq: The Struggle to Build a Future of Hope*, 2006.

Bretherton, C & J Vogler, 'Actors and Actorness in Global Politics. Locating the European Union', in: *The European Union as a Global Actor*, Routledge, 1999.

Brichambaut, MP, 'It's time the EU stopped undermining the OSCE', *Europe's World* 21, 2009.

Brooks, SG, *Producing security: Multinational corporations, globalization, and the changing calculus of conflict*, Princeton University Press, 2007.

Brummer, K, 'Imposing sanctions. The not so "normative power

Europe"', *European Foreign Affairs Review* 14, no. 2, 2009, pp. 191–207.

Brzezinski, Z, *Strategic Vision: America and the Crisis of Global Power*, Basic Books, 2012.

Bull, H, 'Civilian power Europe: a contradiction in terms?', *JCMS: Journal of Common Market Studies* 21, no. 2, 1982, pp. 149–170.

Bures, O, 'EU counterterrorism policy: a paper tiger?', *Terrorism and political violence* 18, no. 1, 2006, pp. 57–78.

Burrows, M, *Global Trends 2030: Alternative Worlds*, US National Intelligence Council, 2012.

Bush, G W, *The national security strategy of the United States of America*, 2002.

Buzan, B & L Hansen, *The Evolution of International Security Studies*, Cambridge University Press, 2009.

Cameron, F, *An introduction to European foreign policy*, Routledge, 2007/2012.

—, *Foreign and Security Policy of the European Union: Past, Present and Future*, Continuum, International Publishing Group, 1999.

Cardash, SL, FJ Ciluffo & J-L Marret, *Foreign Fighters in Syria: Still Doing Battle, Still a Multidimensional Danger*, FRS, 2013.

Carnegie Endowment, *Towards a Euro-Atlantic Security Community*, 2012.

Carrera, S & E Guild, 'Towards an internal (in)security strategy for the EU', CEPS, 2011.

Center for peace and disarmament education and safer world, 'Turning the page: Small arms and light weapons in Albania', 2005.

Chabalowski, M & Korski, D, 'A New Agenda for US-EU Security Cooperation', Documentos de Trabajo, 2010.

Chappell, L, 'Differing member state approaches to the development of the EU Battlegroup Concept: implications for CSDP', *European security* 18, no. 4, 2009, pp 417–439.

Chivvis, C, *EU civilian crisis management: the record so far*, JSTOR, 2010.

Cholewinski, R, 'The EU Acquis on irregular migration: Reinforcing security at the expense of rights', *European Journal of Migration and Law* 2, no. 3, 2000, pp. 361–405.

Cini, M & NP-S Borragán, *European Union Politics*, Oxford University Press, 2013.

Clarke, R, 'War From cyberspace', *National Interest* 2009.

Collins, K, 'Economic and security regionalism among patrimonial authoritarian regimes: the case of Central Asia', *Europe-Asia Studies* 61, no. 2, 2009, pp. 249–281.

Comelli, M & R Matarazzo, 'Rehashed Commission Delegations or Real Embassies? EU Delegations Post-Lisbon', Istituto Affari Internazionali. Working paper no. 11/23, 2011.

Committee of the regions '2012 Annual Report on the Instrument for Stability', COM(2013) 563 final, no. 2013, 2013.

Coonen, SJ, *The Widening Military Capabilities Gap between the United States and Europe: Does it Matter?*, Strategic Studies Institute, 2006.

Cooper, R, *The Breaking of Nations: Order and Chaos in the Twenty-*

*First Century*, Atlantic Monthly Press, 2004.

Cornell, S, *Small nations and great powers: a study of ethnopolitical conflict in the Caucasus*, Routledge, 2000.

Cornell, S E, 'The interaction of drug smuggling, human trafficking and terrorism', *Human trafficking and human security*, 2009.

Cornish, P & G Edwards, 'Beyond the EU/NATO dichotomy: the beginnings of a European strategic culture', *International Affairs* 77, no. 3, 2001, pp. 587–603.

Correlje, A & C Van der Linde, 'Energy supply security and geopolitics: a European perspective', *Energy Policy* 34, no. 5, 2006, pp. 532–543.

Cosgrove, C A & K J Twitchett, New international actors: the United Nations and the European Community, Macmillan, 1970.

Council of the European Union, '2011 Comprehensive Annual Report on CSDP and CSDP-related training', 17438/11, 2011.

–, 'Abstract of 2009 Annual Report on the identification and implementation of lessons and best practices in civilian CSDP missions', 17487/1/09, 2010.

–, 'Civil Military Co-ordination', 12307/02, 2002.

–, 'Council Conclusions and New Lines for Action by the European Union in combating the proliferation of weapons of mass destruction and their delivery systems', 17172/08, 2008.

–, 'Council Conclusions on the EU's Comprehensive Approach Foreign affairs Council meeting Brussels, 12 May 2014', 2014.

–, 'Council Decision 2010/799/ CFSP of 13 December 2010 in support of a process of confidence-building leading to the establishment of a zone free of weapons of mass destruction and their means of delivery in the Middle East in support of the implementation of the EU Strategy against proliferation of weapons of mass destruction', *Official Journal of the European Union* L341, 2010.

–, 'Council Directive establishing a Community framework for the nuclear safety of nuclear installations Nuclear safety directive', 10667/09, 2009.

–, 'Council Regulation (Euratom) No 300/2007 of 19 February 2007 establishing an Instrument for Nuclear Safety Cooperation', 2007.

–, 'Directive 2011/36/EU of the European parliament and of the council of 5 April 2011 on preventing and combating trafficking in human beings and protecting its victims, and replacing Council Framework Decision 2002/629/JHA', *Official Journal of the European Union* 2011.

–, 'EU Strategy against the proliferation of WMD: Monitoring and enhancing consistent implementation', 16694/06, 2006.

–, 'European Council 19/20 December 2013 Conclusions', EUCO 217/13, 2013.

–, 'Fight against the proliferation of weapons of mass destruction – EU strategy against proliferation of Weapons of Mass Destruction', 2003.

–, Council of the European

Union, 'Implementation report on the Council Conclusions on enhancing the links between internal and external aspects of counter-terrorism', 14819/1/12 REV 1, 2012.

—, 'Internal Security Strategy of the EU', 2010.

—, 'Report on the implementation of the European Security Strategy – providing security in a changing world', 2008.

—, 'Six-monthly Progress Report on the implementation of the EU Strategy against Proliferation of Weapons of Mass Destruction', 2012/C 237/01, 2012.

—, 'Tampere European Council', 1999.

—, 'The European Union priorities at the United Nations (2012–14)', 9820/10, 2010.

Court of Auditors, EU assistance implemented through united nations organisations: decision-making and monitoring, 2009.

—, European Union Assistance to Kosovo related to the rule of law, 2012.

—, The Establishment of the European External Action Service, 2014.

Cracknell, BE, Evaluating development aid: issues, problems and solutions, Sage, 2000.

Cronin, A K & J Ludes, Attacking Terrorism: Elements of a Grand Strategy, Georgetown University Press, 2004.

Cross, M K D, 'Cooperation by committee: the EU military committee and the committee for civilian crisis management', Occasional paper 82, 2010, pp. 5–39.

—, Security Integration in Europe: How Knowledge-based Networks Are Transforming the European Union, The University of Michigan Press, 2011.

CSCE, 'Charter of Paris for a New Europe', 1990.

Czosseck, C, R Ottis & A-M Taliharm, 'Estonia after the 2007 Cyber Attacks: Legal, Strategic and Organisational Changes in Cyber Security', Case Studies in Information Warfare and Security: For Researchers, Teachers and Students 2013, pp. 72.

Dahl, R A, Who governs?: Democracy and power in an American city, Yale University Press, 2005.

Damro, C, 'EU-UN Environmental Relations: shared competence and effective multilateralism', in: The European Union at the United Nations: intersecting multilateralisms, Palgrave Macmillan 2006, pp. 175–192.

Dari, E, M Price, J Vand der Wal, G Marlene & N Koenig, 'Csdp Mission and Operations: Lessons learned processes', EXPO/B/SEDE/FWC/2009-01/Lot6/16 2012.

Davutoğlu, A, 'Turkey's Foreign Policy Vision: An Assessment of 2007.', Insight Turkey 2008.

de Vivero, J L S & J C Rodríguez Mateos, 'Maritime Europe and EU enlargement. A geopolitical perspective', Marine policy 30, no. 2, 2006, pp. 167–172.

Den Boer, M & J Monar, 'Keynote article: 11 September and the challenge of global terrorism to the EU as a security actor', JCMS: Journal of Common Market Studies 40, no. s1, 2002, pp. 11–28.

Devuyst, Y, 'European Union's Institutional Balance after the

Treaty of Lisbon: Community Method and Democratic Deficit Reassessed', *Geo. J. Int'l L.* 39, 2007, pp. 247.

Dhaka, A, 'The geopolitics of energy security and the response to its challenges by India and Germany', *Geopolitics* 14, no. 2, 2009, pp. 278–299.

Dimitrova, A & R Dragneva, 'Constraining External Governance: Interdependence with Russia and the CIS as Limits to the EU's Rule Transfer in the Ukraine', *Journal of European Public Policy* 16, no. 6, 2009, pp. 853–872.

Dougan, M, 'The Treaty of Lisbon 2007: Winning minds, not hearts', *Common market law review* 45, no. 3, 2008, pp. 617.

Drent, M, 'The EU's Comprehensive Approach to Security: A Culture of Coordination?', *Studia Diplomatica* pp. 3–18, 2011.

Drieskens E &van Schaik, L *The EU and Effective Multilateralism Internal and External Reform Practices*, Routledge, 2014

Duke, S, 'Diplomatic Training in the EU' in J Bátora & S David (eds.), *European Diplomacy post-Westphalia*, Palgrave, 2015.

Duke, S, *The EU and crisis management: development and prospects*, European Institute of Public Administration Maastricht, 2002.

—, 'Preparing for European diplomacy?', *JCMS: Journal of Common Market Studies* 40, no. 5, 2002, pp. 849–870.

—, 'Providing for European-level diplomacy after Lisbon: the case of the European External Action Service', *The Hague journal of diplomacy* 4, no. 2, 2009, pp. 211–233.

—, *Now We Are One. A Rough Start for the EEAS*, EIPA, 2012.

Duke, S & S Blockmans, 'The Lisbon Treaty stipulations on development cooperation and the council decision of 25 March 2010 (Draft) establishing the organisation and functioning of the European External Action Service', *CLEER Legal Brief* 4, 2010.

ECDPM, 'EU development cooperation after the Lisbon Treaty', 123, 2011.

—, 'The Implementation of the Joint Africa Europe Strategy: Rebuilding Confidence and Commitments, EP, 2014.

Eckes, C, *EU counter-terrorist policies and fundamental rights: the case of individual sanctions*, Oxford University Press, 2009.

EEAS, *EEAS Review*, 2013.

EGS, *Towards a European Union Global Strategy*, UI, 2013.

Eide, K, *Power Struggle Over Afghanistan: An Inside Look at What Went Wrong – and What We Can Do to Repair the Damage*, Skyhorse Publishing, 2012.

Ekengren, M, 'From a European Security Community to a Secure European Community – Analysing EU "Functional" Security – The Case of EU Civil Protection', SGIR Conference, Fifth Pan-European Conference: Constructing World Orders, 2004.

—, 'New security challenges and the need for new forms of EU cooperation: the solidarity declaration against terrorism and the open method of coordination',

*European Security* 15, no. 1, 2006, pp. 89–111.

—, 'Terrorism and the EU: The Internal-External Dimension of Security', in: *The European Union and terrorism*. John Harper Publishing, London 2007.

—, 'Agency and structure in EU foreign policy practices', *Rethinking Foreign Policy* 101, 2012, pp. 81.

Ekengren, M & G Simons, *The politics of security sector reform: challenges and opportunities for the European Union's global role*, Ashgate Publishing, Ltd., 2011.

Ekengren, M, N Matzén & M Svantesson, *The New Security Role of the European Union: Transnational Crisis Management and the Protection of Union Citizens*, Försvarshögskolan, 2006.

Ekengren, M, N Matzén, M Rhinard & M Svantesson, 'Solidarity or sovereignty? EU cooperation in civil protection', *European Integration* 28, no. 5, 2006, pp. 457–476.

Emerson, M, 'EU-Russia – Four Common Spaces and the Proliferation of the Fuzzy', CEPS Policy Briefs no. 1–12, 2005, pp. 1–4.

Emerson, M & J Boonstra, *Into Eurasia monitoring the EU's central asia strategy*, EU Cam Project 2010.

Emerson, M, R Balfour, T Corthaut, J Wouters, PM Kaczynski & T Renard, 'Upgrading the EU's Role as Global Actor: Institutions', Law and the Restructuring of European Diplomacy', CEPS, 2011.

Engberg, K, 'Trends in Conflict Management: multilateral intervention and the role of regional organisations' in: P Wallensteen & A Bjurner (eds.), *Regional Organisations and Peacemaking Challengers to the UN*, Routledge, 2014.

Eriksson, J & M Rhinard, 'The Internal – External Security Nexus Notes on an Emerging Research Agenda', *Cooperation and conflict* 44, no. 3, 2009, pp. 243–267.

EU anti-corruption report', COM(2014) 38 final, no. 2014, 2014.

Euratom, 'Cooperation Agreement between the European Atomic Energy Community and the International Atomic Energy Agency', *Official Journal of the European Commission* INFCIRC/25/Add. 5, 1975.

European Commission, 'Communication from the Commission to the Council, the European Parliament, the European Economic and Social Committee and the Committee of the Regions – Limiting global climate change to 2 degrees Celsius – The way ahead for 2020 and beyond', *Communication from the Commission to the European Parliament, the Council, the Economic and Social Committee and the Committee of the Regions* COM/2007/0002 Final, 2007.

—, 'A comprehensive approach on personal data protection in the European Union', COM 609-2010.

—, 'Evaluation of Visibility of EU external action', 2012.

—, 'Report from the commission to the European parliament, the council, the European economic and social committee and the committee of the regions 2012 Annual Report on the Instrument for Stability', COM(2013) 563 final, no. 2013.

—, 'The EU Fights Against the Scourge of Terrorism', Freedom, Security and Justice – Justice and Home Affairs, 2009 http://ec. europa. eu/justice_home/fsj/ter-rorism/wai/fsj_terrorism_intro_ en. htm.

—, 'The Ethical Justness of European Counter-terrorism Measures', Deliverable 12.2., Work package 6, 'Citizens and governance in a knowledge-based society', 2008.

—, 'CBRN Centres of Excellence: an initiative of the European Union', http://www.cbrn-coe.eu.

—, 'Abolition of internal borders and creation of a single EU external frontier', online 2005, http:// ec. europa. eu/justice_home/fsj freetravel/frontiers.

—, 'Annex to the Proposal for directive of the European parliament and of the council on the coordination of procedures for the award of certain public works contracts, public supply contracts and public service contracts in the fields of defence and security', 2004.

—, 'Commission communication on the implementation of the Preparatory Action on the enhancement of the European industrial potential in the field of Security research, Towards a programme to advance European security through Research and Technology', COM(2004) 72 final, 2004.

—, 'Communication from the Commission on Conflict Prevention', COM no. 211, 2001.

—, 'Communication from the commission to the European parliament, the council, the European economic and social committee and the committee of the regions Towards a more competitive and efficient defence and security sector', no. 542 final, 2013.

—, 'Comprehensive approach to the EU implementation of the United Nations Security Council Resolutions 1325 and 1820 on women, peace and security', 15671/1/08, 2008.

—, 'Consolidated Version of the Treaty on European Union', Official Journal of the European Communities C 325, 2010.

—, 'EU 2011 Report on Policy Coherence for Development', SEC(2011) 1627, 2011.

—, 'EU Plan of Action on Combating Terrorism (revised)', 10010/3/04, 2004.

—, 'Increasing the impact of EU Development Policy: an Agenda for Change', 2011.

—, 'Internal Security', Special Eurobarometer 371, 2011.

—, 'Regulation (EU, Euratom) no. 966/2012 of the European parliament and of the council of 25 October 2012 on the financial rules applicable to the general budget of the Union and repealing Council Regulation (EC, Euratom) No 1605/2002', *Official Journal of the European*

*Commission* 2012.

—, 'Report from the commission to the council and the European parliament EU anti-corruption report', COM(2014) 38 final, no. 2014, 2014.

—, 'STAR 21 Strategic Aerospace Review for the 21st century Creating a coherent market and policy framework for a vital European industry', 2002.

—, 'The EU Fights Against the Scourge of Terrorism', Freedom, Security and Justice – Justice and Home Affairs, available at http://ec. europa. eu/justice_home/fsj/terrorism/wai/fsj_terrorism_intro_en.htm 2009.

—, High Representative, 'Global Europe: A new Approach to financing EU external action', 2011.

—, Communication from the commission on a European Programme for Critical Infrastructure Protection', COM(2006) 786 final, no. 2006, 2006.

European Energy Security, 14, 2012, Greece, Go, 'Informal Meeting of Energy Ministers Athens, 15–16 May 2014', *Energy Security Discussion Paper*, 2014.

European foreign policy unit, Chronology: European Union Foreign Policy – Policy Developments (partial), http:/www.lse.ac.uk/internationalRelations/centresandunits/EFPU/EFPUpdfs/chronologyEUforpol.pdf.

European Parliament, European Parliament legislative resolution of 8 July 2010 on the proposal for a Council decision establishing the organisation and functioning of EEAS.

European Union, 'Peaceful uses of nuclear technology', 2012.

Feinstein, A, *The shadow world – inside the global arms trade*, Penguin, 2012.

Finckenauer, J O, 'Problems of definition: what is organized crime?', *Trends in organized crime* 8, no. 3, 2005, pp. 63–83.

Findley, T, *Unleashing the Nuclear Watchdog. Strengthening and Reform of the IAEA*, The Center for International Governance Innovation, 2012.

Freedman, L, *Strategy: A History*, Oxford University Press, 2013.

Friedman, G, *The Next 100 Years: A Forecast for the 21st Century*, 1 Reprint ed., Anchor, 2010.

Friedman, J & S Randeria, *Worlds on the Move: Globalisation, Migration and Cultural Security*, IB Tauris, 2004.

Fukuyama, F, *The End of the History and the Last Man*, Reprint ed., Penguin Books, 1992.

Füle, S, 'Strengthening EU partnership with neighbours', 2013.

Fägersten, B, 'Bureaucratic Resistance to International Intelligence Cooperation – The Case of Europol', *Intelligence and National Security* 25, no. 4, 2010, pp. 500–520.

Galeazzi, G, D Helly & F Krätke, 'All for one or free-for-all, Early experiences in EU joint programming' ECDPM Briefing Note 50, 2013.

Garfield, R, 'Economic sanctions on Yugoslavia', *The Lancet* 358, no. 9281, 2001, pp. 580.

Gasparini, G, 'Turkey and European Security', *IAI-TESEV Report* 8, 2007.

Gates, R M, *Duty: Memoirs of a Secretary at War*, books.google.com 2014.

Gebhard, C, 'Assessing EU actorness towards its "near abroad": The European Neighbourhood Policy', *Occasional Paper* no. 1, 2007.

Gegout, C, 'The EU and Security in the Democratic Republic of Congo in 2006: Unfinished Business', *CFSP Forum* 4(6), no. 6, 2007, pp. 5–9.

German Marshall Fund of the US, 'Transatlantic Trends 2014', 2014

Ginsberg, R H, 'Conceptualizing the European Union as an International Actor: Narrowing the Theoretical Capability Expectations Gap', *JCMS: Journal of Common Market Studies* 37, no. 3, 1999, pp. 429–454.

Giumelli, F, 'How EU Sanctions Work', *Chaillot paper* 129, 2013.

Glavind, J, 'Effective multilateralism in the IAEA: changing best practice. ' in: *The EU and Effective Multilateralism: Internal and External reform practices.* ed. Drieskens, E, L G. van Schaik (ed.) Routledge, 2014.

Gleditsch, N P, P Wallensteen, M Eriksson, M Sollenberg & H Strand, 'Armed conflict 1946–2001: A new dataset', *Journal of Peace Research* 39, no. 5, 2002, pp. 615–637.

Glüpker, G, 'Effectiveness of EU Conditionality in the Western Balkans: Minority Rights and the Fight Against Corruption in Croatia and Macedonia', *Journal of Contemporary European Research* 9, Issue 2, 2013.

GmbH, P, 'Thematic Evaluation of European Commission Support to Conflict prevention and Peace building', 2011.

—, 'Thematic global evaluation of the European Union's support to Integrated Border Management and fight against Organised Crime Final Report', II, 2013.

—, 'Thematic global evaluation of the European Union's support to Integrated Border Management and fight against Organised Crime', IIIa, 2013.

—, 'Thematic global evaluation of the European Union's support to Integrated Border Management and fight against Organised Crime', IIIb, 2013.

Gnesotto, N, *EU Security and Defence: Core Documents 2004*, Institute for Security Studies, European Union, 2005.

—, *EU Security and Defence: Core Documents 2005*, Volume VI: Chaillot Paper No. 87, European Union Institute for Security Studies, 2006.

Goldmann, K, *Tension and Detente in Bipolar Europe*, Esselte studium, 1974.

—, 'International Relations: an overview', in: *A New Handbook of Political Science* 1996, pp. 401–427.

Goldthau, A & W Hoxtell, *The Impact of Shale Gas on European Energy Security*, GPPi, 2012

Gore, A, *The Future: Six Drivers of Global Change*, Random House, 2013.

Gourlay, C, 'Partners apart: managing civil-military co-operation in humanitarian interventions', *Disarmament forum* 3, 2000, pp. 33–44.

—, 'The European Union as Peacemaker – Enhancing EU Mediation Capacity Background Paper', 2013.

Gourlay, C & A Nowak, *Civilian crisis management: the EU way*, European Union Institute for Security Studies, 2006.

Government, HM, 'Review of the Balance of Competences between the United Kingdom and the European Union Foreign Policy', 2013.

—, 'Review of the Balance of Competences between the United Kingdom and the European Union Development Cooperation and Humanitarian Aid', 2013.

Graf, H G, 'Global scenarios', dandelon.com 2002.

Grand, C, *The European Union and the non-proliferation of nuclear weapons*, Institute for Security Studies, Western European Union, 2000.

Grevi, G & Ád Vasconcelos, 'Partnerships for Effective Multilateralism: EU Relations with Brazil, China, India and Russia' *Chaillot Paper*, No. 109, European Union Institute for Security Studies, 2008.

Grip, L, 'The EU non-proliferation clause: A preliminary assessment', SIPRI, background paper, 2009.

—, 'Assessing Selected European Union External Assistance and Cooperation Projects on WMD Non-Proliferation', EU Non-Proliferation Consortium Non-Proliferation Papers 6, 2011.

—, 'Mapping the European Union's Institutional Actors related to WMD Nonproliferation', SIPRI, 2011.

Groen, L & A Niemann, 'EU Actorness and effectiveness under political pressure at the Copenhagen climate change negotiations', Twelfth European Union Studies Association Conference, Boston, 2011, pp. 3–5.

Groenleer, M L P & L G Van Schaik, 'United We Stand? The European Union's International Actorness in the Cases of the International Criminal Court and the Kyoto Protocol', *JCMS: Journal of Common Market Studies* 45, no. 5, 2007, pp. 969–998.

Gross, E, *EU and the Comprehensive Approach*, Danish Institute for International Studies, 2008.

Gross, E, 'Operation CONCORDIA (fyrom)', in: *European Security and Defence Policy: The First 10 Years*, 2009.

Gross, E, *Security sector reform in Afghanistan: the EU's contribution*, European Union Institute for Security Studies, 2009.

Gross, E & A E Juncos, *EU conflict prevention and crisis management: roles, institutions, and policies*, Routledge, 2010.

Groupe, U R D, 'Real-time evaluation of humanitarian action supported by DG ECHO in Haiti', globalstudyparticipation.urd.org.

Gudda, P, *A Guide to Project Monitoring & Evaluation*, Authorhouse, 2011.

Guicherd, C, 'The Hour of Europe: Lessons from the Yugoslav Conflict', *Fletcher Forum of World Affairs*, 1993.

Guild, E & S Carrera, 'Towards the Next Phase of the EU's Area of Freedom, Security and Justice: The EC's Proposals for the Stockholm Programme', *CEPS policy brief* no. 196, 2009.

Guild, E, S Carrera & A Atger, 'Challenges and prospects for the EU's area of freedom, security and justice: Recommendations to the European Commission for the Stockholm Programme', CEPS Working Document no. 313, 2009.

Guiraudon, V, 'The constitution of a European immigration policy domain: a political sociology approach', *Journal of European Public Policy* 10, no. 2, 2003, pp. 263–282.

Gutner, T & A Thompson, 'The politics of IO performance: A framework', *The Review of International Organizations* 5, no. 3, 2010, pp. 227–248.

Gya, G, 'Enacting the Lisbon Treaty for CSDP: Bright lights or a tunnel?', *European security review* 47, 2009, pp. 1–4.

Gänzle, S, 'The EU's Presence and Actorness in the Baltic Sea Area: Multilevel Governance Beyond its External Borders', *EU Enlargement and Beyond: The Baltic States and Russia*, Berlin: Spitz 2002, pp. 73–103.

Görtz, S & A Sherriff, '1st Among Equals? The Instrument for Stability and Conflict Prevention and Peacebuilding in the EU's new financial perspective', *ECPDM Briefing Note 39*, 2012.

Hagman, H-C, *European Crisis Management and Defence: The Search for Capabilities*, Adelphi Paper 353, IISS, 2002.

Hajnal, P I & S Meikle, *The G7/G8 System: Evolution, role and documentation*, Ashgate Aldershot, 1999.

Hansen, L & H Nissenbaum, 'Digital disaster, cyber security, and the Copenhagen School', *International Studies Quarterly* 53, no. 4, 2009, pp. 1155–1175.

Harrison, L & Callan, T: *Key research concepts in politics and international relations*, SAGE, 2013.

Hart, J A, 'The G 8 and the Governance of Cyberspace', in: *New Perspectives on Global Governance: Why America Needs the G 8*, 2005, pp. 137–152.

Hart, T G, *The Cognitive World of Swedish Security Elites*, Scandinavian University books, 1976

Haukkala, H, *The EU-Russia strategic partnership: the limits of post-sovereignty in international relations*, Routledge, 2010.

Haver, K, T Frankenberger, M Greeley & P Harvey, 'Evaluation and review of DG ECHO financed livelihood interventions in humanitarian crises', aidngolist. org 2012.

Hayes, B & C Jones, 'Catalogue of EU Counter-Terrorism Measures Adopted since 11 September 2001', SECILE project – GA: 313195, 2013.

Hedenskog, J & R L Larsson, 'Russian Leverage on the CIS and the Baltic States', FOI-R--2280-- SE, 2007.

Heinitz, A, 'Migration and Security in the Eastern Mediterranean', DCAF, 2013.

Heisbourg, F, 'The Geostrategic Implications of the Competition for Natural Resources: The

Transatlantic Dimension', German Marshall Fund, 2012, pp. 18.

High representative & European commission, 'Joint Communication to the European Parliament and the Council. The EU's comprehensive approach to external conflict and crises', 2013.

—'For an open and secure global maritime domain: elements for a European Union maritime security strategy', JOIN(2014) 9 final, no. 2014, 2014.

High-Level Panel of Eminent Persons on the Post-2015 Development Agenda, A New Global Partnership: Eradicate Poverty and Transform Economies through Sustainable Development, 2013.

Hill, C, 'The capability expectations gap, or conceptualizing Europe's international role', JCMS: Journal of Common Market Studies 31, no. 3, 1993, pp. 305–328.

—, 'The EU's capacity for conflict prevention', European Foreign Affairs Review 6, no. 3, 2001, pp. 315–334.

Hillion, C & R A Wessel, 'Competence Distribution in EU External Relations after ECOWAS: Clarification or Continued Fuzziness?', Common Market Law Review 46, no. 2, 2009, pp. 551–586.

Hofmann, S C, 'Why institutional overlap matters: CSDP in the European security architecture', JCMS: Journal of Common Market Studies 49, no. 1, 2011, pp. 101–120.

Hoogensen, G & K Stuvøy, 'Gender, resistance and human security', Security Dialogue 37, no. 2, 2006, pp. 207–228.

House, C, 'Maritime Security in the Gulf of Guinea', Conference held 6 December 2012, 2013.

Howorth, J, European integration and defence: the ultimate challenge?, Institute for Security Studies, Western European Union, 2000.

—, 'CESDP after 11 September: From Short-Term Confusion to Long-Term Cohesion?', EUSA Review 15, no. 1, 2002, pp. 5.

—, 'France, Britain and the Euro-Atlantic Crisis', Survival 45, no. 4, 2003, pp. 173–192.

—, Security and defence policy in the European Union, Palgrave Macmillan, 2007.

—, 'The EU as a Global Actor: Grand strategy for a global grand bargain?', JCMS: Journal of Common Market Studies 48, no. 3, 2010, pp. 455–474.

Howorth, J & A Menon, The European Union and National Defence Policy, Routledge, 1997.

Hubel, H, EU Enlargement and Beyond: The Baltic States and Russia, Berlin Verlag, 2002.

Huff, A, 'The Role of EU Defence Policy in the Eastern Neighbourhood', IISSS, 2011.

Hughes, J, 'Reflections on Globalisation, Security and 9/11', CSGR Working Paper No. 105/02, 2002.

—, EU Relations with Russia: Partnership or Asymmetric Interdependency?, Palgrave, 2006.

Huigens, J & A Niemann, 'The EU within the G8: A Case of Ambiguous and Contested Actorness'. College of Europe EU Diplomacy Paper no. 5-2009, pp. 38.

Hunter, R E, *The European Security and Defense Policy: NATO's Companion – or Competitor?*, Rand Corporation, 2002.

Huntington, S P, *The Clash of Civilizations and the Remaking of World Order*, Simon & Schuster, 2011.

Huther, J & A Shah, *Anti-Corruption Policies and Programs: A Framework for Evaluation*, World Bank-free PDF, 2000.

Huysmans, J, 'The European Union and the Securitization of Migration', *JCMS: Journal of Common Market Studies* 38, no. 5, 2000, pp. 751–777.

—, *The Politics of Insecurity: Fear, Migration and Asylum in the EU*, Routledge, 2006.

Hynek, N, 'EU Crisis Management After the Lisbon Treaty: Civil-Military Coordination and the Future of the EU OHO', *European Security* 20, no. 1, 2011, pp. 81–102.

Hänggi, H, 'Conceptualising Security Sector Reform and Reconstruction', Reform and Reconstruction of the Security Sector 6, 2004.

—, 'Making Sense of Security Sector Governance', Challenges of Security Sector Sovernance 2003, pp. 17–18.

IAEA, 'Communication dated 16 November 2011 received from the Delegation of the European Union to the International Organizations in Vienna on international cooperation by the European Union in support of peaceful uses of nuclear energy', INFCIRC/830, 2011.

—, 'Convention on Nuclear Safety', INFCIRC_449, 1994. zzz

—, 'EURATOM-IAEA New Partnership Approach', INFCIRC/193, 1992, text of joint declaration, 1992, http://www.nuclearfiles.org/menu/library/treaties/european-atomic-energy-community/trty_european-atomic-energy-community_partnership_1992-04-00.htm.

—, 'Nuclear Security Plan 2010–2013'.

—, 'The EU's 7th EURATOM Framework Programme (2007–2011)'.

—, EgRttdgot, 'Mulitlateral approaches to the Nuclear fuel cycle', 2005.

—, 'EU Adopts Main IAEA Safety Standards for Nuclear Installations', 2009, http://www.iaea.org/newscenter/news/2009/euadoptsstandards.html.

—, International Atomic Energy Agency (IAEA), 'Medium Term Strategy 2012–2017', 2010.

—, 'Reinforcing cooperation on nuclear energy for peace and development: A joint statement of the International Atomic Energy Agency and the European Commission', Brussels, 7 May 2008, 2008, http://iaea.org/newscenter/news/ pdf/iaea_euratom070508.pdf.

ISIS Europe, 'Securitising Migration: The EU's Approach to Illegal Immigration and the implications on Labour Trafficking ESR 71 – May 2014', *European Security Review* 2014.

Jackson, N J, 'International organizations, security dichotomies and the trafficking of persons and narcotics in post-soviet Central

Asia: A critique of the securitization framework', *Security Dialogue* 37, no. 3, 2006, pp. 299–317.

Jones, A, 'Questionable actorness and presence: Projecting "EU" rope in the Mediterranean', *Political Geography* 28, no. 2, 2009, pp. 79–90.

Judt, T, *Postwar: A History of Europe Since 1945*, Reprint ed., Penguin Books, 2006.

—, *Reappraisals: Reflections on the Forgotten Twentieth Century*, Reprint ed., Penguin Press, 2008.

Jupille, J & J A Caporaso, 'States, agency, and rules: the European Union in global environmental politics', *The European Union in the world community* 1998, pp. 213–229.

Jørgensen, K E, 'Three doctrines on European Foreign policy', Welttrends 12, 2004, pp. 27–36.

— 'The European Union in multilateral diplomacy', *The Hague Journal of Diplomacy* 4, no. 2, 2009, pp. 189–209.

—, *The European Union and International Organizations*, Routledge/Garnet Series: Europe in the World, Routledge, 2009.

Jørgensen, K E & S Oberthür, 'Introduction: establishing a framework for assessing the EU's performance in international institutions", *European Union in International Affairs Conference*, 2010.

Jørgensen, K E, S Oberthür & J Shahin, 'Introduction: assessing the EU's performance in international institutions–conceptual framework and core findings', *Journal of European integration* 33, no. 6, 2011, pp. 599–620.

Kagan, R, *Power and weakness*, Hoover Institution, 2002.

—, *Of Paradise and Power: America and Europe in the New World Order*, Knopf, 2003.

—, *The Return of History and the End of Dreams*, Vintage, 2009.

Kahneman, D, *Thinking, fast and slow*, Macmillan, 2011.

Kaldor, M, *Human Security*, Polity, 2007.

—, *New and Old Wars: Organised Violence in a Global Era*, John Wiley & Sons, 2013.

Kaldor, M & M Glasius, *A Human Security Doctrine for Europe*, Routledge, 2004.

Kaldor, M, M Martin & S Selchow, 'Human Security: A New Strategic Narrative for Europe', *International Affairs* 83, no. 2, 2007, pp. 273–288.

Kantner, C & A Liberatore, 'Security and Democracy in the European Union: An Introductory Framework', *European Security* 15, no. 4, 2006, pp. 363–383.

Kaplan, R D, *The Revenge of Geography: What the Map Tells Us About Coming Conflicts and the Battle Against Fate*, Random House, 2012.

Karatzogianni, A, *Cyber-Conflict and Globalpolitics*, Routledge, 2008.

Karman, T, L Gbowee & E J Sirleaf, 'Thematic Evaluation of the European Commission Support to Respect of Human Rights and Fundamental Freedoms (including solidarity with victims of repression)', 2011, http://www.oecd.org/derec/ec/49682254.pdf

Katzman, K, 'Iran Sanctions', *Congressional Research Service*, 2014.

Kaufmann, D, 'Corruption, Governance and Security: Challenges for the Rich Countries and the World', Available at SSRN 605801 2004.

Kaunert, C, 'Europol and EU Counterterrorism: International Security Actorness in the External Dimension', *Studies in Conflict & Terrorism* 33, no. 7, 2010, pp. 652–671.

Kavalski, E, 'Partnership or Rivalry Between the EU, China and Indian Central Asia: The Normative Power of Regional Actors with Global Aspirations', *European Law Journal* 13, no. 6, 2007, pp. 839–856.

Kemp, W & D Sammut, *Confidence Building Matters. Rethinking the OSCE European Security after Budapest*, Verification Technology Information Centre, 1995.

Keohane, D, 'The EU and Counter-terrorism', *Centre for European Reform*, 2005.

—, 'The Absent Friend: EU Foreign Policy and Counter Terrorism', *JCMS: Journal of Common Market Studies* 46, no. 1, 2008, pp. 125–146.

Kerr, P K, 'U.S. Nuclear Cooperation with India: Issues for Congress', *Congressional Research Service*, 2012.

Keukeleire, S & H Bruyninckx, 'The European Union, the BRICs, and the Emerging New World Order', *International Relations and the European Union* 2011, pp. 380.

Keukeleire, S & J MacNaughtan, *The foreign policy of the EU*, Palgrave Macmillan, 2014.

Khandker, S, G B Koolwal & H Samad, *Handbook on Impact Evaluation*, no. 1, 2009, pp. 1–239.

Khatib, K, 'How Promotion of Political Reform by the European Union is Perceived in the Arab World: The Cases Of Lebanon and the Palestinian Territories', *International IDEA* 2009, pp. 1–16.

Kirshner, J, *Globalizationand national security*, Taylor & Francis, 2006.

Kirton, J, 'From Collective Security to Concert: The UN, G8 and Global Security Governance', Conference on Security Overspill: Between Economic Integration and Social Exclusion, Montreal, http://www.g7.utoronto.ca/scholar/kirton2005/kirton_montreal2005.pdf 2005.

Kirton, J, 'The G8 and Global Energy Governance Past Performance, St. Petersburg Opportunities', a conference on 'The World Dimension of Russia's Energy Security', sponsored by the Moscow State Institute of International Relations (MGIMO), 2006.

Kirton, J & L Sunderland, 'The G8 Summit Communiqués on Nuclear Nonproliferation', G8 Research Group, http://www.g7.utoronto.ca/references/non-proliferation.pdf

Kitt, F, *EU Aid Architecture: Recent Trends and Policy Directions*, World Bank Group, 2010.

Klingebiel, S, *New Interfaces Between Security and Development: Changing Concepts and Approaches*, German Development Institute/Deutsches Institut für Entwicklungspolitik (DIE), 2009.

Kobia, R, 'The EU and Non-Proliferation: Need for a Quantum Leap', *Nuclear Law Bulletin* 81, 2008.

Koops, J A, *Assessing the European Union as an Inter-Organizational Actor: From Policy-Oriented Analysis to Theory-Guided Research*, Vesalius College, 2012.

Korski, D & R Gowan, *Can the EU Rebuild Failing States?: A Review of Europe's Civilian Capacities*, European Council on Foreign Relations (ECFR), 2009.

Korski, D, D Serwer & M Chabalowski, 'A new agenda for US-EU security cooperation', PRIDE, November 2009.

Krahmann, E, 'Conceptualizing security governance', Cooperation and conflict 38, no. 1, 2003, pp. 5–26.

Kronenberger, V & J Wouters, *The European Union and Conflict Prevention*, TMC Asser Press, 2004.

Kuhn, T S, *The Structure of Scientific Revolutions*, 2nd ed., University of Chicago Press, 1970.

Kuniholm, B, 'Turkey's Accession to the European Union: Differences in European and US Attitudes, and Challenges for Turkey', *Turkish Studies* 2, no. 1, 2001, pp. 25–53.

Kuno, Y, 'Multilateral Nuclear Approach to Nuclear Fuel Cycles' in: A Zacarias (ed.), *Current Research in Nuclear Reactor Technology in Brazil and Worldwide*, Intech, 2013.

Kupchan, C A, *No One's World*, Oxford University Press, 2012.

Kusek, J Z & R C Rist, *Ten Steps to a Resultbased Monitoring and Evaluation System: A Handbook for Development Practitioners*, World Bank-free PDF, 2004.

Laatikainen, K V & K E Smith, *The European Union at the United Nations: Intersecting Multilateralisms*, Palgrave, 2006.

Lachmann, Niels, 'NATO-CSDP-EU Relations: Sketching the Map of a Community of Practice', *Notes de recherche du CEPS* I 34, 2010.

Lansford, T, *All for One: Terrorism, NATO and the United States*, Ashgate, 2002.

Larrabee, F S, *Turkey as a United States Security Partner*, Rand, 2008.

Larsen, H, 'The EU: A Global Military Actor?', *Cooperation and Conflict* 37, no. 3, 2002, pp. 283–302.

Laursen, F, 'The European External Action Service (EEAS): the Idea and its Implementation', in: *The EU's Lisbon Treaty: Institutional Choices and Implementation*, Ashgate, 2012, pp. 171.

Lavenex, S & R Kunz, 'The migration-development-nexus in EU external relations', *European integration* 30, no. 3, 2008, pp. 439–457.

Layne, C, 'The Unipolar Illusion Revisited: The Coming End of the United States' Unipolar Moment', *International security* 31, no. 2, 2006, pp. 7–41.

Leen, M, 'Integrating the International Development Goals Into Europe's Trade Policy and Practice. The Challenges of CAP Reform.', *Trocaire Development Review* 2002, pp. 73–86.

Lehne, S, 'More Action, Better Service: How to Strengthen the European External Action Service', Policy Outlook, Carnegie, 2011.

—, 'The European External Action Service Still Suffers From Design Flaws. However, the Euro Crisis Now Offers a Chance for a Re-start', *LSE European Politics and Policy (EUROPP)* Blog 2012.

—, 'Promoting a Comprehensive Approach to EU Foreign Policy', Carnegie 2013.

—, 'Time to Reset the European Neighborhood Policy', Carnegie, 2014.

—, 'A Window of Opportunity to Upgrade EU Foreign Policy', Carnegie, 2014.

Leonard, M, *Why Europe Will Run the 21st Century*, annotated ed., Public Affairs, 2006.

Leonard, M & N Popescu, *A Power Audit of EU-Russia-relations*, European Council on Foreign Relations London, 2007.

Leshukov, I, 'Can the Northern Dimension Break the Vicious Circle of Russia-EU Relations?', in: *The Northern Dimension: Fuel for the EU*, 2001, pp. 118–141.

Levi, M A, *On Nuclear Terrorism*, Harvard University Press, 2007.

Lindell, U, *Modern Multilateral Negotiation: The Consensus Rule and its Implications in International Conferences*, Studentlitteratur, 1988.

Lindley-French, J, *Operationalizing the Comprehensive Approach*, Programme Paper: ISP PP 2010/01, Chatham House 2010.

Lindstrom, G, 'EU-US Burden Sharing: Who Does What?

*Chaillot Paper* No. 82', IISS, http://www. iss-eu. org/chaillot/ chai82.pdf (13.12. 2005) 2005.

Lindstrøm, C, 'European Union Policy on Asylum and Immigration. Addressing the Root Causes of Forced Migration: A Justice and Home Affairs Policy of Freedom, Security and Justice?', *Social Policy & Administration* 39, no. 6, 2005, pp. 587–605.

Lipson, M, 'Performance Under Ambiguity: International Organization Performance in UN Peace Keeping', *The Review of International Organizations* 5, no. 3, 2010, pp. 249–284.

Longo, F, *The Export of the Fight Against Organized Crime Policy Model and the EU's International Actorness*, Routledge, 2003.

Lucarelli, S & I Manners, *Values and Principles in European Union Foreign Policy*, Routledge, 2006.

Lucarellia, S & R Menotti, 'The use of force as coercive intervention; The conflicting values of the European Union's external action' in: S Lucarelli & I Manners (eds.), *Values and Principles in European Union Foreign Policy*, Routledge, 2006.

Lukyanov, F, 'EU: The Partnership that Went Astray', *Europe-Asia Studies* 60, no. 6, 2008, pp. 1107–1119.

Lundin, L-E, *Påverkan genom militärt stöd: sovjetisk militär resursöverföringspolitik visavi Vietnam och Egypten* = [Influence Through Military Support: Soviet Arms Transfer Policy Towards Vietnam and Egypt: four case studies], Doc. diss, Statskunskap, UI, 1980.

—, 'The Charter for European Security from a European Union (EU) Perspective', *Helsinki Monitor* 11, no. 1, 2000, pp. 11–21.

—, 'Security: Bringing Added Value Through the EU. Inaugural Lecture Presented to the National Security Section of the Royal Academy of War Sciences on 22nd April, 2003', 2003.

—, 'From A European Security Strategy to a European Global Strategy: Ten Content-Related Issues', *UI Occasional Papers* 11, 2012.

—, 'The European Union, the IAEA and WMD Nonproliferation: Unity of Approach and Continuity of Action', EU Non-Proliferation Consortium, 9, 2012.

—, 'CSDP Senior Mission Leaders and the Comprehensive Approach: A Need-to-Know Guide', folkebernadotteacademy. se, 2013.

—, 'From a European Security Strategy to a European Global Strategy: Take 11: Policy options', *UI Occasional Papers* 13, 2013.

—, 'OSCE and Transnational Threats', *OSCE Focus Seminar* October 2012, 2013.

— 'The EU as a Regional Organization. Effective Multilateralism in Conflict Management' in: P Wallensteen & A Bjurner (eds.), *Regional Organisations and Peacemaking Challengers to the UN*, Routledge, 2014.

—, 'Effective Multilateralism: the EU Delegation in Vienna' in: J Bátora & S David (eds.), *European Diplomacy post-Westphalia*, Palgrave, 2015.

—, 'The EU, the IAEA and the Comprehensive Approach' in: S. Blavuokos, D. Bourantonis and C. Portela: *The EU's Performance in the Non-Proliferation of Nuclear Weapons*, Palgrave-MacMillan, forthcoming.

Lundin, L-E & Revelas, K 'Security and Democracy: From the Perspective of Commission Officials Working at the Interface between ESDP and Community External Action', *European Security* 15, no. 4, 2006, pp. 423–430.

Luttwak, E N, *The Rise of China vs. the Logic of Strategy*, Belknap Press, 2012.

Lynch, D, 'The Security Dimension of the European Neighbourhood Policy', *The International Spectator* 40, no. 1, 2005, pp. 33–43.

—, 'ESDP and the OSCE', *European Security and Defence Policy* 2009, pp. 139.

MacFarlane, N S, 'The Pre-History of Human Security', *St Antony's International Review* 1, no. 2, 2005, pp. 43–65.

MacKellar, L, A Bartholomew, E Donelli & E Sondorp, *Thematic Evaluation of the European Commission Support to the Health Sector. Final Report. Volume I. August 2012*, aei.pitt.edu, 2012.

Major, C, C Mölling, 'EU Battlegroups: What Contribution to European Defence?: Progress and Prospects of European Rapid Response Forces', SWP research paper, Stiftung Wissenschaft und Politik, 2011.

Makarenko, T, 'The Crime-Terror Continuum: Tracing the Interplay Between Transnational Organised Crime and Terrorism', *Global Crime* 6, no. 1, 2004, pp. 129–145.

Maniokas, K & Žeruolis, D, 'EU enlargement: How wrong blueprint spoils good policy', *Europe's World*, 2014.

Manyin, ME, S Daggett, B Dolven & S V Lawrence, 'Pivot to the Pacific? The Obama Administration's Rebalancing Toward Asia', DTIC Document 2012.

Marchio, R, 'Operation Alba": A European Approach to Peace Support Operations in the Balkans', US Army War College, 2000.

Marsh, S & W Rees, *The European Union in the Security of Europe: From Cold War to Terror War*, Routledge, 2011.

Mattelaer, A, 'The CSDP mission planning process of the European Union: innovations and shortfalls, ECSA-Austria, 2010.

McArthur, S, 'Provincial Reconstruction Teams', http://atlismta.org/online-journals/0607-journal-development-challenges/provincial-reconstruction-teams/.

McGuire, S & M Smith, 'The European Union and the United States: competition and convergence in the global arena', Foundations, 1945(58)58, 2008, pp. 7.

Mearsheimer, J, *The Tragedy of Great Power Politics*, Rev. ed., W W Norton, 2014.

Menon, A, 'From crisis to catharsis: ESDP after Iraq', *International Affairs* 80, no. 4, 2004, pp. 631–648.

—, 'Empowering paradise? The ESDP at ten', *International affairs* 85, no. 2, 2009, pp. 227–246.

—, 'Power, institutions and the CSDP: the promise of institutionalist theory', *JCMS: Journal of Common Market Studies* 49, no. 1, 2011, pp. 83–100.

Menon, A & U Sedelmeier, 'Instruments and intentionality: civilian crisis management and enlargement conditionality in EU security policy', *West European Politics* 33, no. 1, 2010, pp. 75–92.

Méran, F & A Weston, 'The EEAS and Crisis Management: The Organisational Challenges of a Comprehensive Approach' in: J Bátora & S David (eds.), *European Diplomacy post-Westphalia*, Palgrave, 2015.

Meunier, S, *Trading voices: the European Union in international commercial negotiations*, Princeton University Press, 2005.

Meunier, S & K Nicolaidis, 'Who speaks for Europe? The delegation of trade authority in the EU', *JCMS: Journal of Common Market Studies* 37, no. 3, 1999, pp. 477–501.

Middleton, R, P Melly & A Vines, 'Implementing the EU concept on Mediation: Learnings from the Cases of Sudan and the Great Lakes', EXPO/B/AFET/FWC/2009-01 lot 5/16 2011.

Mildner, S-A, G Lauster, W Wodni & G Mounier, 'Scarcity and Abundance Revisited: A literature Review on Natural Resources and Conflict', *International Journal of Conflict and Violence* 5 (1) 2011, no. 1, pp. 155–172.

Mildner, S-A & C Schmucker, 'Trade agreements with side-effects', *SWP Comments* 18, 2013.

Miles, E, A Underdal, S Andresen, J Wettestad, JB Skjaerseth & EM Carlin, *Environmental Regime Effectiveness – Confronting Theory with Evidence*, MIT Press, 2002.

Missiroli, A, 'EU-NATO Cooperation in Crisis Management: No Turkish Delight for ESDP', *Security Dialogue* 33, no. 1, 2002, pp. 9–26.

–, 'EU Enlargement and CFSP/ESDP', *Journal of European Integration* 25, no. 1, 2003, pp. 1–16.

–, 'Strategic Foresight – and the EU', *Brief Issue* 13, 2013.

Mitchell, R B, 'Evaluating the performance of environmental institutions: What to evaluate and how to evaluate it', in: *Institutions and environmental change: Principal findings, applications, and research frontiers*, MIT Press, 2008, pp. 79–114.

Mitsilegas, V, 'Defining Organised Crime in the European Union: The Limits of European Criminal Law in an Area of "Freedom, Security and Justice"', *European Law Review* 26, no. 6, 2001, pp. 565–581.

Mitsilegas, V, J Monar, W Rees, *The European Union and Internal Security: Guardian of The People?*, Palgrave Macmillan, 2003.

Monaghan, A, 'Russia-EU relations: An Emerging Energy Security Dilemma', *Pro et Contra* 10, no. 2–3, 2006, pp. 8.

Monar, J, 'The EU as an International Actor in the Domain of Justice and Home Affairs', *European Foreign Affairs Review* 9, 2004, pp. 395–415.

Moore, W H & D J Lanoue, 'Domestic Politics and US Foreign Policy: A Study of Cold War Conflict Behavior', *The Journal of Politics* 2003.

Moravcsik, A, 'Striking a New Transatlantic Bargain', *Foreign Affairs* 2003, pp. 74–89.

Moravcsik, A & M A Vachudova, 'National Interests, State Power, and EU Enlargement', *Perspectives*, No. 19, 2002/2003, pp. 21-31, Institute of International Relations, NGO

Morsut, C, 'Effective multilateralism? EU-UN Cooperation in the DRC, 2003–2006', *International Peacekeeping* 16, no. 2, 2009, pp. 261–272.

Moser, C & A Winton, 'Violence in the Central American Region: Towards an Integrated Framework for Violence Reduction', Working Paper 171, Overseas Development Institute London, 2002.

Mungiu-Pippidi, A & I Munteanu, 'Moldova's "Twitter Revolution"', *Journal of Democracy* 20, no. 3, 2009, pp. 136–142.

Mölling, C, 'ESDP after Lisbon: More Coherent and Capable?', *CSS Analysis in security policy* 3, no. 28, 2008, pp. 1–3.

Mölling, C & S-C Brune, 'The Impact of the Financial Crisis on European Defence', *EP*, 2011, http://nbn-resolving.de/urn:nbn:de:0168-ssoar-256754

Naim, M, *Illicit: How Smugglers, Traffickers, and Copycats are Hijacking the Global Economy*, Anchor, 2006.

—, *The end of power*, Basic Books, 2013.

Nerlich, U, 'Energy Security or a New Globalization of Conflicts? Oil and Gas in Evolving New Power Structures', *Strategic Insights*, Volume VII, Issue 1, Center for Contemporary Conflict, 2008.

Neumann, I B, *At Home with the Diplomats: Inside a European Foreign Ministry (Expertise: Cultures and Technologies of Knowledge)*, Cornell University Press, 2012.

NewDeal, 'A New Deal for Engagement in Fragile States', www.pbsbdialogue.org/documentupload/49151944.pdf.

Niemann, A & C Bretherton, 'EU External Policy at the Crossroads: The Challenge of Actorness and Effectiveness', *International Relations*, 2013.

Nikitin, M B, 'Proliferation Security Initiative (PSI)', *Congressional Research Service*, 2012.

Nitoiu, C, 'Reconceptualizing "Cooperation" in EU-Russia Relations', *Perspectives on European Politics and Society* 12, no. 4, 2011, pp. 462–476.

Nye, J S J, *The Future of Power*, Reprint ed., Public Affairs, 2011.

Oberthür, S, 'The European Union's performance in the international climate change regime', *Journal of European Integration* 33, no. 6, 2011, pp. 667–682.

OgĞzlu, H T, 'An Analysis of Turkey's Prospective Membership in the European Union from a Security "Perspective"', *Security Dialogue* vol. 34, no. 3, 2003, pp. 285–299.

Ojanen, H (ed.), 'The Northern Dimension: Fuel for the EU?', *Finnish Institute of International Affairs*, 2001.

—, 'The EU and NATO: Two Competing Models for a Common Defence Policy', *JCMS: Journal of Common Market Studies* 44, no. 1, 2006, pp. 57–76.

Onestini, C, 'A Hybrid Service: Organising Efficient EU Foreign Policy' in: J Bátora & S David (eds.), *European Diplomacy post-Westphalia*, Palgrave, 2015.

Orttung, R & A Latta, *Russia's Battle with Crime, Corruption and Terrorism*, Routledge, 2012.

OSCE, 'Astana Commemorative declaration', 2010.

—, 'Charter for European Security', 1999.

—, 'Rules of procedure of the Organization for Security and Co-operation in Europe', MC.DOC/1/06, 2006.

Pabst, M, 'Building Peace and Security – An Assessment of EU Efforts of Capacity-building and ESDP Operations in Sub-Saharan Africa', in: *Foreign Policy in Dialogue* 2008, pp. 29–41.

Panebianco, S, 'Promoting human rights and democracy in European Union relations with Russia and China' in: S Lucarelli & I Manners (eds.), *Values and principles in European Union Foreign Policy*, Routledge, 2014.

Paris, R, 'Human Security: Paradigm Shift or Hot Air?', *International security* 26, no. 2, 2001, pp. 87–102.

Pastore, F, 'The asymmetrical fortress: The problem of relations between internal and external security policies in the European Union', *European Monographs* 40, 2002, pp. 59–80.

Patrick, M, *Defining, Securing and Building a Just Peace: The EU and the Israeli-Palestinian conflict*, Lund Political Studies 2013.

Patten, C, *Not Quite the Diplomat: Home Truths about World Affairs*, Penguin, 2007.

—, *What Next?: Surviving the Twenty-first Century*, Penguin, 2009.

Pearson, I L G, 'Smart Grid Cyber Security for Europe', *Energy Policy* 39, no. 9, 2011, pp. 5211–5218.

Peers, S, 'EU Responses to Terrorism', *Int'l & Comp. LQ* 52, 2003, pp. 227.

Peters, J E, *CFE and Military Stability in Europe*, Rand, 1998.

Peters, S, 'Courting Future Resource Conflict: The Shortcomings of Western response strategies to new energy vulnerabilities', *Energy, Exploration & Exploitation* 21, no. 1, 2003, pp. 29–60.

Petersen, FA & H Binnendijk, 'The Comprehensive Approach Initiative: Future Options for NATO', DTIC Document, 2007.

Peterson, J & H Sjursen, *A common foreign policy for Europe?: Competing visions of the CFSP*, Routledge, 1998.

Peterson, J & M A Pollack, *Europe, America, Bush: Transatlantic relations in the twenty-first century*, Routledge, 2003.

Peyrouse, S, J Boonstra & M Laruelle, 'Security and development approaches to Central Asia. The EU compared to China and Russia', EUCAM Working Paper, 2012.

Piris, J-C, *The Lisbon Treaty: A Legal and Political Analysis*, Cambridge University Press, 2010.

Pirozzi, N, 'The EU's Comprehensive Approach to Crisis Management', DCAF, 2013.

Politi, A, *European Security: The New Transnational Risks*, Institute for Security Studies, Western European Union, 1997.

Portela, C, 'The Role of the EU in the Non-proliferation of Nuclear Weapons: the Way to Thessaloniki and Beyond', PRIF Reports No. 65, Peace Research Institute Frankfurt (PRIF) 2003.

—, 'Where and why does the EU impose sanctions?', *Politique euro-péenne* no. 3, 2005, pp. 83–111.

—, *The Efficacy of Sanctions of the European Union: When and Why do they Work?*, Florence, European University Institute, 2008.

Power, S, *A Problem from Hell: America and the Age of Genocide*, Harper Perennial, New York, 2003.

Prodi, R, 'A Wider Europe–A Proximity Policy as the key to stability', Speech at the Sixth ECSA-World Conference in Brussels, 2002.

Pyati, A & N Hicks, 'Karimov's War Human Rights Defenders and Counterterrorism in Uzbekistan', Human Rights Defenders and Counterterrorism Series 3, Human Rights First 2005.

Quille, G, 'The European Security Strategy: A Framework for EU Security Interests?', *International Peacekeeping* 11, no. 3, 2004, pp. 422–438.

—, 'The EU Strategy Against the Proliferation of WMD: Past, Present and Future', *European Security Review* 25, 2005.

—, 'The Lisbon Treaty and its implications for CFSP/ESDP, Directorate General for External Policies of the Union', Policy Briefing 1, 2009.

Quille, G, G Gasparini, R Menotti, N Pirozzi & S Pullinger, 'Developing EU Civil Military Co-ordination: The Role of the New Civilian Military Cell', Joint report by ISIS Europe and CEMISS, 2006.

Rajendran, G, 'What now for European defence spending?', The International Institute for Strategic Studies (IISS), 2014.

Rashid, A, *Taliban: Militant Islam, Oil, and Fundamentalism in Central Asia*, Yale University Press, 2001.

—, *Descent Into Chaos: How the War Against Islamic Extremism is Being Lost in Pakistan, Afghanistan and Central Asia*, Penguin UK, 2012.

Raube, K, 'The European External Action Service and the European Parliament', *The Hague Journal of Diplomacy* 7, no. 1, 2012, pp. 65–80.

Rees, W, 'The US-EU Security Relationship', *Journal of Contemporary European Research* (JCER)2011, pp. 561.

Reifer, T, 'Geopolitics, Globalization, and Alternative Regionalisms', ASEM 4 People conference in Copenhagen, Denmark, September, 2002, pp. 19–23.

Richardson, J, *European Union: Power and Policy-making*, Routledge, 2002.

Riley, A, 'The Shale Revolution's Shifting Geopolitics', *The New York Times*, The Opinion Pages, 2012, http://relooney.info/o_New_15209.pdf.

Ringe, L F, *The Santer Commission resignation crisis: Government-Opposition Dynamics in Executive-Legislative Relations of the EU*, University of Pittsburg, 2003.

Rodt, A P, 'EU Performance in Military Conflict Management', EUSA Twelfth Biennial International Conference, 2011.

Rose, G, *The Clash of Civilizations?: The Debate*, Council on Foreign Relations, Foreign Affairs 2013.

Ruane, K, 'Agonizing Reappraisals: Anthony Eden, John Foster Dulles and the Crisis of European Defence, 1953–54', *Diplomacy and Statecraft* 13, no. 4, 2002, pp. 151–185.

Rudolph, C, 'Globalization and security', *Security Studies* 13, no. 1, Taylor & Francis, 2003, pp. 1–32.

Rummel, R, 'Die Europäische Union lernt Konfliktprävention', Konfliktprävention zwischen Anspruch und Wirklichkeit, Wien 2007, pp. 39–59.

Santiso, C, 'The Reform of EU Development Policy: Improving Strategies for Conflict Prevention, Democracy Promotion & Governance Conditionality', Centre European Policy Studies, 2002.

Schetter, C J, 'The Bazaar Economy of Afghanistan: A Comprehensive Approach', Südasien-Informationsnetz, 2002.

Schmidt, A, 'Strategic Partnerships – A Contested Policy Concept; A Review of Recent Publications', *SWP*, 2010.

Schnaubelt, C M, 'Operationalizing a Comprehensive Approach in Semi-Permissive Environments, NATO Defense College', 2009.

—, 'Towards a Comprehensive Approach: Strategic and Operational Challenges', NDC Forum Paper 18, 2011.

Schumacher, T, 'The EU and the Arab Spring: between spectatorship and actorness', *Insight Turk.* 13, no. 3, 2011, pp. 107–119.

Scott, A, 'DFID's assessment of multilateral organisational effectiveness: an overview of results', London: Department for International Development 2005.

Security Council Resolutions 1325 and 1820 on women, peace and security', 15671/1/08, 2008.

Shambaugh, D, *China Goes Global: The Partial Power*, Oxford University Press, 2013.

Sherriff, A, 'Security Sector Reform and EU Norm Implementation', Intergovernmental Organisations and Security Sector Reform, Münster: Lit Verlag 2007, pp. 94.

Sherriff, A & V Hauck, 'Study on EU Lessons Learnt in Mediation and Dialogue. Glass Half Full', FWC COM 2011 – Lot 1 Request n°EEAS.K2.002 2012.

Sievers, E W, 'Water, conflict, and regional security in Central Asia', *NYU Envtl. LJ* 10, 2001, pp. 356.

Simms, B, Europe: *The Struggle for Supremacy, from 1453 to the Present*, Basic Books, 2013.

Sjöstedt, G, *The External Role of the European Community*, Gower, 1977.

Skodvin, T & J S Fuglestvedt, 'A Comprehensive Approach to Climate Change: Political and Scientific Considerations', *Ambio* 1997, pp. 351–358.

Slaughter, A-M, *A New World Order*, Princeton University Press, 2005.

Smith, K E, 'Still "civilian power EU"?', European Foreign Policy Unit Working Paper 1, 2005.

Smith, M, 'The EU as an International Actor', in: Richardson, J., *European Union: Power and Policy-making* 1996, pp. 257.

—, 'Toward a Theory of EU Foreign Policy-making: Multi-Level Governance, Domestic Politics, and National Adaptation to Europe's Common Foreign and Security Policy', *Journal of European Public Policy* 11, no. 4, 2004, pp. 740–758.

Smith, M E, 'European Foreign Policy as a Research Field: An Historical and Conceptual Overview', EUSA Conference 2009.

Solana, J, 'A Secure Europe in a Better World' The European Security Strategy 2003, *Natos Nations and Partners for Peace* 2003, pp. 28–30.

Sommer, P & I Brown, 'Reducing systemic cyber security risk', Organisation for Economic Cooperation and Development Working Paper No. IFP/WKP/FGS (2011) 3, 2011.

Spanjer, A, 'Russian gas price reform and the EU-Russia gas relationship: Incentives, consequences and European security of supply', *Energy Policy* 35, no. 5, 2007, pp. 2889–2898.

Spence, D, 'Effective Multi-lateralism: the EU Delegation at the UN in Geneva' in: J Bátora & S David (eds.), *European Diplomacy post-Westphalia*, Palgrave, 2015.

Spence, D & P Fluri, *The European Union and security sector reform*, John Harper, 2008.

Splidsboel-Hansen, F, 'Explaining Russian Endorsement of the CFSP and the ESDP', *Security Dialogue* 33, no. 4, 2002, pp. 443–456.

Starr, S F & S E Cornell, *Putin's Grand Strategy: the Eurasian Union and its Discontents*, Central Asia – Caucasus Institute Silk Road Studies program, 2014.

Statewatch, 'Taking stock of EU Counter-terrorism policy and review mechanisms: Summary of Statewatch's findings for SECILE project', 2013.

Stavridis, S, '"Militarising" the EU: The concept of civilian power Europe revisited', *The international spectator* 36, no. 4, 2001, pp. 43–50.

Steets, J, U Reichhold & E Sagmeister, *Evaluation and Review of Humanitarian Access Strategies in DG ECHO funded interventions*', Berlin: Global Public Policy Institute 2012.

Steinbach, W, 'The European Military-Industrial Complex: Addressing the Determinants of European Military-Industrial Capacity', *The Orator*, http:// students.washington.edu/nupsa/ Docs/Volume4/Wes_Steinbach_ European_Military-Industrial_ Complex.pdf

Stewart, E J, 'Capabilities and coherence? The evolution of European Union conflict prevention', *European foreign affairs review* 13, no. 2, 2008, pp. 229–254.

Stivachtis, Y A, C Price & M Habegger, 'The European Union as a Peace Actor', *Review of European Studies* 2013.

STAR 21, *Strategic Aerospace Review for the 21st century Creating a coherent market and policy framework for a vital European industry*, 2002.

Symeonidou-Kastanidou, E, 'Towards a New Definition of Organised Crime in the European Union', *Eur. J. Crime Crim. L. & Crim. Just.* 15, 2007, pp. 83

Tannous, I, 'The EEAS, EU External Assistance and Development Aid: Institutional Dissonance or Inter-service Harmony?' in: J Bátora & S David (eds.), *European Diplomacy post-Westphalia*, Palgrave, 2015.

Tarschys, D & J Ferrer, 'Investing Where it Matters: An EU Budget for Long-Term Growth', *CEPS Task Force Reports*, CEPS 2012.

Taylor, S, 'Oettinger Under Fire for Nuclear Safety Remarks', *European Voice* 2011.

Tehan, R, 'Cyber security: Authoritative reports and resources', *Congressional Research Service*, 2012.

Teslicko, D, 'The European Union's CFSP: A Lowest-Common-Denominator Approach to Foreign Policy?', Washington Research Library Consortium 2010.

Thomas, D, 'Still Punching Below its Weight? Actorness and Effectiveness in EU Foreign Policy', UACES 40th annual conference, Bruges, 2010, pp. 6–8.

Thorstensen, S & Chitumbo, K., 'Safeguards in the European Union: The New Partnership Approach', *IAEA Bulletin* 1, 1995.

Toje, A, 'The European Union as a Small Power, or Conceptualizing Europe's Strategic Actorness', *European Integration* 30, no. 2, 2008, pp. 199–215.

Toulemonde, J, H Summa-Pollitt & N Usher, 'Triple Check for Top Quality or Triple Burden? Assessing EU Evaluations, Quality Matters: Seeking Confidence in Evaluation, Auditing and Performance Reporting', 2005, pp. 69–90.

Trenin, D V, *Post-Imperium: A Eurasian Story*, Carnegie Endowment for International Peace, 2011.

U.S.-CREST, 'The Nature and Impacts of Barriers to Trade with the United States for European Defence Industries', *ENTR* 08/40, 2009.

Umbach, F, 'Global Energy Security and the Implications for the EU', *Energy Policy* 38, no. 3, 2010, pp. 1229–1240.

Underdal, A, 'One Question, Two Answers', in: *Environmental Regime Effectiveness: Confronting Theory with Evidence*, MIT Press, 2002, pp. 3–45.

European foreign policy unit, *Chronology: European Union Foreign Policy*, LSE, http://www.lse.ac.uk/internationalRelations/centresandunits/EFPU/EFPUpdfs/chronologyEuforpol.pdf

United Nations, *Vienna Convention on Diplomatic Relations*, 1961.

—, *United Nations Convention Against Illicit Traffic in Narcotic Drugs and Psychotropic Substances*, 1988.

—, *The United Nations Convention against Corruption*, 2004.

—, *United Nations Convention Against Transnational Organized Crime*, 2004.

—, *2010 Review Conference of the Parties to the Treaty on the Non-Proliferation of Nuclear Weapons, Final Document*, New York, 2010.

—, *World Drug report*, 2013.

Ury, W & R Fisher, *Getting to Yes*, Harvard Negotiating Project, 1981.

USA, President of the, 'Presidential decision directive Critical infrastructure protection', NSC-63, 1998.

Van Ham, P, 'The European Union's WMD Strategy and the CFSP: A Critical Analysis', 2011, http://www.nonproliferation.eu/documents/kickoff/van_ham.pdf

van Schendel, W & I Abraham, *Illicit Flows and Criminal Things: States, Borders, and the Other Side of Globalization*, Indiana University Press, 2005.

Vasconcelos, A, *A strategy for EU foreign policy*, European Union Institute for Security Studies, 2010.

Vogler, J, *In the Absence of the Hegemon: EU Actorness and the Global Climate Change Regime*, Australian National University, 2004.

Vries, G, 'The European Union's role in the fight against terrorism', *Irish studies in international affairs* 16, no. 1, 2005.

Waever, O, J Sperling & J Hallenberg, 'European Security Identities', *Journal of Common Market Studies* vol. 34, No. 1, 1996.

Wagnsson, C, J Sperling & J Hallenberg, *European Security Governance: The European Union in a Westphalian World*, Routledge, 2009.

Wallace, H, W Wallace & M A Pollack, *Policy-making in the European Union*, Oxford university press Oxford, 2000.

Wallensteen, P, *Understanding Conflict Resolution: War, Peace and the Global System*, Sage, 2011.

Wallensteen, P & C Staibano, *International Sanctions: Between Words and Wars in the Global System*, Routledge, 2005.

Waltz, K N, *Man, the State, and War: A Theoretical Analysis*, Revised ed., Columbia University Press, 2001.

Weiland, H, 'EU Sanctions Against Zimbabwe: A Predictable Own Goal?', in: *Common Foreign and Security Policy: The First Decade*, London: Continuum 2004.

Weitz, R, 'The Netherlands and Afghanistan: NATO Solidarity vs. War Wariness', *World Politics Review*, 2011.

Wendling, C, *The Comprehensive Approach to Civil-Military Crisis Management*, Institut de Recherche Stratégique de l'École Militaire, Paris 2010.

Wennerholm, P, E Brattberg & M Rhinard, 'The EU as a counter-terrorism actor abroad: finding opportunities, overcoming constraints', *EPC Issue Paper 60*, 2010.

Wessels, W & F Bopp, 'The Institutional Architecture of CFSP after the Lisbon Treaty: Constitutional breakthrough or challenges ahead?' *CEPS Challenge Paper* No. 10, 23 June 2008.

Wheaton, J K, J Sperling & J Hallenberg, *The Soviet War in Afghanistan*, Golgotha Press, 2010.

WHO, 'Globalisation', http://www.who.int/social_determinants/themes/globalization

Williams, P D, *Security Studies: An Introduction*, 2 ed., Routledge, 2012.

Wilson, E J, 'Hard power, soft power, smart power', *The annals of the American academy of Political and Social Science* 616, no. 1, 2008, pp. 110–124.

Wishnick, E, *Growing US Security Interests' in Central Asia*, Strategic Studies Institute, 2002.

Wolff, S, N Wichmann & G Mounier, 'The external dimension of Justice and Home Affairs: A different security agenda for the EU?', *Journal of European Integration*, Vol. 31, Issue 1, 2009.

Woollard, C, 'EPLO Review of the Gothenburg Programme', Discussion paper, 2011.

—, 'Policy Paper on Civilian CSDP', *EPLO* 2013.

—, 'The EU and the Comprehensive Approach', *EPLO* 2013.

Wouters, J & S Duquet, 'The European Union and the Risk Posed by Terrorism', Working paper No 122, Leuven, 2013.

Wouters, J, S de Jong & P De Man, 'The EU's Commitment to Effective Multilateralism in the Field of Security: Theory and Practice', Working paper 45, Leuven, 2010.

Wouters, J & F Naert, 'Of Arrest
  Warrants, Terrorist Offences and
  Extradition Deals An Appraisal
  of the EU's Main Criminal Law
  Measures against Terrorism after
  '11 September'', Leuven, 2004.
Wunderlich, Jens, 'The EU an Actor
  Sui Generis? A Comparison of
  EU and ASEAN Actorness*',
  *JCMS: Journal of Common Market
  Studies* 50, no. 4, 2012, pp.
  653–669.
Yergin, D, *The Quest: Energy,
  Security, and the Remaking of the
  Modern World*, Penguin, 2011.
Youngs, R, 'European Foreign Policy
  and the Economic Crisis: What
  Impact and how to Respond?',
  Fride, 2010.
  —, *The Uncertain Legacy of Crisis*,
  Brookings Institution Press,
  2014.
Zagorski, A, *EU Policies Towards
  Russia, Ukraine, Moldova and
  Belarus*, Geneva Center for
  Security Policy, 2002.

Zellner, W, 'Russia and the
  OSCE: From High Hopes to
  Disillusionment', *Cambridge
  Review of International Affairs* 18,
  no. 3, pp. 389–402, 2005.
  —, 'Towards a Euro-Atlantic and
  Eurasian Security Community
  From Vision to Reality', 2012.
Zwagemakers, F, 'The EU's
  Conditionality Policy: A New
  Strategy to Achieve Compliance',
  IAI Working papers 12, 2012.
Zwolski, K, 'The External
  Dimension of the EU's Non-
  proliferation Policy: Overcoming
  Inter-institutional Competition'
  in: *EU External Relations Law
  and Policy in the Post-Lisbon Era*,
  Springer, pp. 357–374, 2012.

# Index